MW00743620

- You Are What You Do - You Do What You Think -

"Lao-Tzu's Shoe"

A Joint Spiritual Journey

****

A present-day teenager confronts
the big timeless questions.

Author: Bob Grawi

You Think What You Believe - You Believe What You Are

Published by: White Bear Enterprises
P.O. Box 106, Florida, NY 10921

****

****

This is the First Edition 2017

****

Library of Congress Control Number: 2016919634
CreateSpace Independent Publishing Platform
North Charleston, SC

ISBN-13: 978-1539871323

ISBN-10: 1539871320

****

With deepest love and appreciation for
My wife Pip for all her work and continuously good spirit,
and in memoriam to:
Suzanne and Julius Grawi,
and Edward and Phyllis Klein,
without whom this life would not be.

TABLE OF CONTENTS

"Dedication" and "Preface to the Forward"

Forward ....Why does this Book Exist? 5

Chapter 1..............................Meaningless and Insignificant 28

Chapter 2........................Everything Ends, but Nothing Begins 61

Chapter 3............................Who Am I? The Circle of Being 89

Chapter 4...Your Sticky Brain 99

Chapter 5...What is Stuff? 113

Chapter 6... What is Non-stuff? 121

Chapter 7..............................Giordano Bruno to the Rescue 130

Chapter 8..The Infinity Within 140

Chapter 9.......................................Duality is Everywhere 164

Chapter 10....................................Joining the Opposites 184

Chapter 11..An End to Dualism 200

Chapter 12..............................Zen, Chan, Huang. and Me 251

Chapter 13..Clearing House 269

Chapter 14...........................Shiva's Dance and Resolution 294

Afterward....................Notes on the Text of Lao-Tzu's Shoe 303

Dedication

This book is primarily dedicated to my son, Ben, for without his bravely persistent questioning and his relentless search for the deepest understanding and truest unfiltered meanings of our common human existence this book would never have been written.

It is also dedicated to all other sincere seekers of deeper spiritual understanding as a thoughtful and useful guide from another traveler somewhere along the way. It contains many original personal insights from my own passage that I still consider to be very important and meaningful. I am passing them along in spiritual communion with you in the hope that you too will find some useful things revealed in it that will also become personally important and valuable for you in your own present-day life journey. Since there is no longer any meaningful bowl or symbolic robe of succession to pass along, may you be able to find some true solace and affirmation in these few heartfelt words I have to offer.

It is also dedicated with great admiration and in loving tribute to the following long dead amazing people I wish I could have known:

Socrates, Giordano Bruno, and Lao-Tzu

****

Preface to the Forward

Speaking personally, I never read the "forwards" of the books I read until after I've finished reading the book itself. This is because I've found that forwards, often not written by the book's author are invariably discussing different aspects of the work that I haven't read yet, and I am in the dark about just how to understand exactly what they are talking about until after I've read the book. So I'll just skip them and go on to read the book. If when I'm done I am not that impressed with what I've read, that's it; it's over, and I won't go back and read the forward at all. But If I really did enjoy the work and I was sorry to see it finally come to an end; then I will go back and read the forward and instead of it being frustrating and opaque, it's just as enjoyable as having a nice little desert after a satisfying meal. So for me "forwards" are misnamed because if I do read them at all, they will always invariably become "afterwards."

This book's forward however, is not that common type of forward. The thoughts expressed in it are not out of sequence and are not repetitive of what will be discussed in the body of the work and they will directly enrich your experience of reading this book. It will also give you a deeper understanding of the characters, their histories, and the background foundation underlying what you are about to read in the body of the work, and the formative reasons of just how and why this book came into being.

Therefore I recommend that you do go forward and read this differently conceived "forward" as an appropriate appetizer, and not to save it as a possible desert to the main meal. There already is a well prepared desert awaiting you as an "afterward" to the main entrée. So what you have before you now is a full three course intellectual meal, so…"bon appétit." Or, you could just skip the forward and read it later if you want to without any big detrimental effect… but in that case you're probably not even reading this now, are you?

Forward

Why Does this Book Exist?

Why are we here? In such a huge universe isn't my life totally meaningless and insignificant? How do I know what's the right thing to do? With so many other people around, what difference does it really make what I do? Is what we're doing now spoiling the future for everybody? Are we all just an experiment in evolution that's bound to fail like so many others before us? Is everything hopeless? Who am I? What do I have to contribute? How can I have less self-doubt and be more sure of myself? What can I wholeheartedly believe in? What's the point of all this? Why was I born? What is the real meaning of life?

These and many other similar existential questions became the arena of many long and deeply spirited conversations I recently had with my teenage son over an extended period of several weeks. They would begin innocently enough in the evenings but would often run seriously and deeply on late into the night. Our intimate talks concerned questions that I hadn't thought about seriously for a very long time, although at one point in my life I did think about them all very deeply and for many years. I had already made my own separate peace with them years before, but now they were all coming back around again through the agent of my son's relentless questioning teenage spirit. Many of these were those very same existential questions I had experienced wrestling with and that were now all of a sudden deeply troubling him for the very first time.

They are all the great timeless questions of the very nature of human existence that must be somehow addressed by every succeeding generation anew. But all too often most people simply try to avoid confronting these huge issues directly and they are usually either nervously joked about and quickly dismissed, or they are just considered to be useless questions impossible to answer and are never brought up at all in any really honest way. They tend to make almost everyone very uncomfortable, and are rarely, if ever, discussed openly in any simple direct and meaningful everyday conversations. They mostly concern subjects that in our culture are in some strangely modern sense taboo, and are usually only taken up and seriously considered at the highest rarefied college academic realms of pure philosophy or comparative religious studies. This is because they are not pointless and useless questions at all. Although they all can sound quite simple-minded and absurdly direct, they are all actually very difficult questions, and there aren't any quick and easy or widely accepted answers to any of them. In addition, no one wants to openly admit their own basic insecurity about all these fundamentally very important matters, or face up to their own doubts and common misunderstanding about the most basic existential truths of our lives. All the proud Emperors secretly wish to quietly remain blissfully unaware that they really have no clothes on at all!

While these questions do also exist in the province of various rigid sets of religious beliefs and dogma, when they are presented to the young in this context, they are only given on a totally "take it or leave it" basis. The only option for them is unquestioned acceptance of their pre-approved given set of answers which require a full belief that these have been transmitted to the select few having been handed down directly to them from the word of God. Without having both a strong faith, and a servile attitude in this inflexible system, and also having an accompanying strong naive belief in angels and in miracles, much of this didactic method is ineffective and can often fall flat, especially when being directly presented for the first time to a questioning young and very intelligent American teenage boy.

As I grew older, my own fascination with these big existential life questions led me on a lengthy personal journey of studying other world religions, during which my growing interests in them became broader and deeper. I read many books on early Christianity, Gnosticism, Taoism, Buddhism, Hinduism, Zen, Chan, and along the way I had some true spiritual experiences of my own. All of which had no direct relationships to any one formalized structured religious practice.

I especially enjoyed my early sojourns through the ancient Hindu Upanishads, the Christian Gnostic Gospels, the Chinese Tao Te Ching, and the Indian Buddhist Diamond Sutra. Then I made my way through the vast expanses of Hindu cosmic vision, and the deep psychological symbolism embedded in the Tibetan Buddhist Wheel of Life thangka, and many of the early Japanese Zen writings of Hakuin Ekaku and others including their Chinese Chan counterparts like Huang Po and their contemporaries. These all seemed to me to be offered up in a much more open and intellectually honest way, and also to be of a more deeply poetic nature than those of our own standard Western spiritual fare. I recognized them as my people for they spoke more strongly and directly to my own awakening and seeking inner artistic spirit. They became my guides and I intuitively accepted them and respected their deep spiritual integrity.

My own direct encounters with the spirit of the Orient continued in other areas as well. In my exposure to Tai Chi and studying Japanese ink brush painting in the art of Sumi-e, I responded directly to the exquisite beauty and dramatic simplicity highly esteemed in oriental art, adding to the clear profundity of what I was also directly experiencing while pursuing these other traditional materials of esoteric Eastern spirituality. As a result of all these gleanings my spirit eventually forged its own idiosyncratic personal amalgam of strong East/West trans-cultural spiritual beliefs. I was finally greatly relieved to have escaped a world of strict religious dogma and to have found within me a deep source of revealed truth and uncompromised spiritual inspiration that I could accept and honor for life.

So, later on in my own life, when I got married and finally at 48 years old had a son of my own, I was determined to remain loyal to these hard won truths that I had acquired over the many long years of my extended solitary inner spiritual journey to the East. I could not in all good conscience choose any of the very limited local parochial institutions to provide for his spiritual education. As a result I did not enroll him in any nearby ongoing organized religious schools of any kind. I basically gave up on trying to direct him and just got out of his way and decided to let him find his own path as I had done. I also must have had some basic underlying faith in Rousseau's noble savage ideals, and I suppose I had also hoped that by the subtle means of some sort of "spooky-parent-to-child-mental-osmosis," some of my own personal spirituality would inevitably rub off on him. But to my chagrin this did not happen in any meaningful way, and it was now all coming around back at me with a vengeance. Perhaps I had done my son a great disservice that it was now too late to correct and I was starting to feel that maybe I had been totally derelict in my parental duties, and that I had made a huge mistake. Perhaps the young do need to rely on some sort of rigid belief structure no matter what the source to give them a feeling of meaning and security in this dynamic world of uncertainty and change that we all inhabit.

But to my general surprise my son did not see it that way at all. He kept on effusively thanking me and insisting many times over about how truly lucky he felt he was as compared to most of his friends by not having been "indoctrinated" in any set of "arbitrary beliefs." I wondered, was he only saying this to assuage my newly found parental guilt? I didn't think so, for he really sounded dead serious in his great appreciation of my total lack of giving him any organized religious training at all during his early formative years.

However, as it appeared to me, the hubris of his youth had led him to adopt a largely unexamined and egotistical attitude of somehow feeling himself generally superior to all the revealed religions in existence. Although he didn't really understand or know much about them, religions just did not seem important or to be necessary and did not make any sense to him at all. He tended to view them all as being childish fables like Santa Claus passed on from the adults of one generation to the children of the next generation, useful in keeping their offspring in line and under control but otherwise totally illogical, unnecessary, completely false, and for him empty and meaningless. So, although I already knew that he had by no means mystically absorbed any of my own spirituality, I was still suddenly taken aback when he proudly declared himself to me to be an atheist. How could I not have seen this coming?

Yet to his credit, he intuitively recognized that there was something very important missing in his own life and this was the force and impetus behind our many recent long late night symposiums. That there existed within him an uncomfortable vacuum which was beginning to trouble him deeply and somehow needed to be filled, and as a result of this he turned hopefully towards me as a possible source of relief and perhaps even of a deeper truth. For my part I was very happy to be there for him to use as a sounding board to explore his long neglected spirituality and to be able to finally share with him some of my own idiosyncratic East/West spiritual synthesis. These far reaching extended spiritual and existential discussions became a strong bonding therapy for the both of us.

This book is the final echo of that mutual father and son search for the real unfiltered deeper meanings of life. It arose not as my own artistic invention, but it really came about only as an afterthought and it is a true remembrance of the many different mindscapes over which our open and frank discussions traveled. It was a very intense experience for both of us. Led largely by my son's own direct questioning and cross-examination of me and my own personally formed beliefs, he directly used our conversations as a way for him to come face to face with his own newly found great endless supply of modern teenage existential angst.

A very large part of his discomfort had to do with his total lack of any satisfying answers to those earlier mentioned big existential life questions… and I was also beginning to feel personally responsible for this problem because when he was younger I hadn't given him any coherent world view to hold on to, and no overarching system of trans-personal values to understand his life or his rightful place in the world. So as a default on his own he had begun to rely totally on the world of science and those things that science could prove without a doubt. There was no room for God, or art, or even the human spirit in this objective model that he had constructed for himself of what was true and real in the greater world around him. What he didn't realize was just how cold, lifeless, and inanimate this objective world view was that he had built up for himself to inhabit, and ultimately how very little emotional stability it held for him. This newly humbled Emperor now suddenly clearly realized that he was in fact naked…

Most of the time my son was a bright busy active, positive thinking, happy and apparently well adjusted person, and a real joy to be with. He was great fun to work with on our many joint creative projects which we always enjoyed doing together. He was very intelligent and he also had a naturally gifted deep sense of spatial design. One time when he was only about three or four years old after playing with a large set of blocks, he left behind structures that were so proportionally balanced and classic that they appeared to me to be a small group of ancient Greek Temple ruins scattered across our living room floor. I was very impressed and affectionately started to call him "Verrocchio" after the renaissance Florentine art master of painting and sculpture who was the teacher of Leonardo da Vinci. He was born Andrea di Michele di Francesco de' Cioni, but he became known as "Verrocchio" which was not his given name. Verrocchio was an honorary nickname he earned in recognition of his great artistic achievement. Pinocchio in Italian means "Pine Eye" Malocchio means "Evil Eye" and Verrocchio means "True Eye." Artistically speaking, even at that young age I could tell that my son had the true eye of a natural born artist.

One of our most hilarious art projects we both enjoyed working on just spontaneously happened when an "artsy" duck shaped cutting board my wife had bought at a craft fair but which had been put together with a weak wood glue, separated into its four component parts after being put through the dishwasher. Then these four wooden duck pieces wound up just sitting on the kitchen table and lying around for a few days. But one day in the morning after Ben had gone off to school I came into the kitchen for breakfast, and instead of a collection of four separate duck cutting board pieces lying there, on the table at my usual breakfast spot there was standing a completely new duck that eventually we started calling "Goosey Longneck."

This duck was so strikingly different from the original cutting board duck that when I saw it I just had to laugh out loud; but it was still a duck! Well, this was interesting… So I rose to the challenge and I took apart "Goosey Longneck" and created my own new duck "Dr. Big Bill" so that he would discover it when he came home from school. Of course my son wouldn't let this one stand either, and next day there was yet another new funny duck sitting at my breakfast spot. This activity became a very enjoyable ongoing diversion and this silent and unacknowledged back and forth duck creation design competition between the two of us amazingly continued on for weeks and weeks. It became a great source of amusement for the both of us. We were each silently working alone and trying hard to surprise and out do the other with our original wacky duck creations. It was a surprisingly fruitful vein! I was so flabbergasted by the amazingly large variety of different ducks we were able to make that in the end I photographed them all, setting them up one by one. Eventually using a computer I even named and catalogued them all into a single graphic image I called "Just Ducky."

During the course of this competitive design process we were each always making our own ducks alternately by having to disassemble the latest duck the other had made, and creating another different new one as ongoing challenges to each other all from just those four wooden duck pieces. They had to be balanced because only gravity held them up; we did not use any glue or tape. The result is that exactly half of the assembled ducks in "Just Ducky" were made by me and the other half were made by my son, Ben. It was a truly mutual collaborative endeavor. Except for the first few ducks I couldn't really tell you now just who had created which of the other ducks except for one. I was immensely proud of my own "Pelly-Can," creation, and I will always be very fond of my son's first duck "Goosey Longneck."

Here is a copy of "Just Ducky" so that you too can enjoy and appreciate just what we were about in these ongoing, oddly amusing, and wacky duck designing activities my son and I were casually engaged in for several weeks strictly for our own personal amusement.

JUST DUCKY *by Ben and Bob Grawi*

Rearrangements of Just the 4 Pieces

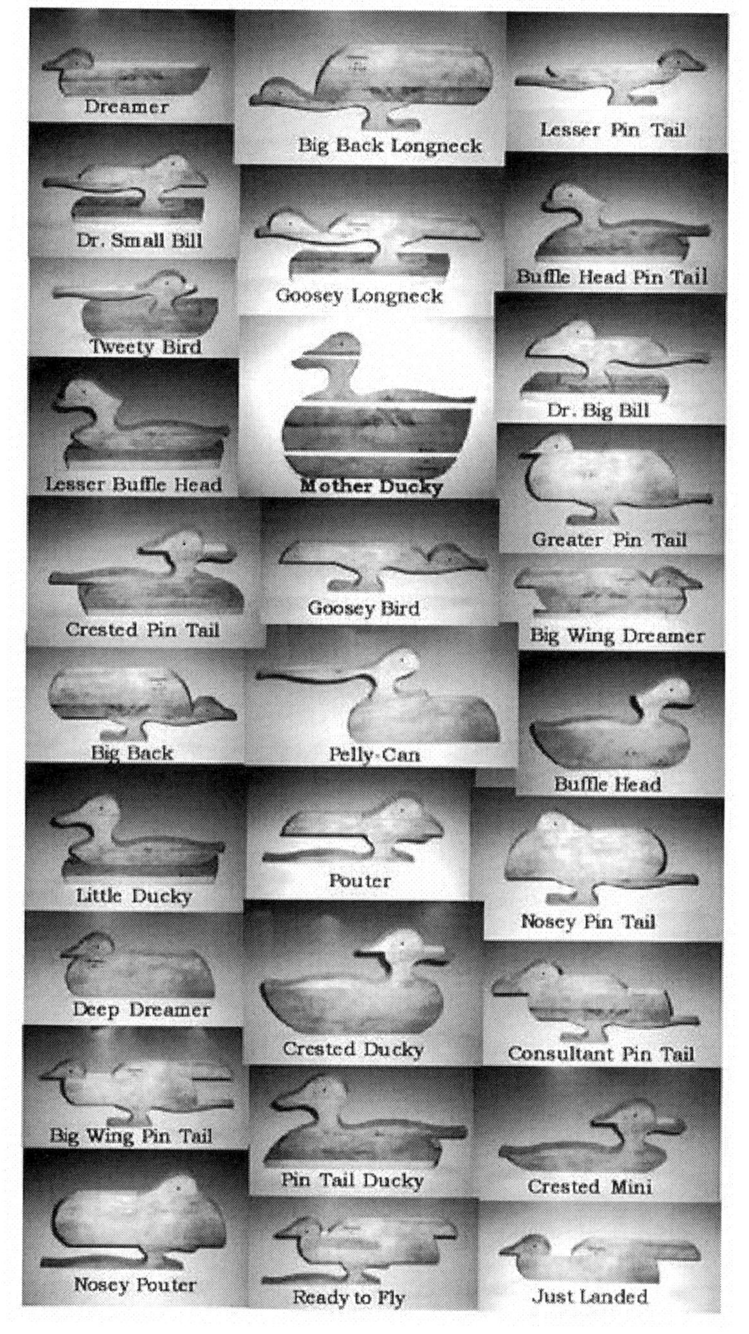

Yes, my son was definitely the creative type, but whenever anything directly opposed him or became somehow emotionally turbulent in his life, perhaps not getting his own way in something he thought was important, or being bullied by a classmate or some such upsetting thing, he would have a very hard time dealing with it and his inner self-doubt would "suddenly go off the charts." He could weather very few disruptions to his sensitive inner core and when they did happen, all at once he'd feel deeply depressed and at odds with everything around him.

His own natural inner joy actually had very little buoyant resilience to it, and it would then simply vanish altogether and all of his normal positive life spirit would suddenly dry up completely and everything around him would dramatically invert so that they would quickly turn from being joyfully positive to abruptly becoming very negative, with everything taking on the bleak appearance to him of being utterly hopeless. Then his own naturally beautiful happy life force would suddenly turn very sad and angry and he would feel totally at odds with himself, and everything else in the world around him would suddenly begin to look empty and totally worthless.

Whenever he was trapped in this sorry state of mind, it would actually become very difficult for us to find out just what had set him off. What event in his everyday life had happened to him to trigger this dreadful mental transformation that was now troubling him so deeply? He would then also silently isolate himself from everything and everyone, his parents included, and he would become deeply withdrawn and inwardly very hard to reach. It was very scary for us when this happened, and although these dramatic emotional turn of events were actually very rare and sporadic, they did occur more than once. His mother with great empathy and patience was usually able to reach him and to eventually reassure him enough of the innate goodness of his own life and of the world around him to bring him back to us and to his normal self once again. This was always a very difficult time for all of us and we had to acknowledge that my son was having some sort of a real on going emotional/spiritual problem in his young life that needed to be taken seriously and meaningfully addressed by all of us with great love and care.

"How was I going to help my own son?" I asked myself.

I thought that surely there must be some simple honest straight forward and direct way for a loving father to give his own young son a deeper and broader spiritual understanding and emotional basis for living his own life that would help bolster him in dealing with these great inner personal temperamental dramas that occasionally seemed to erupt and overwhelm him, and to help him get through them in a less extreme and more balanced way. Surely there must be!

I had to ask myself…"Was this all my fault for not having given him a grounded normal religious upbringing in the first place? And had the time to successfully address and solve this problem already passed? And was it now too late for me to be able to help him get through it?" Hopefully this was not the case.

These were all very difficult questions for me to face personally. They were especially troubling because of the oddly unique religious path I had gone through in my own youth while growing up. For a better understanding of just what this was and why it suddenly all still seemed so deeply relevant, it is important that you should know more about the unique early history of my own family.

My Early Religious Experiences

My own religious upbringing had an unusual ingrained and fractured quality to it that occurred during my early formative years that may have contributed in some ways to the development of this problem in the first place. This odd early discontinuity could be directly traced to my own family's difficult life experiences which were endured during the World War II era. I was born as part of the great post war "baby boom" in America and brought up by my parents in a small rural town in upstate New York. But my father was born in Germany at the turn of the previous century on a small rural family farm and cattle ranch in the town of Neheim, Westphalia. It was in many ways a rich experience as their fragrant livestock barn was attached right to the back of their large family farm house. Of course there were always many flies associated with their farm animals, and as a result he had an easy folk remedy for itchy fly bites. You licked your finger and placed it in a sugar bowl, then rubbed the bite welt with the sugar crystals sticking to your finger. This in itself felt very good and the sugar left on the bite drew out the poison and stopped the itch fairly well.

One of his other boyhood tales my father shared with me was also about the flies on their family's cattle farm. As a kid he'd made a precocious business deal with his own father that he would earn one pfennig (1¢) for every 100 dead flies that he could produce. So you can just imagine how many flies there must have been to make it profitable, and as a result he became very good at catching flies bare handed, a talent he never lost. Of course it was a better deal than it sounded like since there was no real overhead and I also suppose 1¢ was worth a lot more then than it is now... Anyway he soon mastered a highly developed technique whereby he would not attack a sitting fly directly, but he'd snatch them right out of the air by coming up very quickly from behind and slightly above them, resulting in their mid-air capture as they were in the process of instinctually flying away and trying to escape from his threatening approach. In this fly catching scheme the fly's own natural escape mechanism, a hard-wired nearly instantaneous reflex which normally works well enough to enable them to usually evade looming death from the more common direct frontal swatting attack, was being cleverly subverted and actively turned around and successfully used against them. For now their normally quick irresistible response of flight to safety only resulted in their flying directly up and into his grasp of doom. It was a feat that required perfect timing, and even in his older years he could still effectively demonstrate it as often as required. I now realize that my father was actually employing the classic Taoist strategy of immersing oneself "into the Tao of the fly's innate nature" and working "in sync" within the ongoing natural forces at hand to solve the vexing problem of how to profit from more easily catching horse flies!

However, later on in his own adult life, he was the one who would have to successfully escape from looming doom. He had already left the family farm behind and had gone off to Leipzig University and after graduating from medical school had become a successful practicing doctor who was living well in the German city of Dresden. My father was also personally very brave and in his university days he'd actually been involved in a real life sword fight. It was a classic formal duel over the honor of a woman, and he had a half-moon scar on the tip of his nose to prove it. His bravery would soon be put to an even more difficult test in 1939.

After witnessing the anti-Semitic Nazi demonstrations of *kristallnacht*, he was just barely able to escape from the fast escalating horrors of pre-war Germany and the Nazi's final brutal persecution of all the Jews there. As a deeply religious Jew and a 40 year old already well established physician, he was very lucky at the very last minute to be able to immigrate to the United States bringing along with him his young German wife on the steamship S. S. Normandy. It was a very narrow escape, and in this life wrenching process he would lose all of his money and personal property, and he would also have to leave behind everyone else in his large immediate German family, all of whom would be eventually murdered with great efficiency in Adolf Hitler's many gas chambers of the holocaust. Although he never talked about it, this of course was very difficult for him, as he was also an honorable war veteran who had been forced to serve in the German army during World War I. He never forgave his native country and he also never went back to visit Germany again during the rest of his life.

My father was brave and very intelligent, and well educated in the long standing classic European academic traditions and he was fluent in four different languages – German, Hebrew, Greek, and Latin. He was already a licensed practicing physician in Germany, however when he came to America he still had to work very hard for several years to learn English from scratch and to be able to speak and write it at a very advanced technical level. This was necessary for him to continue working in his chosen profession, since he was now again required to pass the medical licensing boards here, but which were only allowed to be administered in the English language. My mother was also working very hard during this period as a seamstress in the garment business in New York City to help support them both. He was finally very proud after many additional years of near poverty and hard work, to have become a licensed medical doctor once again for the second time in his life. Now he also spoke English, had a home here, and they both had just become newly naturalized United States Citizens and were now starting to raise a family of their own. At this point in his life my father wished most of all only to assimilate and become as fully an American as possible. Always grateful to America that had saved them both from the horrors of the Nazi domination and plundering of war-time Europe, they even named their first born son, my older brother, "Franklin" after the U.S. World War II president FDR.

My brother was born in 1942 during the war, and I was born in 1947 as part of the post war "Baby Boom" in America. My father delivered me at home in the upstairs of our house which he had converted into his own private medical clinic. I like to say that he did the whole job from start to finish! He named the clinic "The Henrietta Grawi Memorial Hospital" dedicated to honor his mother whom he had lost with the rest of his entire family to the Nazi Holocaust.

He himself had only recently barely escaped with his life and his wife from the brutal Nazi anti-Semitic persecution in Germany in 1939. He had witnessed the total eradication of the long established Jewish culture there, the mass destruction of synagogues, and the confiscation of all Jewish property. He had learned first hand of the "final solution" gas chamber murders of all his own beloved family, and the systematic state level genocidal industrial killing of six million other innocent European Jews. Understandably this was the reason why he was very cautious now about publicly expressing his own strong Jewish heritage here, and for a long time he quietly remained a withdrawn non-practicing "Closet-Jew."

Curiously and inappropriately, this reminds me of an old Jewish insider joke, a shortened version goes something like this:

Moesha speaks to the Lord

Moesha, a religious Jew has a deep spiritual question that has been troubling him for a very long time and he wants to have a personal audience with God. So he goes out into the desert and prays constantly in the hot sun and fasts for many long days on end, punishes the flesh and finally has a vision of the Lord before him.

Moesha prostrates himself on the hot sand and says, "Oh Great One and Only God, Holy Father and Ruler of the Universe, I, Moesha, your lowly undeserving supplicant, the only son of Jacob the Levite, wishes to ask you just a very simple little question." Abjectly pleads the sunburned starving dehydrated Moesha.

"You have been very patient, Moesha," says the Lord in a deeply resounding voice, "and you have performed many holy deeds and caused yourself great suffering… I have seen all this and I have taken pity on you and therefore I now reveal myself. Rise up Moesha and tell me what is it that you wish to know that is so troubling you?"

"I wish to know for the sake of my own sanity, if it is absolutely the truth what is written in the Torah. Are the Children of Israel really and truly your chosen people?" Moesha asks God.

"Why yes, my son, of course it is true what is written," God answers, "the Jews really are my chosen people."

"Well…" Moesha gets up his nerve and bravely asks the Almighty, "Maybe you could just do me one little favor then, for your poor undeserving servant Moesha? Maybe you could just go ahead and choose somebody else for a little while?"

****

Whatever Happened to Christmas?

At home when I was growing up we yearly had our own great fragrant live evergreen Christmas trees. We hung up our oversized brightly colored and embroidered red and green Christmas stockings on the fireplace mantle with care, and late at night while we were sleeping on Christmas Eve, Santa Claus came to our house too, just like he was supposed to, coming down the chimney and filling up all the stockings with many small gifts for everyone. There was also of course the amazing pile of big presents under the tree on Christmas morning. My brother and I would play all day long with our classic holiday Lionel Train set which we often fought for control over. (He usually won because he was five years older than me.) And outside there were the many great wonderful brightly colored neighborhood lighting displays that were festively sprinkled all over our small town visually transforming the bleak clear cold winter nights into a cheerful real country folk art celebration. Our big dining room table always held savory memories for me too especially because my mother was a great German cook! At home we also created our own decorations for our Christmas tree including multi-colored glued together construction paper chains, hand cut out fancy white paper snowflakes, and popcorn and cranberry string ornaments. We kept all of them, the tree stand, the colored lights, the blown glass ornaments and the tinsel too, in cardboard boxes labeled "X-Mas" on the highest shelf in the dining room closet during the rest of the year. Of course Christmas for a young boy in America is a very exciting time and it was definitely my favorite holiday! Thanksgiving came in a distant second.

In my younger years, when I attended Church Street Elementary School, we would have whole student body assemblies in the spacious central atrium just before winter break. Hundreds of us kids would all be sitting there in rows on the steps of the three long and wide central branching staircases. Altogether we would sing the traditional holiday Christmas Carols led by our wonderful young music teacher as she stood all alone with a pitch-pipe directing us from the common central landing. It was our own small town school's community sing-along just before winter vacation, and everyone's excited pre-Christmas voices would fill up that cavernous space with the great joyful resounding musical reverberations of Jingle Bells, Noel, Silent Night, etc. I have come to love them all and as a musician I still like to play them with my wife every season as a part of our own ongoing holiday tradition.

The Fracture Occurs

But after spending many years here and becoming an American citizen, my father must have slowly come to understand and realize at the deepest of levels that his new home country, The United States of America, was not at all like his native Germany. America was truly a free country and that no religion here, not even Judaism, would be persecuted as it had been for so many centuries throughout Europe. Then suddenly one year in my mid-childhood, unaccountably a very dramatic big change happened — "the fracture" took place in our family.

From then on there were to be no more Christmas trees in our household anymore, and everything else about Christmas was all of a sudden "*verboten*" and not to be brought up or even mentioned anymore. All of it just totally vanished overnight from our lives never to reappear again. And instead of the "X-Mas box" full of our oversized stockings and all our homemade Christmas ornaments, out of the closet came three metal menorahs. And after dinner the lighting of the candles for Chanukah, to our shaky rendition of the old Hebrew hymn "Moau Tzur" – "Children of the Martyr Race" – which my father would begin singing with great gusto and we would usually be a half a beat behind him just trying to keep up. We lit the candles, one more every night, and sang this hymn for the eight days of Chanukah. My father lit a large old tarnished classic eight armed cast brass beaded menorah, and my brother and I dutifully following his lead lit our own separate candle displays in two other small identical, modern, rather cheaply stamped out flat tin ones. In our darkened dining room, the candlelight of these three softly glowing menorahs after dinner on the cleared off dining room table were beautiful in their own simple way, but they couldn't really "hold a candle" to our old Christmas trees! What ever happened to Santa

Claus? He still seemed to visit all my friends and our neighbors... Had we all of a sudden somehow been mistakenly dropped from Santa's "Nice List" and added to his "Naughty List?" None of this that I can remember was ever openly discussed at our home.

Today my wife who is actually half-Jewish, but was raised as a Christian, and I do joyously celebrate Christmas in our own small family home once again. And yes, she has insisted on our having a real live Christmas tree with all the trimmings which I am glad to set up in the music room and help transform with our own especially meaningful decorations that we have assembled and add to every year. Yes, and even Santa Claus has had a rebirth too, for the benefit of my son when he was young. I feel it is not right to pass up this amazing country wide celebration that in its season so completely dominates everything all around us from the broadcast media, movies, printed newspapers, the shops and villages, and even the junk mail! To not take part in celebrating Christmas is to reject something fundamental about our American culture and its history.

Annually during the months of the "American Christmas Season," many Jews have a difficult love/hate relationship with this time of year. I also for a time was one of these confused souls. It is a hard, isolating, and an unnecessary thing to be an outsider at Christmas time as many Jews silently feel that they are. But in my own strange case I have finally come to a fully conscious peaceful understanding, acceptance, and dare I say, enjoyment of it all. So, from a purely Jewish perspective on Christmas, here is what I have come to accept as my own fully conscious personal resolution of this overwhelming and recurring Jewish-American seasonal dilemma, perhaps there may be some solace in this for others as well.

First of all, was not Jesus himself a member of the tribe of Israel? He certainly was. And didn't he also greatly reform, preach, and work tirelessly against many of the problems that already existed in the Judaism of his day? Yes he did. And didn't this pro-active work include throwing the money lenders out of the Synagogue? It surely did. And even more importantly, he is also absolutely the one who single handedly brought about the hugely important transformation of the Old Testament's fearsome Jewish vision of Almighty God as an all powerful smiting, jealous, and vengeful Deity; into our present day image of the much more truly loving and forgiving God of the New Testament. And didn't he accomplish this amazing feat all on his own by just simply pointing out in a forthright way that God is our father, and we are his children? Yes, that's right. And doesn't a good father love all of his children? Of course he does. And certainly everyone already knows and understands this to be true. This alone is one of the most wonderfully benevolent and bountiful spiritual gifts that has ever been bestowed upon the human race. His legacy is also especially meaningful, far-reaching, and enduring because of all the important work taken up by his disciples. With great dedication and untold personal suffering so many generations of his followers have continued to be inspired by his life and to actually spread his teachings, along with the Jewish ideal of monotheism all around the world and thereby greatly help to truly civilize the rest of the planet. Now really all of these very important things have just got to be more than enough very good reasons for everyone, Jews and Christians alike, to rejoice in celebration of the birth of Jesus… Hallelujah!

For me and my own strangely convoluted religious path, these are all strong arguments that ring of profound truth and are the seminal spiritual links between all Jews and Christians. And during the holiday season this realization gives me a feeling of great peace and joy, and isn't that what Christmas is really all about? Joy to the World, Christ is born. Monotheism will be spread across the Earth far and wide; its civilizing effects will be felt well beyond just the Jewish people, Merry Christmas to all, and Happy Chanukah too!

Of course this was not my own father's life long perspective.

He was brought up strictly as a devout and persecuted European Jew – historically persecuted mainly by Christians – and he could not even countenance the existence of a Jewish born Jesus as necessarily being an actual historical person. He once told me that there were no independent references to Jesus in all the Roman records of the times. For him and other strictly religious Jews, Jesus may not have really existed at all, and certainly is not the savior – simply because the world is still in such a huge spiritual mess. They are all still patiently awaiting the appearance of their own messiah to come save humanity from itself, and strangely enough the Christians too are also still waiting for Jesus to return and finish the job.

The Plot Thickens

After this sudden abrupt change in my mid-childhood, I was then brought up as a Conservative Jewish boy in America. I now had to go to Hebrew School twice a week after regular school, and learn the Hebrew alphabet: "Aleph Bet Vet, Gimmel Daled Hay, Vav Zayin Chet Tet Yud…" and how to pronounce all the strange new Hebrew sounds. We learned how to recite the words of the Torah, but we never really learned Hebrew. We only learned how to ape the sounds of Hebrew without any real understanding of the structure or meaning of the "empty words" we were speaking. The English translations of the Hebrew texts were of course printed on the facing pages in the prayer books. But in our local Conservative Jewish congregation, many of its members were also immigrant Jews from Europe who could read Hebrew nearly as well as my father could, so the actual service itself was totally conducted in Hebrew. This was probably a very similar thing to what many Catholic kids in our town, my best boyhood friend Butch being one of them, had to go through at that time also with the Catholic Church's ongoing usage of the ancient Latin liturgical language.

We then held weekly family Friday night Sabbath dinners at home and said the Hebrew blessings over the candles, the wine, and the braided challah bread, one solitary loaf of which was baked specially for my father once a week on Fridays by the local bakery. I attended Sunday school and Friday night and Saturday morning synagogue services with my father. On the way he'd often stop the car to pick up some poor elderly Jewish immigrant men from their homes in other parts of town in order to make up the Saturday morning minion – the ten adult Jewish men needed to read aloud from the Torah and to conduct the service according to ritual religious laws. In our small town on Saturday mornings a minion was not that easy to come by, and my father was instrumental in keeping them going.

At our traditional home Seder my father chanted all in Hebrew and at very high speed fluently and in record time the whole Passover Haggadah – the Exodus story of Moses leading the Jewish people from slavery out of Egypt. Since I was the youngest I had to sing in Hebrew "The Four Questions" too. My father also often led the small isolated rural Jewish congregation when there was no rabbi, and after a while I could sing all the sacred Hebrew songs by heart, just like an opera singer performing phonetically in a foreign language. At 13 years old I performed my Bar-Mitzvah well, mostly from rote memory. I successfully chanted the "empty words" of that week's Torah reading and from a disinterested observer's perspective I must have looked like a devout new adult member of our small rural Jewish community. I certainly was well trained in all the right moves.

But it did not stick. For me it was all forcefully externally imposed mumbo-jumbo and an enormous obligatory ordeal that when it came my time, I decided that I was not going to perpetuate it by forcing it upon my own son. By the time Ben was born, both my parents were deceased, so I didn't have to explain this decision directly to anyone. Although this was a conscious decision I made, it did not come about without a lingering sense of some amount of doubt and guilt. For over 5,000 years my ancestors had successfully played catch with the religious ball from generation to generation, and finally when it got to be my turn, I dropped the ball…

Without a structured religious upbringing, there are many cultural and literary religious references that will often come up in the course of everyday life that even an intelligent young boy will not know anything at all about. So I made it an important part of my son's upbringing to clarify and discuss any biblical references that arose naturally, but only from the historical point of view of our Western culture.

Since my own interests in other world religions had already developed by this time and were broad and deep, we were basically able to cover Genesis, Exodus, and early Christianity in this process. We also discussed Mohammad, the Buddha, Confucius, Lao-Tzu, and Socrates, among others. All of which took place without any particular order or our participation in any formalized weekly religious observance. I was now no longer a practicing Jew, but I was not an agnostic, and I was definitely not an atheist either.

Again the question, "How was I going to help my own son?"

The rest of this book is all about the big questions in life that often go unanswered, or never even get properly asked, and is the result of my deep love for my own son by trying to deal directly and seriously with these big difficult existential issues. We both honestly entered upon a long and open ended serious dialogue which was led mostly by his direct "no holds barred" questioning of me and my beliefs, and by my fullest possible answers to his questions which were very soon coming directly from the depths of my own being. I soon began to realize that in trying to help him by freely and objectively examining his feelings and sharing with him some of my positive gleanings from my own un-nameable spiritual beliefs, I was also in the process renewing mine. It was a deeply exhilarating experience for me to be able to bring my own long held inner spirituality back up to the conscious level, and then to also be able to examine and dissect it all for his benefit.

Now many months after our lengthy father and son explorations of inner space, I am writing down this account of our journey in book form because many of our highly spirited verbal exchanges kept coming back to me and returning fully complete and in a new clearly defined focus. They seemed to still have a very strong resonance for me in my present day adult life, and during this process I was also able to further develop some of my own earlier rudimentary ideas into more fully completed forms. This writing process also gave me the opportunity to include some deeply formative experiences and additional pertinent background material on various other spiritual and historical subjects. It also allowed me to present and comment on several of my own deeply personal spiritual epiphanies. Some of these subjects may not have actually come up during our conversations, but their inclusions, sprinkled here and there where appropriate, do substantially enrich the work. It also became very important for me to be able to openly share my own personal perspective on all these life essential spiritual beliefs with my own son, and it was really exciting to be able to hear his spontaneous and honest responses to them all — since I had never had the opportunity to have this same kind of a direct open personal communion with my own father. It was also wonderful that it all came about so naturally and unforced through Ben's own initiative. We were both ready for it and it was long overdue, and in the end it was a very gratifying experience for both of us.

I also feel that this record of our discussions may possess some deep meaning, and therefore may have some utility, or maybe just some parts of it may prove helpful to some other people who are currently embarked on their own inner spiritual journeys in this confused and disjointed modern age we live in. Especially now in the present moment, when many of the formal and rigid aspects of our long established traditionally organized religious institutions are losing their power and seem to be in a slow process of crumbling and breaking down around us. It may also prove entertaining and useful for others to consider the spiritual wrangling that my son and I engage in here in the course of our ground level, open, give-and-take discussions that we had on these big timeless existential subjects. Although the basis of some of these arguments can go way back to the ideas of several early philosophers and mystics from the far distant past, I feel that they all still have great vitality and still may rightly hold some important basic pragmatic truths for all of us even now many centuries later while engaged in our present daily lives.

To this day when I fill out forms I'll enter "Jewish" or "Hebrew" in the box entitled religion. The real answer would never fit into their tiny boxes. Although it has a very long and tortured history, Judaism is basically a very beautiful, direct, and open religion. It requires believing in one God, living your life in accordance with the Ten Commandments and the other laws of

Moses and most of the old Hebrew prayers are simple affirmations of praise for creation and for the Creator. Nothing too strenuous for the mind, like virgin births of Man-God-Son, no tri-part God-head, and no once in a lifetime Hajj pilgrimage to the Holy Land is required.

I am always amazed that all of our three main established Western religions – Judaism, Christianity, and Islam – all stemmed from that first Old Testament Jew, Abraham. The world would definitely be a different place without him. As a young rebel and iconoclast, from the true meaning of that word – "idol breaker" – he allegedly went on a rampage and wrecked havoc by personally destroying many of the assorted local deity's clay idols. This was reportedly done by him as a service to the one true God and was his first pro-actively symbolic deed as the historic founder of Jewish monotheism. Today he would simply be arrested as a public nuisance, put in jail and fined for destruction of private property. Then he would probably have been given a low dose of social worker therapy to try to make him a more docile and conforming citizen, and put on an early work release program with a three month period of public service required, perhaps helping at the library or the local property disposal center.

"3 Bubbles 3 Mirrors Yantra"
from the author's "Bubble Series," a linoleum print

Chapter 1
Meaningless and Insignificant

Although we both don't know it yet, my teenage son casually begins what will become our first of many long late night highly spirited and far ranging conversations concerning the many questions he has about life that have just recently begun to trouble him rather deeply. Innocently enough out of the blue, he directly asks me just four simple words that are quite possibly "the mother of all existential questions."

He asks me:
"Why are we here?"

I answer him:
"Because this is our home, this is where we live. You are here because you're my son. I am here because I am the son of my parents, and your grandparents who came from Germany and settled here. That's the easy answer. But if by your question you're asking me for what reason are we here, well that's a different kettle of fish entirely… Perhaps you are searching for a *"raison d'être"* as I once did…"

My son says:
"What do you mean? I don't get it. Why were you were looking for a raisin to enter? Dad, that doesn't make any sense at all."

I say:
"Raisin to enter? Ha, ha, ha! No, no. Not "a raisin to enter," ha, ha, that's very funny – that would be hard to find! It'd be worse than trying to find "a needle in a haystack" which is at least possible. But what I said was a *"raison d'être,"* it's not English, but French, so it threw you off. It simply means "a reason for being," or finding something important to give your life real meaning. You should learn this phrase *"raison d'être,"* every cultured person knows it. Just say it, *raison d'être."*

My son says:
"Raison d'être."

I say:
"Yes, that's right; it's an important idea that comes from the European enlightenment period in France. It's an expression of our deep modern existential angst, and it just seems to me to be the kernel of what's been bothering you lately."

My son says:
"Whatever…Raisin to enter, *raison d'être,* I don't really know what it is… What's the matter with me? I just feel very restless all the time and it's like I'm looking for an answer to something, but I don't even know what the right question is. Everything's so strange out there and I don't seem to fit in well anywhere. There are so many really big questions floating around in my head that seem to have no real answers, and nobody's paying any real attention to them at all. Everybody is just busy doing their own thing. Sometimes everything all of a sudden just appears to me to be so totally pointless. It's all very frustrating and I don't really get what it's all about. Dad, can you help me and tell me what's really going on here? Is what I'm feeling right now modern existential angst?"

I say:
"Well, whatever it is, it's not pointless! There's nothing wrong with you. Right now you're at an important developmental stage of searching for the truth of your own life. That's what's happening. It's not a simple question and there's no easy answer. Every seriously self-aware person goes through this and each one of us has to find our own answers to the meaning of our own life. Everyone's an individual and you need to find your own unique personal answer, one that you can fully believe in. No one can do this for you. This will become the firm armature that you'll build the rest of your life around. It can also be a dangerous time for if you just give up trying; your life really can become pointless. You don't want that to happen. I'll try to help you out all I can, if you'd like that. But it's your life and this is your time to cope with it now and it's not an easy quest.

But know this; that it's the most important and worthwhile thing that you can accomplish on your own right now."

My son says:
"So what you're saying is that you basically went through all this too? But I can't believe that you could have felt the same way that I do right now… Is that possible? But that must have been a long time ago. How did you manage to deal with it? Can you really remember just what it was like for you and what finally got you through it? I'd really like to hear your take on all of this."

I say:
"I think you're just beginning to question a lot of things that you never really considered before. What you're in the process of going through is a rite of passage from your trusting childhood self leading you on to your eventual mature adult manhood. These deep existential questions were always there, but they really didn't matter that much to you when you were young. Now they are asserting themselves and have become important and there's really no evading them anymore. They can be very personal and even painful to deal with. There's no crib sheet, and no one can give you the answers. You've got to find your own honest answers. It's very important. There's a lot that you have to confront and figure out all by yourself.

"Eventually in my own search I found solace in the thoughts expressed in the prose poem "Desiderata" by Max Ehrmann which has these all embracing and heartfelt lines in it:

> "You are a child of the universe,
> No less than the trees and the stars,
> You have a right to be here."

My son says:
"That sounds good. I like that."

I say:
"But of course there's much more to it than that! So, let me try now to give you a better answer in my own way. Let's see…to

Ehrmann's beautiful poetic sentiment, which is truly fundamental, but also really very incomplete, I'd like to add these far more basic and mundane things that to me are also quite important to acknowledge:

1. **We are all made of this world:**

"This is self-evident; we are all indigenous natives, not invading aliens. We have been created over billions of years by the still ongoing forces of evolution from the common stuff of this Earth."

2. **We are all made for this world:**

"This is also at the elemental level. We all breathe air, we drink water, and we eat local plants and animals. We have evolved in conjunction with our surroundings and we are an integral and important natural part of the total ecology of planet Earth. To put it simply, we belong here."

3. **We all only get here through an act of love:**

"Egotism is never justified in anyone, for no one of us is self created. No one fertilizes his own egg, gestates it, and gives birth to himself. We all graciously and humbly owe our existence to an act of love however great or small between male and female parents who also have parents of their own, etc, etc... We all have a genealogy and a long heritage, whether we know it or not. Most of us can never really repay the love given freely to us by our parents, and we can only hope to repay it forward to our own children."

4. **We are all best suited for the times we are born into:**

"This happens naturally as we become educated and grow into adulthood. We absorb and are made to study what our earlier predecessors have worked hard to attain and have handed down to us. We do not have to independently discover the usefulness of fire and the wheel. We have the collective benefit of all those who have come before us. This is the direct result of our human language and culture. We naturally fit into our own time. For us the radio and recorded music have always been there, for you, our children, the personal computer and cell phones are natural. We may not approve of everything, but we do fundamentally understand it all and feel at home in the present here and now."

5. We all have something important that we can do here:

"Although this is not necessarily given, nor easy to find; but when we do find our true calling in life we will feel that what we are doing is the best thing possible that we can do with our lives. This becomes our own more personally derived and practical answer to your basic question of why we are here. We will want to concentrate our energies on doing this revealed thing, and when we are not doing it we will have the nagging feeling of shirking our responsibilities. Just what this important thing is, is necessarily an individual judgment. What's very important to one person may not be important at all to another. This naturally creates a world of great richness and diversity.

"And that at the moment is my best response to your very short, and basically very deep existential question of just why we're all here. What d'ya think?"

My son says:

"OK. So I'm a child of the universe… I'll buy that, but so what! The universe is so hugely immense, and it just seems to go on and on forever and ever in time and in space! We only exist for a very short time as the very smallest most minuscule part of it all. We are merely tiny creatures inhabiting the outer crust of our Earth, an average sized rocky planet circling around our Sun, an average sized star, one of billions and billions of other stars, two-thirds of the way out on the galactic disc of the Milky Way, an average-sized spiral galaxy, one of billions and billions of other galaxies in a vast infinitely expanding universe of cold black empty space. Does the universe even know or care that I exist? How can it? Child of the universe? More like an abandoned orphan if you ask me… We are all so small and insignificant that we really are just totally meaningless."

I say:

"Whoa! Take it easy there fella… This feeling of being abandoned, meaningless and insignificant that you've just expressed is very serious stuff. We've got to dig you out of this hole! It can be very dangerous and even life threatening, but it's really not all that uncommon. As I see it, this basically comes from that small self-centered ego part of yourself... Your ego feels threatened by the fact that you are so totally dwarfed by the grand immensity of the universe and it therefore feels that it can never become anything very important given this huge setting. And basically your ego is suffering and feeling sorry for itself because all it wants is to become self-important and to be recognized as being something very special. It's the old common "Big fish in a small pond vs. Small fish in the big ocean" syndrome, and unfortunately in your extreme case your ocean is absolutely the biggest ocean of them all, it's the infinite universe! Still, you should try to overcome this feeling; it's really just a very negative, childish, and selfish response you're having to the presence of the greater reality outside of yourself. Relax – so you're alive in the big universe, big deal. Just enjoy it – it's really the only place to be."

My son says:

"Yeah, maybe so… But when I look at all those big and beautifully detailed astronomy pictures of all the many different huge galaxies of billions of stars just floating and spinning around in black empty space; the Milky Way, Andromeda, the Sombrero Galaxy, after that first impression of just how absolutely beautiful they all are passes away, I immediately begin feeling totally dazed by it, and it all spins out of control and all at once it just starts to suddenly collapse and close in on me. Then it completely physically overwhelms me and I begin to feel personally beaten down, squashed to almost nothing; in a word "meaningless." I'm in trouble, it's way beyond me, and there isn't really anything I can do about it. It all becomes very disturbing and depressing to me and then it just stays there bottled up inside me for some time. And it's not even a conscious thought that I'm having, it's just an uncontrollable physical reaction to something so overwhelming that all by itself is happening to me. Then I feel so totally oppressed by this paralyzing feeling of absolute and total insignificance that I almost have a hard time just simply breathing. I have to immediately turn away and try very hard to think about something else, something mundane and completely different. But it haunts me still and it remains there underneath everything else, that hollow feeling of my life and everything else all around me actually being totally meaningless. It's hard to get motivated about anything under these circumstances. How can I go about changing these out of control things that just, all on their own seem to be automatically happening to me?"

I say:

"Yes, that's a very good point, and you've just described it very well. But it's not really so hopeless as you make it sound… The way out is for you to bring it all up to the conscious level out in the open, like we're doing right now, and seriously think it all over and talk about it too. That's always the best way to go about affecting any long term change in your emotional outlook. You've got to confront it head on and come to a better, fuller and deeper more conscious and reality based understanding of just what all the issues are here, and then really think them all the way through. I really don't think that you've done that yet, so let's just do it right now."

My son says:

"Sure, but how exactly do you go about doing that? Don't you see? It's just the way I'm made up isn't it, and the way I naturally feel about everything? Isn't that just basically who I am? How can I possibly go about changing that? I don't really get it..."

I say:

"OK, I understand your confusion here and maybe I can help you out; I'll certainly try. I've worked out things like this before, even on myself… I went through a period in my own life I like to call my "fuck-me stage." There were things deep within myself that when I looked at them I just didn't like and I instinctively knew that many of them were outrageous and plain wrong. They were bad ideas, bad attitudes, and bad habits I had simply absorbed from my surroundings as I grew up. These were things that I had never questioned before, and they were all suddenly rising up to the surface directly confronting me and they often embarrassed me. I was embarrassing myself! It was an odd feeling to be so very disturbed and angry with my own self. Who was to blame? Just who was it really that was so embarrassed and angry at whom? Good question… So I took a hard line and said right to myself, "Fuck me!" and then I went about changing the complicated confused me I was, into the truer simpler me that I knew I ought to be. I spent the time and put my own house in order. I worked hard to understand and straighten out all the messed up stuff that was conflicted deep inside me. It was my own self-work and internal purification struggle and it took me quite a while and it was not an easy thing to do, but I sure learned a lot doing it. So I really do have some first-hand experience in this field and I think I can be of some real help here."

My son says:
"Gee, fuck-me, huh? That sounds pretty radical."

I say:
"Yes, that's right, and it was. But like I said, the best thing for us to do here is to just lay it all out bare and consciously think about your problems all out in the open, in a very straight forward, honest, and a more deeply open way. So let's both of us just do that together right now. I'll help you to get started with the basic process."

My son says:
"All right, I'm game, count me in. Have a crack at it. Let's see what you can really do to help me out here."

I say:
"Look; first off you've got to understand that everything you feel comes from something that at one time or another you've swallowed whole and taken deeply within yourself, oftentimes without your even thinking too much about it. Yes, the universe is really a very large place and teeming with possibilities. You can't change that one bit; it's just an indisputable fact of reality. Yet this is having the undesirable effect of making you feel depressed and making you think that you and everything else in the whole world is ultimately worthless and meaningless. But why? We've got to try to further understand the roots of this in a more properly reasoned way of just why this very negative emotional response is actually happening to you. That's the first thing we've got to do."

My son says:
"OK, I get what you're saying. Go on..."

I say:
"So this is the way I see it… The higher truth here is that this really shouldn't be making you feel so sad and depressed at all; but rather the more healthy natural response to it all would be that you should be feeling glad and excited about being alive and being a real conscious part of such an amazing and miraculous thing as the universe! It's really awful in the original sense of that word — meaning inspiring and full of awe! The universe is not actively opposing you and beating you down to nothing as you've just described it, and your active fantasy of anthropomorphizing it by saying that the universe *doesn't care* about you at all, is just making it all the worse for you. *The universe doesn't care about anything!* It's way beyond *caring.* The universe in all its glory just miraculously exists, and it is here for you and me to live in, experience, explore, and enjoy.

"Far from actively opposing you, the universe is actually actively supporting you all the time in many different ways, and you couldn't possibly even be here alive having these thoughts right now without its existing in just the amazing way that it does! It's really a great gift and you should try to see it that way. You should completely open yourself up to the truth of this reality, and be more appreciative of all those necessary facts that make our lives here even possible. You should re-think these things over again by yourself; it's one of the unresolved divergent aspects of what's disturbing you. But there's good news too. The good news is that you do intuitively feel this ontological conflict deep within yourself which is why you've brought it up in the first place and why we're talking about it right now. And that's good too."

My son says:
If everything's so good, like you say, then why do I feel so bad?"

I say:

"Hey, we're just getting started here, so let's focus in on that now. Listen, what all this means is that you have to realize that there is something that's gone wrong, that's askew and fundamentally unresolved deep inside of you. This is your problem. You've got a classic advanced case of psychic cosmic indigestion. You've unknowingly swallowed up and incorporated some basic misunderstanding about the true nature of yourself and the true nature of the universe at the deepest belief level of your being, and this inner conflict is now rising up to the surface, to extend our gastric metaphor, just like cosmic acid reflux disease… And that's good too, because that's how we can recognize that this problem really exists. If you just silently swallowed this thing whole and kept it submerged within yourself it would continue to fester and it could possibly ruin your life. That's why I said it was serious. People who deeply believe that their life is totally meaningless can for no apparent reason at all suddenly wind up doing absolutely crazy disastrous things. You don't want to be one of them! Once in a while you'll hear about it in the news, and the reporters will go ask their neighbors what went wrong? What was the reason that something so terrible happened there? And no one will ever really know why and it always seems to be just a totally unexpected and an unexplainable meaningless tragedy!

"So this potentially very dangerous feeling of everything being meaningless has you hotly in its grip and it's starting to take over your spirit simply because of the grand size of the universe and your ego's seemingly impossible task. And believe it or not, you're also partly enamored and fascinated by this. There's a certain romantic heroic quality about you struggling against the universe, while at the same time it's torturing you and making you feel meaningless and insignificant too. But you don't really see all its implications yet and you're still wondering just what's the meaningful part that you can possibly play in all of this…Right?"

My son says:

"OK, I'm following you so far, and what you're saying is all kind of interesting… and you're actually starting to scare me a little bit too…but I still really don't see what we can possibly do about it?

I say:

"Well, we've made a little progress here anyway… So let's just keep on delving a little more deeply into it. Perhaps now we should start concentrating our efforts on that one key word that we've both used here several times already, and that word is "meaningless." Meaningless is a human word. We humans are really the only ones around that create meaning in this world, and perhaps even in the whole universe. Without us there really is no meaning at all… So, this is yet another one of the basic sources of your anxiety that you aren't really facing up to properly, and that we'll also need to directly look into at a deeper level too. You see we humans are full of meanings; we're really very meaningful, we're not at all meaningless! Now we're starting to get somewhere, so let's just take it a little further still…"

My son says:

"Wait a sec. What do you mean by saying that we're the only thing that means anything in the universe? Are you serious? You can't be discounting everything else in the whole universe! That's one of the wildest thoughts I've ever heard. You can't possibly believe that's true now, can you?"

I say:

"Sure I can, but I only said perhaps…Meanings are not given, meanings are created. Look, it takes a conscious rational intelligent being to create any meaning at all. How many other rational intelligent life forms do you know of that are living somewhere else in the universe right now? None, right? They all only exist in science fiction stories and as special effects in movies like "E.T. the Extraterrestrial." Actually I'm among those people like that wonderfully tragic 16th century itinerant Italian Benedictine monk Giordano Bruno who believes that there are other exo-planets outside of our own solar system, and that many of these do have other native intelligent life forms inhabiting them. And that there are many and they are all widely scattered about throughout the universe somewhere. But now even four centuries after Brother Bruno first formed this original earthshaking concept, although it's not exactly "meaningless," it's still really only a vague and unsubstantiated belief.

"No one has ever proved anything like it yet. Actually though, since Bruno's time we have recently found a few large exo-planets outside our solar system in very nearby stars, but even with all our space probes and our advanced technology we have yet to recognize any other life existing outside of our own Earth. There's actually an award that exists called "The Bruno Prize" named in Giordano's honor that is offered for anyone proving that other intelligent life exists outside of our solar system, but, of course, so far it hasn't been awarded to anyone. So, believe it or not, it's still actually possible that we really are the first and the only rational ones capable of producing meanings in existence in the entire universe! This of course is a very big interesting and controversial question, but for us here it's only a small side track; so let's just keep working on that one key word we've just identified, you know, "meaningless," OK?"

My son says:

"Sure, but some time in the future I really would like to keep on talking some more with you about other intelligent life in the universe. I've already read some interesting speculative discussions and even some statistical analysis about the probability of other intelligent extraterrestrial life existing and the other closely related probability of our actually being alive at the same time and then also the possibility of our being able to find it and then even theories about how we should go about making contact and even trying to communicate with them. There's also a big astronomical organization I know of that's called The SETI Project – Search for ExtraTerrestrial Intelligence – which right now is scanning large sectors of space using modern radio telescopes that are all hooked up to computers that are analyzing and listening for any possible intelligent electromagnetic signals beamed out from any other advanced civilizations that might possibly exist somewhere else in outer space. All the distances involved are so astronomically great that this seems to be the most practical way of going about the search. It's even been mostly automated and is still ongoing, but apparently without any success as yet."

I say:

"That's right; so far it seems like nobody's home but us... that's kind of *significant*, don't you think? OK, don't worry; we'll definitely talk some more about Giordano Bruno's ideas a little later. He's really key and is an important historical figure that many people don't know very much about. He believed that an infinite God would surely only create an infinite universe, also with infinite numbers of other populated worlds in it too. He lived long ago during the Renaissance just after Copernicus and he incorporated Copernicus' ideas with his own and greatly expanded them to be much more aligned with the way that we presently understand the basic structure of the universe today. He was a true visionary way ahead of his time. Tragically he got burned alive at the stake in Rome in the year 1600 for his efforts, and he is today considered a martyr for intellectual free thought, although the Catholic Church still considers him just another heretic. But let's get back on track now and keep on exploring our own also very interesting subject of meanings..."

My son says:

"I've never heard of Bruno whatever his name is... He sounds like an interesting fellow. How did he get himself into such hot water?"

I say:

"Burned, not boiled, although I guess either one would do! They certainly had no lack of imagination on different horrible ways to torture and kill people back then. Yes, it was very bad for him, tragic really. He had great intellectual integrity and true vision in a time when the Catholic Inquisitions held unquestioned power. During his trial he never recanted his beliefs and as a result he suffered the ultimate consequences. But he is still held in great respect by some very intelligent people who honor him even to this day, and especially on February 17th the historic day of his immolation. It's really a long and very good story with a very sad ending, and he also had other original advanced philosophical ideas too. We'll talk some more about them later; but let's finally get back to our present also good discussion too, all about meaning..."

My son says:
"OK, but I'd really like to hear some more about him too."

I say:
"Sure... So, what does anything really "mean" anyway? It's all up to us. Even when we're all speaking the same language, each person will put their own personal spin on the words they use. They'll judge the meanings of the words by how they've heard them being used before during their own past experiences and other factors. Realistically it's what most discussions are finally all about. Here's the kind of deeply meaningful questions that can come up for discussion in some very good conversations:

"What do you really mean by *free will?"*
"What do you really mean by *the truth?"*
"What do you really mean by *happiness?"*
"What do you really mean by *meaningless?"*

"If everyone could totally agree on exactly what all the words they were using really meant, then they probably wouldn't have much of anything left to argue about. But of course they can't, don't, and won't. So although the words we all use are apparently the same, everyone in some way or another has their own individual unique subtle vocabulary in play all the time."

My son says:
"That's really an odd thought... So what you're saying here about meaning is that when people disagree and argue, the problem isn't actually that they are holding different conflicting ideas, but it may just be that only the words that they are using seem to have different underlying definitions for each of them? So that even the same words that they're both using don't necessarily mean the same things to each other, and that their whole conflict could be resolved if only they would just agree on what exactly their different words really meant? Is that it?"

I say:

"Yes, that's certainly a big part of it. The problem often isn't what they are apparently arguing about, but what they believe to be the underlying meanings of the abstract words that form the basis of their disagreement. Yet this subtle root problem is often very far from their focus, so that the arguments continue to circle around each other and often remain unresolved."

My son says:

"Wow, I get it. That's great stuff! I never really thought about it in that way before, but I can see the truth in what you're saying. I'm definitely going to use that idea next time I'm arguing with my friends! That will give them something to think about!"

I say:

"OK, So far so good… But I've got to do everything I possibly can to break the hold that this very stifling feeling of everything being meaningless has over you. It's very important for your own well being that we break you out of this debilitating existential trap that you've been caught up in! But I can see now that this won't be too easy and it's definitely going to require some very strong medicine. Hmm…

"So, let's see now, "*meaningless*"… OK, let's just focus in on what exactly is the full meaning of that one word "meaningless" – of having no meaning. Hmm… Like what are all the ramifications and the full implications of it? Hmm… What can we definitely say about the full overall meaning and implications of everything being totally meaningless and therefore having no meaning at all, and what exactly in the end does all that really mean? I don't know… Hmm…"

My son says:

"I smell the wood burning… Dad – I don't really get what you're driving at… Just what do you think you're going to accomplish with all this weird meaningless stuff – like just focusing on what that one word *"meaningless"* really means anyway?… It's meaningless, it doesn't mean anything! I can't see the point of it…It just doesn't really seem possible to me that there can be very much of anything there… if there's even anything there at all … This whole approach just seems totally meaningless to me! Ha, ha, ha… Hey, that's kind of funny, isn't it? We're both like just caught up in this one big weird endless meaningless loop! I don't really get it…What are you up to? Why are you even going through all this dumb meaningless stuff anyway? Get real Dad; there really can't be anything very meaningful there at all now. Can there be? I don't think so… Please if you don't mind, I think you're on a wild goose chase; just wake me up when it's all over."

I say:
"Hey, I'm doing all this just for your benefit kiddo; so don't be a little twerp! Just because you don't see it, that doesn't mean that there's nothing there. Have some patience please! I'll grant you, this one's a little strange and it really isn't all that easy too, ya know… But I just know that there is something meaningful here. I can feel it… It's kind of like a riddle within a conundrum… It's got a certain quirky puzzle like quality to it that seems almost like some new kind of Zen koan or something. Hmm… Yes, I like that idea…

"Wow that is a rather interesting possibility though… I hadn't really considered it from that angle before… I don't know. Hmm… Well, that's kind of an odd bit too, isn't it? Yes, but I like it! Hmm… Well yes, maybe if…

"Yes! That's it…Yes! It's all good and it's really very interesting too!"

My son says:
"Whatchagot?"

I say:
"Listen up Sprout…Sometimes we've got to be creative and think a little outside the box here. Now we're going to try out something that's brand new just for you… It's some strong medicine I've cooked up that just might do the trick. Might be just what the doctor ordered to help you overcome your own self-described present

overwhelmingly "meaningless" condition. Let's just see if you can swallow this medicine whole too. Try to follow along and think this thing through with me now, and I just hope that you'll be able to understand and really appreciate what it's all about, and that you'll also be able to see the real beauty of it – OK, here we go:

> ***"If you really and truly feel that "everything is meaningless," which is just what you've been telling me, right? Then you've also got to understand and accept what follows directly from that idea, which is this: that that basic fact itself – that everything is meaningless – is also meaningless too! It simply has to be, right? Just like everything else that is also meaningless! It just can't possibly be the only thing that has any real meaning if everything is meaningless! Now can it? Of course not! And that's good news too! Because if it is essentially meaningless that everything is meaningless, then it's still quite possible for things to actually have great meaning! And they do!"***

My son says:

"WHAT? Are you NUTS? How can that be true? You really need to have your head examined! Are you seriously trying to tell me right now that things HAVE meaning BECAUSE everything is meaningless? That just can't be, Dad! What's gotten into you? That has got to be the stupidest and most totally idiotic thing I've ever heard anyone say in my whole entire life! That's not only illogical, but I think I'd really have to call that idea completely "ANTI-LOGICAL!" Not only does it totally ignore basic logic which is the very cornerstone of all our critical modern human thinking. BUT it also directly flies in the face of one of the most fundamentally basic concepts of General Mathematical Set Theory itself which clearly states that... If there is a set "A," then there must also exist a complementary set "not A." And that then, everything that exists has to be EITHER in set "A" OR in "not A." What you're now actually saying to me right here is this: that "A = not A." Dad, did you just hear that? That was Euclid rolling over in his grave!"

I say:

"Ha, ha, ha… That's a good one too! But you're right, that's just how fundamental it is! I was afraid that you wouldn't really get the gist of this… But I didn't think you'd totally fly off the handle and even go and tell old Euclid on me! Listen, I just told you that this was going to take some strong medicine. And it IS a little like breaking Euclid's prime axiom of identity… But to be more accurate, what I'm saying is actually a little more subtle than that.

"To break you out of your stifling self-defeating conundrum, what I'm really saying to you in all seriousness now is this: that EVEN IF we do accept your premise that everything is meaningless, BUT THEN just on account of what that REALLY MEANS and what are the TRUE OVERALL IMPLICATIONS of it, that in its fullest realization it also finally results in the total meaninglessness of all things being meaningless too, and that therefore things really CAN STILL have meaning! Don't you see, that's the real BEAUTY of it! So here's what we can truly say is the full and total meaning of this idea of "Everything being meaningless," which is this: that yes, IF you like, everything CAN be meaningless; but it DOESN'T mean that things HAVE TO BE meaningless, because as we've just pointed out, "IF everything is meaningless it is THEN also ultimately meaningless that things are meaningless too, which then CLEARLY ALLOWS for meanings to still exist! Get it? That's really it in a nutshell…"

My son says:

"You're the nutshell, or maybe I should just call you a nut case!"

I say:

"No, no, don't you see? This is actually a very good result for us! For now this very odd yet clearly demonstrated truth that we've just firmly established here should be able to ultimately shatter your previously ill conceived idea of a totally "meaningless world," and open you up to what in reality is the really very meaningful world that actually already exists all around you. And this will greatly enhance your freedom and it should also open up for you new vistas of many other meaningful new experiences, and it will also provide you with some necessary extra personal space so that you'll be able to breathe a little easier too!

My son says:

"Clearly demonstrated? That would be nice, but give me a break; I know you're trying to help me out here, but your being so deeply caught up in this crazy "meaningless/meaningful" concept of yours… you've got to admit that it's really way out there. I'm sorry, but I can't really see how it makes any sense at all, Dad…"

I say:

"Don't you see? What I've just proven to you even by starting out from your own ideas is that in fact everything is not meaningless! And I have been very clear and rational all the way through this explanation and you now have no option but to agree with me that it's NOT at all "ANTI-LOGICAL," whatever that is; but that it's really ONLY LOGICAL! And therefore I can say to you Q.E.D. which stands for what our old Greek friend Euclid himself used to add to the end of all his geometric proofs, *"Quod erat demonstrandum."* – That which was to be demonstrated. Hah!

My son says:

"Oh really? I don't know… Don't get me wrong Dad, I do very much appreciate all the thought and trouble that you've just put into this very strange idea of yours… and right now I can't really refute what you've been saying; but it all still really sounds like very shaky logic, and it also all seems in some ways down right sneaky to me… It's still a little hard for me to totally wrap my head around just what you've done here… It seems an awful lot like an end run…or circular reasoning to me or something like that. I don't know… I can't really see the whole thing all that clearly yet, and I'll just have to wait a little while till it clears up some more and then I'll have time to sit down and quietly re-think everything all over again…"

I say:

"Don't bother… Meaning is all important. Things are not meaningless. Don't you see? It's just the opposite; everything has meaning, and not just one meaning either. Meaning is rampant and it doesn't even exist as its own simple separate thing. People are always bringing their own meanings into play and overlay them on all their own experiences and on all the different things that are happening around them too. Many different people are walking around in many self-created yet different meaningful realities simultaneously, all the time, all over the place. It may seem strange to you, but the same exact thing can have many different meanings to many different people. We humans are hard wired to constantly automatically give meanings to everything! As I said we humans are really a very meaningful life form, and we're all totally chock full of meanings, and you are too. Unfortunately the deeper you delve into just what meaning itself really is and how it comes about, the more elusive it can become. In the end it remains an individual judgment of your own self-created inner spirit. Nonetheless it is not arbitrary and it forms the whole weave and fabric of each person's perceived reality, and is the basis of how we can come to understand complex ideas and even how we come to know or understand anything at all."

My son says:

"I don't get it. I don't feel like I'm really doing anything at all most of the time. But you're saying that while I'm just hanging out and having fun with my friends, or even when I'm just walking around all by myself, that all the while I'm actually really very busy internally creating many meaningful things about everything that's happening all around me all the time. Do you really expect me to believe that?"

I say:

"Yes, definitely. Not only are you the constant creator of myriads of different meanings every day and throughout your life, but you are also always involved in the active process of mining all those meanings you have already created to help you navigate your way through the complexity of living your everyday life as a human being. If you ever lose access to all these meanings, by a brain injury, or a stroke, or slowly like an Alzheimer patient does, then you will also simply lose this basic ability to consciously do what's required to get around in the real world.

But not only are you always making and using your own meanings, but you also mean just what you are too. What do I really mean by this? Just that people will judge the meaning of what you have to say in the light of their own opinions of just who they think you are. They will judge your meanings by what you mean to them! This is perhaps one of the best features of our legal system; the fact that in a jury trial, the jury must sit and listen to each witness and judge for themselves how to evaluate their testimony and just what weight to give to it. To pass judgment is the final act in a long series of the application and evaluation of many linked meanings concerning the many different aspects of the thing being judged. In the end the jurors must decide on the meaning of the entire case before them by evaluating and distilling everything they've just heard over weeks of testimony down to just one very meaningful word: either "guilty" or "innocent."

"Unlike our British-based legal system with its many different levels of courts and its organized due process of multiple appeals; in our own inner lives we often never get the chance to review or appeal any of our own personal judgments of our own experiences once we've made them. We just gather them all within ourselves and they become incorporated as part of our own ongoing identity and so too become a part of the controlling forces in the subtle invisible background level of our lives.

"They all just quietly accumulate and sit there and remain permanently part of the resources that our inner being has to work with. It only gets to work with what we give it. That is unless we decide to actively look within ourselves and try to perform some kind of conscious self-work evaluation of our own mental condition and thinking process. But this is a rare thing. Then if we can take this objective approach, and if we are serious and persistent we can actively work within ourselves and we may be able to find out just what we've at one time swallowed whole that makes up this universally important yet almost entirely invisible background environment that actually forms the basis for all our decisions and the real groundwork of our own individual character. What exactly are the buried roots of our own long standing beliefs that at one time we swallowed whole which are still actively involved in forming and directing our own feelings and are making all our important ongoing thoughts and decisions? Do you really know what they are?"

My son says:

"Dad, are you really serious? I just don't understand what you could possibly mean by all this… I'M THE ONE directing MY OWN feelings, and I'M THE ONE making ALL OF MY OWN important ongoing thoughts and decisions, ISN'T THAT RIGHT? Really, WHO ELSE COULD IT BE? Or as you might colorfully put it: I'M THE SOLE CAPTAIN IN COMMAND OF MY OWN SHIP! Come on now, just what the heck are you talking about here?"

I say:

"Yes you are, but not in the way you think you are. There is a complex undercurrent of random beliefs that you don't realize you have unconsciously identified with and have incorporated deep within yourself over time that are all playing an important role in directing everything you think about and do. You need to examine and understand what these basic underlying assumptions are that are silently at work within yourself to become a more unified and consciously life affirming human being than you are now. You are presently actively stumbling over problems within yourself that you are unaware of and that you don't really understand. You have to become deeply introspective and work it all out to have a chance at finally becoming consciously your own true self."

My son says:

"What do you mean? I am already my true self. Are you saying that I'M NOT REALLY TRULY ME? Come on now, I don't think so… That's not possible. This is all nonsense. I feel very much EXACTLY TOTALLY JUST LIKE ME! Believe me, I'M 100% ME. Who else could I be?"

I say:

"You are not the me that you potentially fully could be, the whole conscious self-unified me that you should be and deserve to be. Very few of us are… and this will not, and does not happen on its own. It requires conscious effort. Self-realization requires true self-knowledge, that's the only way it comes about. The process that lies before you is the self-work, should you take it up; and it is the most essential part of becoming a fully conscious, unified, meaningful and empathetic spiritual being. Old Socrates, that original fully self-aware Athenian of the 5th century BC, who once profoundly remarked that, "The unexamined life is not worth living," still smiles his tacit approval on all our efforts in any such activities as these. This is exactly what he recommends we should all be doing to live a life "worth living" and it still rings true! For this is the real way out, of leaving the isolating dark shadowy cave and coming out into the unifying clear light of self-realized consciousness. Socrates, that long dead Greek of old, was a trailblazer and he'll always still be there encouraging us and cheering us onward towards this end."

My son says:

"Dad, how come you're always talking about these old long dead people like they're your best friends and are all still alive and just might be sitting right in the next room about to walk in here and have a cup of tea with us?"

I say:

"Because for me they are. They are my true intellectual partners and they are all still alive within me. I know them better than some of my own real living friends right now. In my mind Socrates is really cheering us onward toward doing the self-work of examining our own inner selves to live a life worth living. This is everyone's own perpetual independent study assignment given directly to us from Socrates of long ago. And this is exactly what we've been trying to do here in the current curious case of the basically unresolved internal existential conflict between you and the universe. Ain't that right, Socrates?"

(Socrates doesn't answer, but he's smiling and nodding up and down in total agreement. He knows full well that I'm just another one of his many latter day acolytes.)

"I think we've done well here shedding some light on a few of the more critical points of the problem at hand. You are truly an amazing, beautiful, significant and meaningful part of this miraculous universe that we all inhabit. Don't you ever doubt that. And you shouldn't really have any direct emotional conflicts about your being here either. Do you love your mother who brought you to life? Do you love the universe that sustains your life?"

My son says:
"You know I love mom very much."

I say:
"What about me?"

My son says:
"Dad…"

****

More on What Meaningful Means

This above discussion about the meaning of things reminds me of a period in my life when I was becoming an artist and learning about the fine art of painting. I would go to many galleries and art museums and I would often stand before a great oil painting in a public place and wonder just what to make of it. How was I supposed to judge this work of art, what meaning did it really have? I instinctively knew that the work must be of some importance since it was considered worthy of public display, but exactly in what ways? Is it good? Is it great? Is it a masterpiece? Or could it even be perhaps just bad art masquerading as good art just to make money? How could I tell what exactly it was? What was to be my basis for understanding it?

While standing there as a rank novice, but also being a sensitive observer held in its aura and not knowing exactly how to evaluate this painting for sure; others with more formed opinions would also come up to it within my earshot, and as I stood there I could hear them commenting to their companions about the qualities that they saw in this very same work of art:

> "Oh, look at this; it is from his earlier period, see how crude his colors are."
>
> Or
>
> "This is one of his more vibrant and bold works, see how the colors vibrate against each other."
>
> Or
>
> "Here he is still under the influence of his teacher; he has not yet fully matured and realized his own true style."
>
> Or
>
> "Notice the whimsy in his original brush work, a true master."
>
> Or
>
> "Here he is totally out of control, they shouldn't even hang this piece, and it's just another one of his pot boilers he churned out."

All these people were commenting on the very same painting that I was standing in front of too. What is it? Is it crude? Vibrant and bold? Not yet realized? Does it have original whimsy? Is it an out of control pot boiler? What's a pot boiler anyway? The painting was just silently hanging there on its own, still the same, it hadn't changed one bit. What was going on here? Why did so many different people see the same thing in so many different ways?

This painting, as all works of art, has more than one meaning. In this as with all things whose meaning requires individual subjective judgment, people bring to it all their own past knowledge and experiences, and it becomes an active theater of self-revelation. Everyone's own deeply formed beliefs, opinions and prior judgments of similar things are brought to bear – the total accumulation of their own unique internal set of "non-stuff" – is called forth into action and at the same time is clearly revealed.

I too would one day also become part of this ongoing chorus of critics and form my own strongly held personal opinions of just what it was. This is the end result of the natural process of aesthetic maturation. As you mature you'll eventually find out at a very deep level just who you uniquely are and what you feel is worthwhile; just what it is that you value above all else, and you will develop a lasting respect and deep admiration for those things that intrinsically possess and exhibit these same values too, be it artwork, people, politics, or otherwise. You will find yourself irresistibly drawn to them. You'll naturally feel communion with those artists whose creative oeuvre unmistakably represent these same aesthetic values in their work. Great art is always a symbolic representation of our deepest values. Stand quietly for a while in front of an interesting painting in a busy metropolitan art museum sometime and then creatively eavesdrop and see for yourself what it means to different people. You may be amused, surprised, and perhaps even amazed.

I remember one time being in the Museum of Modern Art and standing in front of the surrealist René Magritte's famous painting "The Empire of Light" and in the midst of admiring it, when a father and daughter came upon it too. This masterpiece is an odd nocturne where the sky above is bright but the street scene below is dark. In it centrally located is a streetlight that is painted so well that it appears to be actually turned on and gently illuminating the evening village scene around it. "Is that a real light?" the wide-eyed young girl asked her father. "No," was all he said. But I looked at her kindly and explained it a little better, "That's real light you're seeing, but it's not a real streetlight."

But it is also important to question just what is the meaning of meaning, and just how stable are the meanings that we attribute to the things that we think we already understand and know what their meanings are. Even the long established meanings of those things we have directly experienced in our own personal lives, are not really simple fixed things and over time these can dramatically change too. As we ourselves mature and evolve spiritually, our own understanding of these deeper things also matures and develops simultaneously, just like our aesthetic judgments of paintings as well as other things in general.

Sometimes as you get older and become an adult you may hear a song, or see an old movie, or re-read a favorite old book that you loved and may not have looked at or even thought about for many years. Often times you'll find that you will now experience it from a new and different perspective and that you will come away from the experience with an altered opinion of the value and meaning of that same work of art than the one that you'd previously held for all these intervening years. I once had the personally very upsetting experience of bringing some good friends of mine to see a revival of an old independent art movie that I thought was really great, and I wound up squirming in my seat in the dark because I now thought it was so very dreadful! This at first may puzzle and then even embarrass you, as it did me… What's going on here? Obviously the work of art hasn't changed; but its meaning to you has greatly changed simply because in the interim you yourself have greatly changed! So we've got be careful in the meanings we ascribe to things and even to the meanings of things in our own past direct personal experiences. This is of course especially true in our youth as we are gaining many new experiences in the world and our values are in the active process of maturing within ourselves.

This is one common and useful way to receive some direct feedback about your own spiritual growth. It is not an easy thing to gain an objective external perspective on yourself and the changes that occur in your inner belief values, since your own judging mind is also contained within them. These unexpected changes in the values of things we have already experienced and judged once before in our own past can offer us a rare clear window into our own inner spiritual development which is normally hidden from us. When these things happen to you, you should take a moment to reflect on your own spiritual growth. How and why do you now perceive it from a new point of view and give it a different value? What has changed within yourself to account for this, do you understand it and is it an overall positive change? It can be a very useful and an important self-revealing tool on our own spiritual journey, especially since in our own minds we tend to think of ourselves as being much more constant and unchanging than in truth we actually are.

My son says:

"Jeez Dad! We can't go around doubting everything we think we already know… Where would that lead us? Obviously into much more self-doubt which is just what I'm trying to overcome here. This idea isn't very helpful to me at all… I thought you were trying to help me out to get a better grip on things, but it seems to me that you're now undermining everything totally by saying that meaning itself is a very slippery thing. But I don't really buy that because every time I look things up in the dictionary everything there is really very specific. Definite words always mean definite things… What the heck are you talking about now?"

I say:

"Ah yes, words…Clever…Words are the cultural tools we all share in common. But meaning in life is what you build with those tools. Just because the tools appear to be stable doesn't mean that the structures we build with them will be stable too, and everything will warp and become unrecognizable over many intervening years. You aren't old enough to have experienced that yet. The language structures written down and left behind may still be in tact, but all the unspoken principles and the underlying assumptions leading up to their specific choice and use in its creation will be lost forever. Language is not a static thing either, but it is also a living thing that changes and evolves over time in its own way parallel and organically with its parent living human cultures. This is always a natural ongoing process and there's no way to stop it. Everything including language is in a constant state of evolution."

My son says:

"Everything is evolving all the time?"

I say:

"Yes, of course. Evolution is not just an abstract concept in biology. You'll understand this more clearly as you get older. You'll actually see it happening in the real world all around you. And there is no stopping it either. It is a reflection of the great Tao in the process of ever newly unfolding itself. You will see many instances of this in your own lifetime.

"But it's strange to think about the very abstract nature of what words are. It's fun to sometimes try to hear your own native language as a foreigner does – it's not that easy to just hear the sounds of it without attaching any meaning or content to it. Or you can choose any multi-syllable word and just say that same word rapidly out loud repeating it over and over again many times in a row. Very soon it will start to spontaneously disassociate and crumble and disappear right in front of you. It will soon become what it truly is, just an irrational weird group of sounds that you will find yourself babbling out loud for no apparent reason at all, and its normal meaning that was just recently so clearly solid and obvious will simply evaporate.

"But although this is the strange underlying truth of our language, its real foundation is based on use; the unstated cultural acceptance of its universal usefulness and the fundamental understanding that it is the most important thing that we all share in common. It is all we really have for the surface rational mind to hold on to and to be able to properly orient itself to the conditions of life present in the real world around us. No matter what else you may think, language is truly humanity's greatest invention. It is also the essential portal between the two different infinities that we all are constantly and simultaneously living in."

My son says:

"I don't really ever think of language as an invention…In fact I can't even remember not knowing it. It just seems to have been naturally in my head all the time. Yes, I learned how to spell and how to write, but did I ever really learn language? I can't even remember, I don't think so…But in English classes in school they make it so overly complicated by trying to rationally explain everything about it and just how it all works together with so many rules and a bunch of other made-up words like subject, predicate, gerund, prepositional phrase, transitive or intransitive verb, subjunctive tense, present progressive, pluperfect, and so on and on… They've created another whole complicated different language just to explain the original language that everybody knows already, and then they give you all these additional crazy complicated rules about it too. It's really bizarre when you stop and think about it."

I say:

"Well, that's just what academics naturally do; it gives them all a *"raison d'être."* Remember what that phrase means? Yes, words like "subjective, objective, adjective, adverb, dependent clause" and all those others you've mentioned and many more are really invented "meta-words," or words about words, and you'll never hear them used in any other context. In fact every profession has its own dedicated jargon and becoming a member of it, like becoming a doctor, a lawyer, a plumber, or a stock broker means that essentially you have to learn a whole new and very specialized professional language, new words with ever finer and more precise meanings to them. This new language will then appear totally opaque and incomprehensible to any non-members of that occupation, and that exclusivity is also a very important part of it. I find it funny that when you tell a doctor what's wrong with you, usually he'll simply repeat what you said to him in Latin, and that's the diagnosis! They'll also say other meaningless things to you like "Drink plenty of liquids." That's really the only thing I drink, what's the alternative, to drink plenty of solids?

"Unfortunately the overall trend now appears to be that the more and more you study the narrower and narrower your focus becomes until finally you know almost everything about almost nothing. That's what it means to be educated these days. It wasn't always this way… Whatever became of the ideal of expanding our knowledge and finally gaining wisdom? I guess wisdom is not a saleable commodity any more, and the marketplace is king! But we are once again straying from our own topic of interest here…

"Going back to what you've just said earlier, it's not really that meaning is a slippery thing, or that we shouldn't trust our own beliefs, but more that it's an ever evolving thing too. And it is a thing that depends very much on each person's uniquely created inner reality of what they know and understand to be the meanings of their own present realized truths. Unfortunately these truths are not in any sense universal, but are all of an individually formed nature, and as we have just seen these truths also are not static but they too are ever evolving within each person's inner spirit as it develops over time."

My son says:

"Wow Dad, are things really all that complicated? I just don't think so. In fact I never even think about all these little subtle things about language and meanings that you are bringing up right now. And I don't think anybody else really does either. Aren't you just completely over analyzing this whole thing? I just think you're in it way too deep and that you're totally blowing it all out of proportion."

I say:

"Well, I'm trying to be as clear as possible with you, and the deeper you go, the deeper it gets. Just determining the meanings of many different things is one of the main ongoing jobs of our inner autonomous spirit. This very important functioning may all normally happen without your giving it too much thought. In fact you may not even be aware of it at all. Maybe that's what you're saying right now… And it may seem to be happening more or less automatically, all on its own just below the conscious level for you. But consciously understanding just what's really going on inside your mind, well that isn't quite so simple, and that's what we're trying to do here.

"This autonomous inner spirit that we all possess is in fact independent and it doesn't blindly obey the wishes of even our own conscious mind, but it develops all on its own and in its own unique true way. If you can through your own self-work become a whole empathetic spiritual being it will unite and become one with your purified and unified conscious mind. This is the great enlightened goal that we all should be striving for – self-realization and self-unification. Try to become one and whole within yourself. But if you are not successful you will still be split apart and remain an internally divided being whose conscious self has become divergent and separated from one's autonomous inner spirit and this can only result in continuing inner turmoil. You'll be a sitting duck, and you will be very embarrassed if Socrates ever comes around your way again and starts asking you about the weather or some other mundane thing.

"As your inner spirit matures and develops, so too in a similar manner, will the many different meanings that you ascribe to the world around you. They will also simultaneously evolve too, seemingly automatically all on their own. You should be aware of this odd often hidden nature of the self and to be able to allow for it when necessary and to act accordingly."

My son says:
"So all that's what's the meaningless meaning of what meaningful really means is, is it, Dad?"

I say:
"Don't be cavalier about it; this is serious stuff, or rather "non-stuff!" Most people never even approach this level of understanding of just what their life is all about, or even can be all about. I hope that all this long and very convoluted discussion we've just been having has helped you to see more clearly, understand and appreciate the great importance and also the very subtle nature of just what that abstract thing that we simply call "meaning" truly is. Do you really get the deep meaning of just what being meaningful really means? And how chock full of meanings everything actually is, and just how much you will be throwing away if you ever find yourself falling back into that stifling condition you were in of believing that "everything is meaningless?"

My son says:
"Well, you've certainly given me a lot to think about."

I say:
"If you ever again truly believe that everything is meaningless then your life will become meaningless too at that very same moment. I hope that you can now see this as a very dangerous, even deadly and self-defeating existential trap you were in. Do you really understand how very serious this all can be? I've been working very hard here to try and get you out of its clutches. I've done my best and

I hope that now you've got a better and deeper awareness of what all these very important issues are."

My son says:
"OK Dad, I'll give it up to you… After all this, I've got to say that you definitely have that one word "meaningless" pretty well covered. I like what you've said and it does make me feel a little better about everything… But what about that other word, "insignificant?"

I say:
"Well, if you're meaningful you are not insignificant."

My son laughs:
"Ha ha ha… That's too easy, Dad!"

I say:
"OK, Sprout… You've got the rest of your life to make yourself significant to others. Go ahead, go on out there and see what you can accomplish! Good luck! Do your best, and along the way try to meet and get involved with other bright creative people too. There's a lot of positive synergistic energy to be found in real honest friendships with good people. Have fun when you can, but don't get too distracted, and always try to keep your eye on the big picture too…

"Also please remember that no matter what you do, and no matter whatever happens to you out there, you will always be very significant and meaningful to me."

Chapter 2
Everything Ends, but Nothing Begins

My son says:

"But we have been created by evolution, by mere chance. What possible deep meaning can mere chance have?"

I say:

"You're right, and Charles Darwin agrees with you. We have developed through the process science calls evolution, and it is foolish to argue against it. And it is also true that the driving forces of evolution are random chance mutations. This again is what science directly tells us. But you must understand that evolution is not what we are; it is only the mechanism that has brought us about.

"Yes indeed, you are absolutely right that the input of evolution is governed by pure chance as far as which genetic mutations occur and when; but don't forget that the outcome of evolution results from the concurrent external forces of natural selection. This is the all important other complementary part of evolution that's not governed by chance. We have been selected by nature over many thousands of generations as the latest and the best of our species. Humans are perhaps the most highly re-engineered and mutated life form that has ever appeared on this earth. Through this outlandish process of both invisible random chance molecular events, and overcoming severely selective natural survival pressures, we have developed the uniquely important ability of adaptively changing our own environment and even ourselves to form a better fit. That's what is really so special about us humans."

My son says:

"Sometimes when I hear the news about how our developing human activities are negatively affecting our own local environment and are even impacting the whole Earth's ecosystems, I feel like it's all totally hopeless. Even when all the scientists agree and are saying one thing, the politicians are not listening to them, and everything just keeps on going like nobody's navigating and we're all just cruising along towards a cliff at top speed on autopilot and no one seems to care. Everybody just keeps on doing what they've always been doing. Then pollution, population, global warming, and all sorts of things just keep on slowly building up all the time, and we all know that there are critical levels and tipping points somewhere, eventually something has to give...Things often seem to be totally out of control but nobody's really paying any attention to the whole process of what's actually happening. It seems like everyone has blinders on and is just looking out for themselves. They all just want to be the lucky ones. It makes me feel like there is something extremely dysfunctional in mankind in general and that we're all just an ongoing experiment of nature that's eventually surely going to fail, and then we'll all become extinct just like the dinosaurs and like so many other species before us. Don't you ever feel that way too? Why was I born? What's really the point of all this?"

I say:

"Whoa! Buck up, Sprout...Why were you born? That's a terrible thing to ask your own father! You were born simply because of your mother's and my love for each other. And now we both love you very much too. Are you really asking me what's the point of all this love? Really? What's the point of a beautiful flower? What's the point of a beautiful painting? Just beauty itself is the point! Love and beauty, just by the very improbability of their existence, enrich all who come in contact with them. The more love and beauty there can be in this world the better off the world will be. When there is total love and true beauty everywhere we will all be back in Eden. And now you also have the chance to participate and even to contribute in creating more of it. We've invited and escorted you into this world to be here and share with us the many beautiful and loving experiences of a lifetime! What greater gift can there be?

My son says:

"I know, I know...I'm sorry, Dad... I really am thankful to be here, but it's just all so complicated...There are so many things happening to me all at once..."Love is all you need," but is it? That sounds so very simplistic and purely romantic. Will love and beauty cure and heal the planet? I don't realistically see how they can."

I say:

"Yes they can, if it's the right kind and there's enough of it. Don't think that love is small and ineffectually weak; it is really enormous and very powerful… and love has the unique advantage in that by its expression it naturally creates more and greater love in others and not its opposing forces as hate and fear do. Love is like light, and fear is like darkness. The darkness can never ever overcome the light. If the light goes out, darkness will be there, but even a single small match will always cause eons of darkness to simply vanish."

My son says:

"Yes, that's all very beautiful and poetic, but it's really only another one of your metaphors. It just might make you feel better, but it's not really going to accomplish anything."

I say:

"Right, it's still up to us to do things. But to really count, what we do must be based on something true and profound. I recently asked you if you loved the universe…all these problems you're troubled by can be solved if we all could just learn to love the universe a little more and not see it as only an inanimate stage. These problems were mostly created by warped introverted love of self, money and power. Some wouldn't even call these things love at all, but they are not looking deep enough. These people have cut themselves off from real love and as a result, much of this introverted love comes from an isolated survivalist fear of shortages and from their ego-centric concept of being in a struggle alone against the world. To quell this fear they start wanting more and more stuff to shield themselves with, but it's never enough. It becomes their unfulfillable quest, and they view life through the lens of "an us verses them" mentality. We're still caught up in the mindset of what the great president FDR once warned us about, "The only thing to fear is fear itself." Real love, sharing with others, all of life, the Earth, the Universe, and more is what is lacking. If we really all could accept and understand that the Earth has truly been given to us as our sacred trust, and learn to live accordingly… Yes, love can save our planet... Take heart. You're not in this alone; we're all in it together. Always have been and always will be."

My son says:

"I know, I know, but just look at the history of it all. Mankind is constantly pushing everything to the brink, including biological diversity, the climate, water quality, and population. Dad, it's really already become pretty bleak now, hasn't it?"

I say:

"The American Indians already long ago lived this great truth I've just mentioned. They felt and understood their oneness with nature and tried to walk in peace with the Great Spirit. They didn't even have a concept of private property, for it was totally inconceivable to them that anyone could own what the Great Spirit has freely given to all. The phrase "Indian giver" is totally misunderstood by most people. Among the Indians things were not owned individually, but held in community. So if you needed something an Indian had, he would gladly give it to you, but if he needed it again in the future he naturally expected you to give it back to him. We can still learn from their example how to live more lightly and in greater harmony with nature. The Indian's way was right and in natural harmony for his time, but we must learn how to do this in a new and different modern way. And you're right, now it does seem like we are pushing nature to its limits and it is offering us a stark ultimatum.

"But this gift of a lifetime you possess also comes with great responsibility... What you do with your life is naturally framed by everything that is currently happening right now in the context of our present-day world. The point of all this that you're now complaining about is: to help you find and actualize your own true self and in so doing to become an active conscious living and loving part of the ongoing story of creation; for you to experience and contribute your own true self in your own unique way to the Greatest Show on Earth; to become an active responsible contributing member of the Universe in its active and present form; and for you to be able to offer up your own direct input and to share in helping others to bring about its future reality. The most important thing is for you to feel that what you are doing matters, to yourself, to others, and to the universe."

My son says:
"I am not responsible for the future of the Universe! Come on now, give me a break…You're really going off the deep end here. As far as I know I didn't ask to even be here, but maybe I'm wrong… Yes, there are a lot of problems in our modern world that need our attention… and yes, now thanks to you and mom I'm now also a part of all this too. But just put a lid on it Dad, you have a tendency to always exaggerate everything to the ultimate. Let's try to keep it a little more in perspective here… How can I possibly have anything at all to do with the future of the Universe?"

I say:
"I didn't say that the future of the Universe depends on you, but you are certainly a living conscious part of it. You are a unique meaningful individual part of the whole that is also at the same time aware of the rest of it – how else could we even be having this conversation right now? The more you understand and accept this fact and what it means, the better off you'll be."

My son says:
"That's really a very grand vision of what one person's role in life is all about. To me you're being overly dramatic here and much too romantic. It's like you're presenting me with some kind of a corny overblown plot in a bad musical… "*Let's all get together and save the Universe! Da da da dat dat dat!*" Do you really believe all this? Get real. Be honest, tell me the truth. Do you really think about all these grand things when you're making your own daily decisions in your own everyday life?"

I say:
"I do really believe that this is the ultimate and highest truth of our existence here, and I'm always being honest with you, don't ever doubt that please. No, you don't have to be conscious of this whole, as you put it "grand vision of things" all the time. But it is something that you need to think about and make your peace with deeply at

least once, and then put this reality into active practice by creating the ongoing positive life-affirming inner habits of your daily life. This may all seem very abstract to you now, but it is how you live your life and it will all become very important to you in the end. The way you live your life will determine your fate. No doubt about it.

"In the beginning you must realize the deep nature of what it means to be alive and to then try to become a responsible person. That's what you're struggling with right now. Then you'll need to form the deeper automatic internal belief structures in your own being that will unconsciously respond in the right way to the events in your everyday life that will be happening to you. That's what it means to be a responsible person. As a very simple "no-brainer" example of what I'm talking about here – you shouldn't have to consciously think about all the ecological arguments for recycling every time you are about to throw something away. But at one time or another you just need to reach the full understanding that this is the right thing to do both for yourself and for the planet, and then develop your own ecologically positive long-term recycling habits. This should then become imprinted as one of your own automatic behaviors, and it will then subtly add to your own perceived self-worth. You will then have escaped some small amount of our universal human environmental guilt."

My son says:

"What do you mean by environmental guilt? What am I guilty of? I just got here; I didn't start all this stuff! You sound like a religious nut talking about original sin. Why are we always all being made to feel guilty of something? It's just a way to make everyone cower and toe the line and that makes it easier for the powers that be to dominate us, don't you think?"

I say:

"Look, you've got to face the facts that we humans are basically an exploitive group. We are very successful animals and we have now developed the modern scary unanticipated potential to unintentionally wreak havoc upon ourselves and the planet too. Our great recent success story has also paradoxically become our greatest imminent danger. No, you didn't start it, but now you're here and you're one of us, and that definitely makes you part of it all. Over most of our species' collective history this potential danger was greatly minimized since our numbers were so much smaller. When we acted exploitively, it was not on a worldwide industrial scale, but on a much smaller local scale too, and it was by means of much more forgiving natural methods. But now that our amazing present-day technologies have become so much more efficient and highly developed since the industrial revolution, this is no longer the case. As they say, "the chickens are coming home to roost..." All those things you just mentioned earlier are now seriously coming into play at a very large trans-national scale and are beginning to threaten the earth's life sustaining ecosystems worldwide. All the old methods and goals that have worked so well in the past have brought us to the brink of the next level. But there is still a lot of inertia in the old systems and there is no operative consensus on just what the right path to that next stage should be.

"To me the greatest and most important ideas now are how to use our modern advanced technology, not to capitalistically maximize profit and perpetuate endless growth; but instead how to achieve a steady state economy with renewable natural non-polluting energy systems and total recycling that will allow most of mankind to live an essentially non-exploitive existence in relative comfort without in the process completely "soiling our own nest."

My son says:

"Yeah, I completely agree with you. You're right. But isn't the economic capitalistic deck stacked against us? And who is actively doing the work necessary to actually get there?"

I say:

"Buckminster Fuller, with his popularization of the concept of "Spaceship Earth," was an early 20th century visionary and practical inventor in this field. He was able to foresee many of the coming new developing problems and environmental concerns. He spent much of his life's energy contributing to solving many of these threatening dilemmas which he saw looming on the horizon, not only technologically but also philosophically.

"When I'm working on a problem I never think about beauty. But when I've finished, if the solution is not beautiful I know it's wrong." **– R. Buckminster Fuller**

"He actually had a very broad view of humanity's potentials and of the emerging serious consequences of our technologies. But none the less he also still held great faith in the possibilities of using these very same developing technologies to overcome these difficult problems in mankind's future.

"Buckminster Fuller led a very interesting and productive life. You should read more about him someday. But at one point early on, he was so economically frustrated and having such a very hard time just making a living that he actually considered committing suicide so that the money from his life insurance policy could help out his family. Strong social and financial pressures had made him consider that maybe he was worth more dead than alive!

"At this low point and in his darkest hour he relates having had a profound overpowering spiritual vision of being suspended within a sphere of light and being directly told that he did not have the right to kill himself, and that in fact his life was not his own to take but that it belonged to the universe. And that his intuitive insight and design ideas were correct and that they were important and that he should continue on living and working hard on all the things that he thought were the most important for humanity's future and not to pay so much attention to his own present temporary material condition."

I also once had the pleasure of hearing him speak live and although he was very old then, and he also complained that he was receiving a local radio station on his hearing aid; his performance was still very energetic and inspiring. I particularly remember him describing in detail the historical evolution of the wheel, one of man's earliest inventions; going from dragging things on the ground with straps, to moving large loads by putting them on platforms with many long log rollers underneath.

Rolling friction was so much less than sliding friction that once you had the platform or cart, and the log rollers in place, men with straps or animals in harness could move great heavy cargos with relative ease. It didn't take that much of an imagination to look at the round end of a rolling log and see a wheel. The real trouble was that the cart kept rolling over and leaving its "wheels" behind, and then the logs/wheels had to continually be brought forward from behind the cart to the front of the cart over and over again to keep it going. So, the more subtle real truth of the matter was that the big invention was not really the wheel, but the hole in the middle of the wheel and the axle, so that the cart could finally bring its wheels along with it!

These first wheels were very large thick and heavy. They were usually round log sections or double or triple cross layered solid wooden discs nailed and hammered together with just a hole in the middle for the axle. Although crude at the time this was still a major innovative advance over log rollers. The wheel and axle had come into existence, a great innovation that would be passed on to future generations, and would be used by them in countless new and unforeseen ways. Where would Leonardo DaVinci have been without the wheel?

This first solid or multi-layered wooden wheel over time eventually evolved into the spoked wheel, where about 80% of the wood material wasn't needed anymore. In this wheel, the load continually pole vaulted, or in effect stilt walked from spoke to spoke as it was rolling along. For this wheel to work it structurally needed a tight steel rim band going all around it to hold it together and a strong well made central hub to support the spokes. This hub was then greased and fitted to a stout strong axle. This was the wheel of the Conestoga Wagons. In this wheel, the wooden spokes were under compression and still needed to be thick and strong enough to support the whole load directly on their own, like the legs of a table. This spoked wheel was still just as strong as the earlier solid ones, but it now used much less wood and already had become 80% lighter than the old multi-layered solid wooden ones.

Then came the wire-spoked bicycle wheel. In this wheel amazingly 99% of all the material had been successfully removed! Now the heavy wooden spokes were replaced by many light steel wire spokes. These wire spokes were no longer strong enough to support the load under compression but they were now designed to support the weight under tension. The load was now in effect being transferred over an endless series of sequential trapezes which were always hanging the load from the upper wheel rim, so that the bicycle wheel basically functioned like a rolling suspension bridge. This new wheel was still very strong, and it was also the lightest wheel ever! Its much more highly engineered design used only a very small amount of materials and it had a lighter metal axle that incorporated steel ball bearings to greatly reduce the friction which also made it much more efficient. Over time through human technological ingenuity, the wheel had greatly evolved, but of course it was still only a wheel!

In his speech, Buckminster Fuller used this description of the evolution of the wheel as a metaphor for how we should go about solving today's problems. He called it the "ephemeralization" process, or doing more with less by better design. He firmly believed that all our present day difficulties that were created by our advanced technology and by our exploding population growth could also all be solved by technological means if they were socially directed towards the right goals. He did not live to see the digital cyber revolution that's now going on, but it is certainly following his predictions as so many of the earlier analog physical inventions are now being replaced by more ephemeral digital means.

Buckminster Fuller's own great breakthrough design of the geodesic dome that he is best known for, like a soap bubble, uses the least amount of material to efficiently enclose the most volume of space possible. If in the future we ever do colonize other planets, Fuller's geodesic domes will probably be the first permanent human structures built there. He also created the one piece bathroom, his dymaxion automotive designs, and many other design innovations.

My son says:
"Yes, that's all good stuff, I've heard of Buckminster Fuller, they even named a new spherical carbon molecule "Fullerene" after him because its structure closely resembles his geodesic domes. But don't a lot of our present day problems already come from modern designs? And is there really so much more left to improve upon that we can save the planet or really have any great lasting effect?"

I say:
"Good question…nobody knows what's around the next innovative design corner. I believe in Buckminster Fuller's vision of the potential creative power of properly directed human design, and I also believe in its infinite possibilities. And I remember exactly the moment when I woke up to this truth. It was in the spring of 1973 as I was walking through Fann's Department Store in Rosendale, New York. There I saw for the first time on display a camouflaged painted new compound hunting bow and arrow set for sale in the sporting goods section. This stopped me dead in my tracks. In the box was an ingeniously designed and very powerful new bow. The design of this bow used cams, or off-centered pulleys that had a built-in variable mechanical advantage which made drawing the string initially very

hard, but at full draw easier to hold when aiming. This is exactly the opposite of the ordinary traditional bow, and because the bow string was now part of a pulley system it had an added mechanical advantage too so that it also possessed much more power. Wow! Someone had just totally re-designed the bow and arrow, arguably one of mankind's first important inventions! This fact alone shocked me to the core and opened my eyes. If the bow and arrow, an invention that had been around since the dawn of man, could be so radically re-designed and improved upon, what else couldn't be?

"Using less material in better designs, recycling the materials we do use, and creating renewable energy sources, and better housing and land use are all key elements to a stable future. Your generation will have an important role to play in this ongoing human re-design drama to make these things possible. Otherwise to me the future looks bleak with many resource based wars on the horizon. It seems like we've already had some of these over world oil supplies. We still have a long way to go, but now intelligent people realize that the Earth should not be seen as an unlimited resource to be continually plundered and exploited. "Spaceship Earth" is a closed limited irreplaceable system that has evolved over billions of years to support the life that it does today and that we must not use up all its natural potential simply for our own immediate materialistic aggrandizement."

My son says:
"Yes! That's exactly what I'm so worried about. It seems like all the economic and materialistic systems now have so much monetary and political power that they can practically control virtually everything that is happening just to maximize their own self-interests and profits. And now this way of doing business is expanding worldwide and even China and India with their huge populations are also getting into the same old game and it's even spreading to Africa... How do we go about changing the ongoing inertia of such a huge system that just wants to keep on gobbling up everything in sight, and to keep on going full speed ahead with little or no regard for any of the negative consequences it is leaving in its wake?"

I say:

"Yes, that's exactly the problem! Everything everyone does is additive to the whole system, nothing is subtractive. It's all mathematically just like one big integral or infinite sum over all of mankind's activities, but there is no controlling formula and nothing is fixed or pre-set. We are always evolving, and even though it looks to you like everything is on autopilot and out of control, in reality things are always in a state of flux. It is not uncontrolled and at every point along the way there are conscious decisions that are being made by someone in charge. But it is also true that there certainly are many negative forces around us that are also at work that can give you pause, make you question yourself and sometimes feel depressed, and yes, even cause you to temporarily lose hope. But these are the normal pains and problems of existence and are to be expected and are more universal than most people generally will admit. This can also have its positive component too and infuse us with greater energy in the long run to work on it. But conditions are always in flux and changing; and we have the unique capacity for culturally understanding our own situation and the possibility of self-correcting any of the negative forces that are in play. This of course is not always easy to do, or even necessarily a sure thing… nothing important ever is… but it is not hopeless.

"All these facts are true in both our own individual lives and in the life of the greater world around us. You should understand that all the things that people are doing now that negatively affect mankind's future in one way or another will not last forever. All of these things will eventually come to an end, for good reasons or even for no good reason at all. Resources will dry up, or new approaches will become feasible. In the big picture I am from the school of thought that believes that everything eventually ends, but that nothing ever really begins."

My son says:

"Wow Dad, that's really crazy too! Wouldn't that mean that everything will eventually just peter out and grind to a halt, and finally flat out completely stop and end? I can't think of anything that's dumber and more depressing than that idea is… I'm swimming in doubt here and I thought you were trying to help me to get out of my funk and to see the brighter more hopeful side of things. This idea of yours that nothing ever begins is like handing me an anchor instead of a life jacket... Come on now, can't you do better than that..."

I say:

"I'm not trying to help you out to become mindlessly happy – you can take a pill for that. But watch out when it wears off! All I want is for you to see the whole big picture as best as I can show it to you, and then for you to decide for yourself. Maybe this isn't exactly the right time for you to grasp the broadest outlines of all these things that I'm trying to share with you right now. It can all be a little disorienting, even overwhelming and confusing...But this actually happens to be the best time for me to express it to you as honestly as I can, and to lay it all out for you in just the way that I see it. Very soon you'll be out in the big jungle on your own, but now while you're still here for a while at base camp, I'm trying to do my best to prepare you for the journey and I'm shooting for big game now, and this will probably our last safari together..."

My son shouts:

"Lights! Camera! Action! Zoom to close-up! The Great White Hunter is out on his Final Safari with his only son in deepest darkest Africa and he is showing him the ropes of just how to survive all on his own out there in the biggest most dangerous jungle of them all...Cut! Print!

"Holy Cow Dad! You really are a hopeless romantic...It's no wonder I saw that you were really crying the other night while we were both watching that old black & white film "Captains Courageous." I know you said that you are at heart an artist and that you feel things more deeply than most people do, but this idea of yours that "nothing begins" still sounds awfully dumb and totally hokey to me... Really, I'm amazed. Sometimes you can just say the oddest things!"

I say:

"No, no, you just don't get it yet, that's all… Hey! Come on now "Captains Courageous" with Spencer Tracy and Lionel Barrymore happens to be one of my all time favorite old movies! When you were little I even used to lie down on your bed and sing you to sleep with that song from it "Yea ho Little Fish" that Spencer Tracy, as Manuel the loving Portuguese fisherman, sings to the spoiled rich boy, Harvey, when they're both on evening watch together in the cockpit of the Gloucester fishing schooner *We're Here*, while cranking on his dead father's old hurdy gurdy:

"Yea Ho, Little Fish"

(Chorus and a few verses)

Chorus: Yea ho, little fish,
Don't cry, don't cry.
Yea ho, little fish,
You'll be whale by and by.

Some Verses:

Watch out little fish,
We're fishing for you,
But you can swim away
Deep in the blue.

You go to fish school
And you learn from a book
How not to get caught
On the fisherman's hook.

You'll swim all alone
And look for a home
You'll find a cute fish
Have little fish of your own.

Said cabbage to fishcake
Who lay on one dish,
I beautiful cabbage
You only poor fish.

You just swim around
The fisherman's bait,
You won't end up
On the fisherman's plate.

And when you're a whale
You'll grow a big tail
And swim far off shore
Where no fishermen sail.

Yea ho, little fish,
Don't cry, don't cry.
Yea ho, little fish,
You'll be whale by and by.

"I even made up a whole bunch of these extra verses for it too so that you'd always fall asleep before I got to the end of the song. You were such a great little kid and I really loved putting you to bed and singing that song for you...Remember? "Captains Courageous" is a very beautiful book by Rudyard Kipling, a favorite author of mine, and it's a very loving movie too, with its heart in the right place. It also has a lot of great exciting Grand Banks fishing scenes and some amazing schooner sailing footage in it too. This was the real thing – no CGI back then. It's really a marvelous movie. I always enjoy sharing my favorite things with you, and maybe one day you'll feel things so deeply that you'll want to cry too... I hope so. Anyway..."

My son says:

"Yeah, I remember you singing that little fish song...I liked it with you lying there right next to me putting me to sleep. I remember your singing and feeling your breathing and everything. Sometimes I even tried to match your breath in the same rhythm. It was all very warm and it felt so safe and nice going to sleep that way. I guess you liked being a father and all that... But "Nothing begins?" Really? That just seems so lame to me Dad... You say the strangest sounding things to me sometimes. I'm listening, but I still just don't get it!"

I say:

"OK, look, I can understand how this idea that nothing begins may at first sound quite strange to you. How can this be? Like you said, wouldn't this mean that everything finally would just stop altogether? But no, it doesn't mean that at all. You still really don't understand what it's all about. So let's look more closely at this big strange idea that "everything ends but nothing ever begins" so that you can understand just how big and beautiful an idea it really is, and just what it actually does mean in this phenomenal world that we all live our lives in.

"This statement doesn't mean that, "There's nothing new under the sun." New things are happening all the time and seemingly at an ever increasing rate, while at the same time other older things are continually winking out of existence. This is true not only for new products and inventions in the world of "stuff," but also even for biological life in general. Just think of how long the dinosaurs were around and how many different species of them there were, and now there are none of them left. In the 18th and 19th centuries the oil industry was very large and profitable then too, but it used to be based on catching whales and rendering their blubber into barrels of whale oil that was used mostly for oil lamps and lubrication, but now you can't even find any whale oil to buy in the store anymore. In the big picture there is always a slow constant turnover going on. I have even heard the statistic that 99% of all species that have ever lived are now extinct. How can this be? Does this mean that all life is hopelessly doomed?"

My son says:

"I've heard that before too. When you think about it that really does sounds dreadful… Do you actually think that that can be true? And if it really is, what do you think that it actually means? It certainly doesn't sound very hopeful for us humans, compared to the dinosaurs we've only been here a relatively short period in geologic time… Dad, you're not really helping me out very much here, this is all still very depressing and it really doesn't make me feel any better about everything…"

I say:

"No it isn't depressing, it's just because you still aren't getting it, that's all. Just relax now and listen…Look; it's not really anything scary like that at all. This is just a huge statistic taken over an extremely long period of time – actually since the very beginning of life on Earth, and it just might be true. Over time many species have gone extinct, yes, maybe even 99%, and new ones have replaced them. The fact that 99% of all species that have ever lived are now extinct is not a catastrophe; it's just a measure of how far we've advanced through the process of evolution. I don't know of anyone who has ever done the study, but probably over any smaller more reasonable time periods the number of species times their populations has been more or less stable based on the carrying capacity of the Earth at that time. Life on its own tends to proliferate and to fill up all the available niches. There has always been a full ecological web of life interacting with other life forms since the first big bloom of life on Earth. It just keeps on evolving over time to ever increasing levels of interaction, complexity, and of beauty. This is just what evolution does; this is what it's all about. And you're just the latest volunteer."

My son says:
"I've never heard about the evolution of beauty theory before, Dad. Did you just make that one up?"

I say:
"OK, you caught me. It's just my old artist's bent coming through again, but I do believe it's true. Just look at the Pterodactyl compared to the Bald Eagle, Neanderthal women compared to Marilyn Monroe, look at the Model T Ford compared to the Jaguar XKE. You get the basic idea, right? Some things are just true and you know it in your gut, but I would really hate to have to try and rigorously academically defend this thesis...

"The first thing that you'd have to do would be to come up with some definition and a way to objectively evaluate just what beauty is. I'm afraid I couldn't do that any better than the Supreme Court judge that was involved with a case about whether or not something was pornographic, who said, "I can't really tell you just what pornography is, but I know it when I see it." Ditto for me and beauty!"

My son says:
"OK, I'll overlook it this time; we'll just let that one slide. But let's keep on going – you were talking about old species dying out and the evolution of new species beginning, and somehow also saying that nothing ever begins. Let's see you get out of that one..."

I say:
"Right...Throughout evolution new species are periodically coming into existence. We are a new species "Homo Sapiens" that never existed before. But where did we really come from? Are all these new species really something totally new? Or aren't they all just developments from earlier species in constant change and

evolving? One old established species blurs into another "new" one and then the old one disappears. There are always "missing links" of the intermediate forms that can't be found or studied in this process. You can't say exactly when the new species began, as it arose incrementally and slowly from the ranks of the earlier one. But you can pretty accurately say when the old one became extinct since after a certain time it is no longer found to be present in the geologic record. It's gone for good, period. No more dinosaurs, no more Neanderthals. Everything ends, but nothing begins. See?

"Creation did not just happen in seven days and then was all over as it's written about in the Old Testament, but creation has never stopped and it is still on going! It's an ever continuing process that's still happening to this day through the ever advancing and adapting process of evolution in all its forms. This of course was Charles Darwin's great insight and contribution. The new has its source in the old and the old eventually dies out and becomes extinct. The new also over time eventually becomes old too; this is all a direct expression of the great nature of things. It is the way of the world, the Tao of existence. I also see it religiously as one of the holy seals of creation that cannot be circumvented or changed.

> ***"To everything there is a season, and a time for every purpose under heaven…*** **– Ecclesiastes**

"Sounds corny, but there is no escape from this omnipresent evolutionary trait and it even holds true in the non-living world of human innovations as well. The automobile did not just spring into existence fully formed from the horse and carriage, but first there were many separate people tinkering around with their own different versions of the "horseless carriage." All inventions have in them a seed from an earlier form or idea. If a new invention is so much superior to the earlier form that it totally replaces it, then that earlier one is no longer made and it "dies out" and becomes an antique, or becomes in an analogous inanimate way "extinct," since now no one will build it anymore because nobody wants to buy it anymore. They all greatly prefer the latest new thing. The old thing has served its timely purpose and now it is no longer needed. Nobody's making ice boxes anymore because everyone naturally prefers the inherently better modern refrigerators. You can't go down to the neighborhood armory store and buy a new suit of metal armor made up just for you, or a coat of chain mail anymore because bullets and gunpowder weapons have made them obsolete; but you can now buy a new Kevlar bullet proof vest. These are just some other instances of the fact that the closer you look, the more it is apparent that "everything ends, but nothing ever really begins!"

My son says:

"I think that these times we are living in now are the greatest of all times ever for new inventions. I'm happy to be living in such exciting innovative times. Just think about what my small cell phone can do. It's a phone, a still camera, a movie camera, a calendar, clock, an alarm clock, a GPS navigation system, an email portal, it's a reference library, a star and constellation locator, I can play chess with people far away, it has access to a huge music collection, and much more. Every day more new apps are coming out that enable me to do ever more neat stuff right at my fingertips! Every year or two a new generation of computers comes out that are even faster and have much more memory, new operating systems, better games with better graphics, and they can handle more complex programs too like very realistic flight simulators... Boy do I love those flight simulators! I feel like I've actually flown helicopters, been on World War II fighter plane missions from aircraft carriers at sea, flown international commercial jetliners and navigated them across continents all while sitting right at my own desk. I've even calculated and launched rockets into stable outer space orbits; I really had a hands-on experience and learned an awful lot of neat real physics about how orbital mechanics works in that program!"

I say:

"Yeah, that's all great stuff. But my father also lived his life through a period of an extraordinary bloom in human innovation too. He lived his life through probably the greatest period of changes that had ever occurred before. He was born before the Wright brothers flew, and lived to experience the first Apollo manned landing on the Moon, and to see it broadcast in real time on live TV. These were not clever new cyber things, but real historical events. These and many other apparently new things occurred within his life span too. This was also true especially in medicine his own chosen field of endeavor with the advent of antibiotics which revolutionized medical care. Before antibiotics, doctors had been extremely limited in what they could do to fight off infections. They basically just had to rely on and encourage the body's own natural defenses, which often were not up to the task and this resulted in many unavoidable patients' deaths. This all suddenly changed and became preventable with the advent of the new antibiotic therapies.

"But even that first antibiotic, penicillin, it did not really begin either. Even though it became the first antibiotic to ever exist, it did not come into existence as a totally new thing. It was not created from nothing. In fact, it was only accidentally discovered by Alexander Fleming in 1928, because he had carelessly left a Petri dish open one night and it had by chance become contaminated with *Penicillium notatum,* the mold that naturally produces the active penicillin enzyme. His real genius was that he was able to recognize in this mundane situation, something that was completely new. When he returned to the lab early that fateful morning and saw that accidentally left open contaminated Petri dish, he didn't just automatically wash it out and start his original experiment all over again, as many less observant people might have done. But he was able to stop, look, and amazingly recognize just what it was that he held in his hands and the great future potential of what his dumb careless "housekeeping error" actually contained.

"Penicillin already existed in the form of an enzyme which was naturally excreted by a common bread mold that had evolved to normally produce it in order to defend itself against competing bacteria in its own natural micro-environment. About his fortunate chance discovery Alexander Fleming said, "When I woke up just after dawn on September 28, 1928, I certainly didn't plan to revolutionize all of modern medicine by discovering the world's first antibiotic, but I suppose that was exactly what I did."

"Fleming won the Noble Prize for his work and in recognition was knighted by the Queen. Sir Alexander Fleming, a humble man, would later also observe, 'One sometimes finds what one is not looking for.' It was the first antibiotic ever and it only needed to be recognized, isolated, and manufactured which started a whole new class of wonder drugs which in turn totally revolutionized modern medicine. Many people who previously would have surely died could now be easily saved.

"Your example of cell phones is yet another contemporary instance illustrating in a dramatic new way this same idea that nothing begins. It was something very exciting when cell phones first came out, and they seemed to be something totally new too. Imagine after over one hundred years of using wired phones connected to the wall, then walking around with your own personal phone in your pocket! But they also had their predecessors. Cell phones were really just a combination of the earlier inventions of the telephone, radio, and the computer taken to the next higher level with state-of-the-art electronic miniaturization and cellular networks. Now they are starting to digitally gobble up many other separate earlier analog inventions too that had already pre-existed independently on their own, like traditional cameras and photography. Photographic film is now in the process of becoming "extinct" too.

"This is just one more instance of Bucky Fuller's predictions of the continuing process of "ephemeralization" that's going on right now. Just think what happened to computers; going from the original 1951 UNIVAC I, that weighed 29,000 pounds with rooms full of 5,200 vacuum tubes that also needed large air-conditioned cooling systems to work; being transformed to everyone walking around now with a much more highly powerful interactive personal computer right in their pockets too. Talk about 'ephemeralization,' this will definitely change our society in many unanticipated ways. It's happening already…Time to adapt again!"

My son says:
"Yeah, I just recently went to a computer history museum and they had a lot of the earlier systems there as exhibits. They actually

started out with the abacus which no one knows how old it really is. There were very many different interesting earlier machines, and there were even large totally mechanical ones there too. The big old electronic vacuum tube models like the UNIVAC you were just talking about were called "main frame computers" and they mostly used reel to reel tape to store data, and like you said, they took up major parts of buildings. Everything there on display was totally obsolete and none of it was being made anymore, even though some of the stuff there were breakthrough inventions of only about 50 years ago!"

I say:

"So maybe now you can better understand just what the big idea that "nothing begins" really does mean. Even when apparently new things like cell phones or even new living biological species appear, they don't just pop into existence on their own fully formed from nowhere. When we really deeply look at it, it's apparent that everything always has its own roots and its own origins in something else that has already existed earlier. Nothing comes from nothing. Everything that exists now forms a continuum from earlier previously existing things. Everything somehow or another originates from something else before. See! Nothing ever truly begins!"

The Ouroboros: Symbol of Infinity and Eternity

My son says:

"Well… What about me? I have a birthday. I began, didn't I?"

I say:

"No you didn't. Before you were born, you grew from the union of two very small separate living biological cells, one given from me, your father, and another one from your mother. An act of love between two people, your parents, brought these separate cells together. But even those egg and sperm cells were already there and existed independently alive on their own before your actual conception. So you did not really begin either but you are also the direct result of the continuation of other pre-existing life. Go back as far as you wish… further and further, everything comes from something else before. You may think that your life began at your birth, and that penicillin began when Alexander Fleming first discovered it in 1928, but you'd be mistaken. If you really look deeply enough at everything, nothing truly ever begins. Do you get it now? Can you now see the transcendent beauty of it altogether?"

My son says:

"I'm not really sure of what you mean by transcendental beauty, but I think I'm finally starting to see just what you've been driving at. It's very odd… Nothing really begins… Hmm… So what you've been trying to say to me all along here is that although many new things appear to be constantly popping up into existence, like new cell phones and new computer games, that for me in my world all these new things really do begin. After all I've spent time standing in big lines at the mall waiting for the stores to open to buy them when they first come out. But for you they really don't begin there because they are all linked in some definite generative and causal way to pervious things that have already existed in the past. That there always is some direct or hidden linkage of every new thing to something else that already existed before it. So that all these new things that appear to be just popping up around us are really continually in the process of growing out of all the other earlier things in the past that were already here. And that therefore even though all these new things are really new things that had not existed before, they never really began because they couldn't have come into being without springing from the roots of these earlier things in the past. Nothing comes from nothing; everything comes from something, so nothing ever truly begins! – Oh Wow! That means that everything that exists today is totally linked all together in one long chain to everything else that has ever existed before. What a strange idea…I've never really thought of it in that way before."

I say:

"Yes, that's right; now you're starting to get the big picture. That's the transcendent beauty! The biological continuum from generation to generation through everyone's family tree is a fairly obvious example of this, but the branching tree of evolution linking birds, fish, reptiles, mammals and all, showing the flow of species, orders, phyla, and even kingdoms together is truly one of the great creative works of the human mind. It is the biological equivalent of chemistry's final organization of the Periodic Table of the Elements. But even that's not the end of it, and there actually is still really much more transcendent interactive linkage happening all around us in the universe everywhere…

"Even our own solar system itself did not just begin, but it too came from earlier cosmic precursors. Our Sun and planets came from a gravitationally collapsed dust cloud floating around in outer space which itself had come partially from previously existing other stars that had become violently exploding super novas. These earlier generations of stars forged in the heat of their exploding deaths, the higher atomic weight elements beyond iron that they then forcefully scattered throughout space in all directions. Their death throws seeded the proto-dust cloud which would then eventually collapse and become our own solar system with these necessary higher atomic weight elements. Without these needed heavier elements existing because of those earlier generations of super novas, the development of our own present-day life forms here on Earth would not have been possible.

"Everything, including even our own solar system, comes directly from something else that already existed earlier. Can you now see the great and beautiful truth of this big transcendent idea that "Nothing Begins?" All of creation and everything in it exists as one long unified and evolving continuum. Everything continually flows out from something else that existed before it and at some point in their existence they were all interconnected and joined. Pull on any one thread and you will pull on the whole tapestry of creation. This is yet another derivation of what the mystics throughout time have always been telling us all along "All is One" – "Shema Yisrael!"

My son says:

"Dad, you're making my head spin…That's some humongous tale in the telling, a very large tapestry indeed you've just been weaving. OK, maybe after all, when you do think about it in the very biggest possible way "nothing begins" isn't quite as dumb of an idea as it originally sounded… That is after you explain it all…but it sure does take an awful lot of explaining to clear it up…By the way, what was that last weird "Shema Yisrael" bit you tacked on? You just said it at the end of everything and I don't really get what the reference is or what you really meant by it."

I say:

"Oh, of course, you wouldn't understand that… that's Hebrew. That's the remnants of my Jewish upbringing bleeding through again…"Shema Yisrael" is the most fundamental prayer of the entire Jewish faith that begins with those two Hebrew words. The Shema is the statement of their basic core belief of monotheism. The prayer begins, "Hear O Israel, the Lord our God, the Lord is One."

My son says:

"But, wait a sec. What about the Big Bang Theory? If nothing begins, what about that? Surely the Big Bang began, didn't it? I mean it began all of a sudden with a very BIG BANG! Right? You're not really saying that that didn't happen either, are you? Wasn't that really the beginning of just about everything else?"

I say:

"Maybe… Science can only go back as far as the Big Bang which they claim, like you just said, was the ultimate beginning of everything. It is amazing just how much they have been able to piece together and figure out what may have happened so immensely far back in time. This has been accomplished mainly by viewing all that can be seen with cameras, telescopes and spectroscopes, and then painstakingly developing and re-inventing cosmologic theory after theory to try and keep up with and explain all their continually advancing and often newly unexpected astronomical findings that may seriously conflict with their previous theories. All these theories are just that, theories. Even scientists will tell you that they haven't reached any firm conclusions yet. They are constantly going back to the drawing board… But they really do deserve a lot of credit for their combined work of so many dedicated scientists over so many generations working to try to understand and describe the scientific truth of the Universe as we know it, and even today it still exists as a largely unresolved work in progress. But don't ever ask them what came before the Big Bang. They will just look back at you with the blank stare of a deer in the headlights.

"But the Hindus actually do have their own mythic answer to this question. I believe that the Hindu vision of time and the multiplicity and complexity represented in their art and the detailed richness of the architecture of their temples is unsurpassed by any other culture. Contained within their vast vision of time is their own cosmic creation cycle story. They believe that what we are all living in now is not the one and only universe, but it is actually the eighth creation of the Universe and that in time it too will totally destroy itself all over again.

"To the Hindus the Universe symbolically arises anew from the rhythmic dancing and drumbeats of their eternal Lord Shiva's cosmic dance, and it actually pulses in and out of existence over and over again throughout the eons of boundless time. The drum which Lord Shiva holds in one of his four arms is irresistiblially calling us forth into existence, and then finally he brings about our ultimate destruction by the all consuming fire that he holds in another of his dancing arms. He is the cosmic Lord of the Dance, and we and all the atoms in the universe are forever rhythmically engaged in his cosmic dance of eternal creation and destruction.

"It is also part of their belief that when the Universe is created it begins in total perfection. But from then on it starts to slowly degrade itself, and continues to only get worse and worse. Until finally, mostly as a result of the misdeeds of mankind generation after generation, it completely and utterly destroys itself and everything in it by means of Lord Shiva's all consuming fire of destruction.

"Then once again, through the creative actions of Shiva's eternal dancing and his irresistible drumbeats of creation, the universe will spontaneously re-form itself and arise anew once more from its own dust and ashes – just like the Phoenix Bird of ancient Greek mythology, only on a much grander scale. Perhaps the big bang is just another one of Shiva's cosmic drumbeats. As a result the universe is again reborn anew and refreshed once more existing in total perfection only to begin another of its long epic cycles of existence."

***"You are from dust and to dust you will return."* – Genesis**

"But believe it or not as far as evolution is concerned, you are the latest and the greatest."

"Peek-a-Boo"
from the author's "Transformative Figures Series," a stone lithograph

Chapter 3
Who am I? The Circle of Being

Yes, according to evolution you are the latest and the greatest; but who are you really?

My son asks:
"The world is full of so many other people already; how can it possibly make any real difference what I do?"

I say:
"What you do may not change the world overall by very much, but what you do does have a very important and significant effect on you yourself and on all the people around you whom you know and who know you. At the most basic level it clearly defines who you are to yourself and to the rest of the world."

The Circle of Being

You see an interesting looking stranger at a party. You ask someone you know, 'Who is that over there?' They say, 'Oh, that's Mary, you'll like her. She's a teacher.'

This is the most obvious outer layer of being – You are what you do. If you teach, you are a teacher. But why is it really that you do what you do? Why does Mary teach?

You don't just do things arbitrarily, especially those things that you eventually become known for. At some point in time you must have thought deeply about it. You do what you wind up doing because there is something about it that has captured your imagination and attention and you have already been thinking about it for some time before. You have internally decided that for you it is something that you can do with your natural abilities, and it is also something worthwhile doing, and it is personally important for you to do it well. It's something you feel connected with and it utilizes some special area of your natural interests and it also stimulates new experiences in things which you have already been focused on in some deep way. It may even have the potential in the future for providing useful practical support for your life needs. Pursuing it further does not deplete you but actually gives you more energy to keep on pursuing it. It has become a fruitful vein for you and it continues to lead you on.

And just what is it that directs what you become interested in pursuing and thinking about? You don't just think deeply about random things. You think about and are concerned with all those things that in your heart of hearts you believe are important to you, to your ongoing physical existence, to your interests and your life's work, things that will contribute to your future well being in some real and meaningful way. These are the things that over time you have come to realize are very important parts of your life and that you have knowingly put your faith in – they are the things that you most deeply trust and truly believe in. They are not just things which have captured and absorbed your attention for a little while, but they must also give you something back in return that you are able to use in your real life and you can build upon. To you they have positive intrinsic value in themselves and you consider them to be important in their own right, and they also have a relationship to your ongoing developing spirit. In the best case they will contain and embody deep things that have been personally revealed to you. They have the potential of becoming your life's calling, and as a result it also satisfies one of your deep existential drives. They are the worthwhile things that have come into your life that you have come to identify yourself with and they are the things that you value most highly and that you truly believe in.

And just what is it that you finally can really know, trust, and truly believe in? Right here is where the magic dwells, for this is the keystone and the essential part where the snake eats its own tail and closes this existential circle of being... Because what you deeply understand and know better than anyone else in the world is the inner truth of your own life. What you finally truly trust and believe in is just what and who you are. What you finally truly and fully believe in – are your own beliefs!

This creates what I've come to call "The Circle of Being" at its simplest level:

"The Circle of Being"

You are what you do.
You do what you think.
You think what you believe.
You believe what you are.

All these parts dynamically interact with each other to make up your essential character as a human being. They also unite to form the ground for the emotional basis of how you feel about yourself and everything else too. If there is dissonance between these elements; for example, you are not doing what you believe in, then you will not feel good about who you are, and maybe it's time for you to re-think things… but if you're living your life well and there is harmony between all these elements then things are good in your life and you're feeling connected to yourself and also to the world around you. Musicians call this harmonious feeling being in the groove – you're "feelin' groovy."

My son asks me, 'What difference does it really make what I do?' It makes a big difference to who you are. In fact if you change any of these linked parts in your own "Circle of Being," all the rest will change too, perhaps not quickly but they surely will change in time. What you do, what you think, and what you believe all have an affect on who you are and who you will become, both to yourself and to others.

The parts of this interactive circle all function independently but are also fundamentally linked. Changes in who you are do not necessarily happen in one direction only, but can happen through the action of changes in any single one of these elements and their affects will then ripple through the whole system. Changing what you think can change what you do; changing your beliefs will change what you think; changing what you do can change your beliefs, etc. All the entry points are equivalent and not hierarchical, and all are mutually interactive with each other and always function in concert to produce your unique character and result in your current state of mind.

You will not always believe in what you believed as a child, you will not always think the thoughts of a teenager, and you will not always act the same way in similar circumstances as you have done in the past. As you mature and develop your own thoughts and beliefs, your actions and behaviors will also begin to advance and develop in other new ways too. Your being will change and evolve over time. Just how it changes is of course ultimately up to you. There is no escaping your own responsibility for who you are. This is yet another of the holy seals of creation.

As you progress, the "Circle of Your Being" will also begin to rise in value and quality and it will start to become more of what we could call "a Spiral of Being," in essence still circular, but evolving to higher levels as you internally develop into a deeper, broader, and more fully conscious self. This rising spiral traces your individual development as a consciously growing spiritual being. This is the direct result of the active evolving process of your maturing inner spirit. It is the cumulative result of "the way" you have chosen to make your own life manifest. It is the Buddhist philosophical subtext of Jack Kerouac's breakthrough American novels "On the Road" and later "The Dharma Bums," both early important classics of the Beat Generation which were greatly influenced by Buddhism. The Beatniks and their followers the Hippies were American sub-culture movements that were both deeply concerned with their own personal spiritual development.

For the Buddhists everyone in life is always somewhere along "the way" on their own particular karmic journey through their own present human existence. This is one of their most fundamental concepts, and the Tibetan Buddhist "Wheel of Life" thangka is a beautiful complex artistic representation of this deeply held spiritual idea. It is an important thangka, or spiritual painting, depicting the many spiritually different ways of being alive in this world.

The Tibetan Buddhist "Wheel of Life" thangka

The artistic design of the "Wheel of Life" thangka is of a very formal and stylized symbolic nature. It is one of their highest artistic achievements, and is an extremely stunning visual example of Tibetan Buddhism's very beautiful and rich religious culture. Tibetan monks make these thangkas the way medieval European monks made and copied illuminated manuscripts.

So we do not exist as just one fixed unchanging thing, but we have built into us the possible continuing evolution of our own inner selves. But if we do not self-examine who we are, what we do, or what makes up our thoughts and our beliefs, we probably will not grow in this dynamic positively directed way, and our being will most likely remain more or less stagnate and fixed at some more basic ground level of existence. This is the realm of people who have become bored with their own life, and as a result their own life also becomes boring to themselves and to others. It becomes almost impossible for them to open up to having any truly new experiences. This is the very definition of boredom. Unfortunately, I feel that this is a common condition for very many middle-aged people here in the West. These people are all sorely in need of a direct wake-up call from Socrates. He was a very early great teacher. We'll talk more about his method of stirring things up a little later. Unfortunately, he has long since taken down his shingle and gone out of business. But even after all these centuries he still does have his admirers, active adherents, and followers… Count me in.

In addition, we must realize the important fact that it is also possible to devolve instead of evolve. This is really the saddest condition found in people who have never achieved any real objective perspective on themselves. They are obsessively totally locked within themselves and have never questioned their own motives ever in their whole life, and if they are selfishly directed they can eventually find themselves falling into an ever-descending downward spiral of being. As each descent becomes easier they also become less amenable to change. This will also build up over time and they can eventually feel blocked on all fronts and it may finally become too painful and difficult for them to even continue living and as a result it can all end very badly for them and the people around them.

Surprisingly this condition is not limited to fully mature adults only, but it can even occur in the young as well, as we all have witnessed in the many desperate high school students' final vengeful acts of striking out in mass killings and suicidal incidents that have happened all too often in our culture recently. These are definitely the hopeless acts of people who must feel themselves totally blocked on all fronts without any real hope at all, and at the end of their ropes. But here again finally there is no escaping your own responsibility for who you are, and what you do.

The amazing Tibetan "Wheel of Life" thangka also clearly illustrates these two contrasting conditions of the growing human spirit. In the second ring of the wheel there is an equally divided lighter half and a darker half. The lighter half shows rising evolving beings ascending higher, while the opposite darker half of the ring depicts descending lower devolving beings. The differences of course are the individual life paths chosen by them. There is no final escape from the karma you are constantly creating. You are the one fully responsible for who you are and who you are becoming.

In the central hub of the wheel are depicted "the three poisons" that keeps the wheel of reincarnations turning – these are the iconic images of the pig, the snake, and the rooster. The pig is symbolic of greed and selfishness, the snake of anger and hatred, the rooster of pride and desires. To Buddhists these three poisons are the ignorant forces of Samsara, or the potent forces of the world of delusion that ceaselessly keeps the karmic wheel of life turning.

This significant and compelling Tibetan Buddhist masterpiece thangka is often found displayed at the entrances to Buddhist temples and Tibetan monasteries and exists in many different versions expressed in a variety of original artistic styles. But its substantive contents are fundamentally the same and it contains an overall symbolic representation of the essence of Tibetan Buddhist philosophy. In all its forms the iconic and very colorful Wheel of Life is being held firmly in the grip of Yama, the three eyed Tibetan lord of death and impermanence. He is the embodied symbol of our transitory existence in this world.

As an object of meditation it is a representation and distillation of very many different Buddhist spiritual concepts concerning karma, and reincarnation into the many different realms of being, and the ever-present transcendent Buddhist path to enlightenment that exists in all of them. Religiously symbolic illustrations of these ideas and many of their different aspects and their sources are collected together and integrated artistically into the Tibetan "Wheel of Life," one whole complex and deeply mystical artistic image.

The Tibetan "Wheel of Life" thangka exists basically as a very colorful, fearsome, and very elaborate spiritual cartoon. It was originally designed, I'm sure, as a helpful teaching device for illiterate worshipers. If you can learn and explain what the meanings are of all the various symbolisms in this complex colorful spiritual thangka you will have learned and understood a great deal about Tibetan Buddhism. I keep one on my wall just to remind me of the big picture.

Who Are You Really?

If and when you finally do become truly self-aware, you will then come to the full realization of what your actual human spiritual condition truly is – that as you exist naturally you are not a finished product but are only a raw material of nature. You will then clearly see that up till this moment you have been living your life in a random accumulative manner and in the process becoming an unformed haphazard composite; a conglomerate of many disparate components. Some of which may even consist of unrecognized self-contradictory elements, all of which have become part of you and have been unwittingly stuck together in an awkward uniquely personal assemblage by the tenacious glue of your own unconscious psyche. And your resulting being now consists wholly of the sum of all these unbidden and randomly acquired parts. These are elements which have all come from many different unrelated sources and have been combined, unexamined, unrefined, and un-unified to form the underlying complex chimera-like nature of your own present personality. You may then have the opportunity to clearly understand that this is actually your true present condition, and that it is also the shared common condition of most of humanity around you. The world at large is altogether in a big mess, and so are you.

Suddenly you will realize that continuing along your old accustomed path and doing nothing to change your present condition is no longer even an option. In fact, it is not even possible. If you do nothing actively in this regard you will still necessarily wind up doing very many different things in the course of the rest of your life anyway, and because of this, your being will certainly unavoidably develop and randomly accumulate additional new changes over time in one way or another. We are all karmic beings. Karma happens; there is no way around it. This is yet another one of the holy seals of creation that cannot be circumvented.

Now you will suddenly realize that you are at a spiritual turning point, and you will deeply understand for the first time that you have within yourself the possibility of consciously self-directing your own spiritual growth and evolution. Isn't this really a much better option for you to now become a knowingly involved active participant in your own future spiritual development? Of course it is! Learning mastery over how we become who we are is our greatest responsibility and it is also the greatest potential freedom that we can possess. This is the way out and paradoxically it is also the way in.

Up to this moment you have been living your life in an open accretion mode of existence. You have been indiscriminately and haphazardly collecting your own unique personal life experiences. The karma that you have already created from your earliest stages of development onward in this aggregation sleep-walking mode still actively exists within you. And it will still exercise its influences over your behavior until you have successfully performed your own healing self-work. But at least now you have finally seen the truth of the matter.

Once you have left the cave, once you have awakened to who you actually are; you can then no longer remain blandly unaware. This is what being awake really means. You now understand that the sum total of what you have been living has been basically a self-indulgent and passively unexamined life. You are coming face to face with the unvarnished chimerical truth about the state of your own inner being. This is the great awakening, and coming to the end of self-delusion. And this really isn't a pleasant new-agey feel good experience. In fact it's just the opposite. This is when the self-work truly begins. This is what Socrates tried so hard to instill in the minds of the young citizens of Athens that got him into such trouble with the governing authorities of his day. Those in power will always prefer the somnambulant status quo and a servile complacent citizenry to a self-aware involved and questioning populace.

We will be focusing on and discussing how we can individually grow spiritually and how we can gain conscious control over the direction of our own internal spiritual growth in positive trans-personal transformative ways during the course of this work. This is what living a spiritual life is really all about. This sudden awakening is the first step; the important dawn and the beginning of lucid living.

We began this chapter with the question, "Who are you?" A better way of asking this same question would be: "Who have you been, who are you now, and whom are you actively in the process of becoming?"

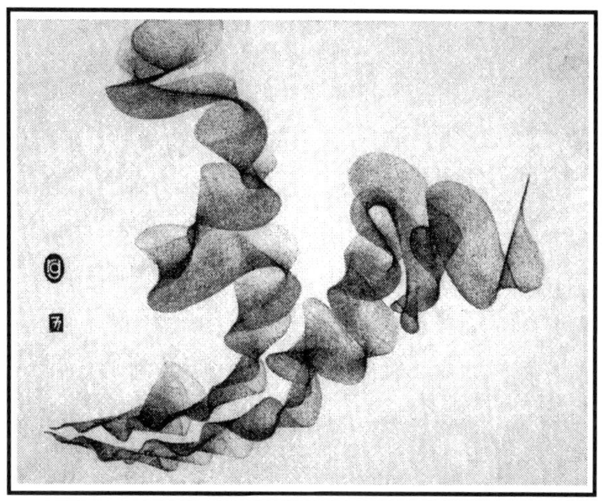

"Come Fly with Me"
from the author's "Nippon Homage Series," charcoal on rice paper

Chapter 4. Your Sticky Brain

My son says:

"Where does our individuality really come from? What really makes me so different from everybody else? How come I'm just the way I am today? Why do I seem to be so different from everybody else? What makes us all become so uniquely ourselves?"

I say:

"We are all distinct individuals and we have all been given our own unique lives to live. No two of us can ever have exactly the same experiences in life, even if we do walk that proverbial mile in someone else's shoes. In fact according to that old Greek philosopher Heraclitus of Ephesus, not even you yourself can experience exactly the same thing ever again:

"You can't step into the same river twice." **– Heraclitus**

"All in this world is uniqueness and ever flowing change, everything, everywhere, all the time, and all around us from snowflakes to ourselves. Why should this be so? I don't really know, but it definitely is so, and you must accept it for what it is. All I can say about all of this is to echo the traditional Islamic expression of universal praise…although culturally since 9/11 it has come into disrepute, but I think it still applies here – "Allah Akbar," God is great!"

I have a book entitled "Snow Crystals" by photographer W. A. Bentley, a serious man who took nothing for granted. At one time or another someone must have said to him probably in an offhand way that no two snowflakes were exactly alike. But W. A. Bentley was not like everybody else either, and so for years he dedicated himself to taking thousands of detailed photographs of individual snowflakes on his own just to make sure. During cold winter snow storms while they were falling in the air, he went out and caught individual snowflakes before they hit the ground on black velvet pillows. Then still in the freezing cold with a large bellows box camera, inspired lighting, and the right close-up lenses, he enlarged, photographed, printed, and catalogued them all according to their general characteristics and in order of their increasing complexity. This was no easy task and is a remarkable revelation of nature's true diversity and it is also a testament to one man's shear dogged determination. But after 50 years of doing this he finally had to give up his search for two identical snowflakes with the end result being that no two of his thousands of individually photographed and catalogued snowflakes were exactly the same. It is a very beautiful impressive and inspirational book in any case and I do recommend it to all. But sometimes I do wonder what would have happened if he actually had found two identical snowflakes? (It certainly would have been easy enough for him to fake it!)

Twelve Random Snowflakes

Photographed by W. A. Bentley

Anyway, next time you are peacefully at a window silently staring in awe enjoying the pure silent poetry of a pristine virgin winter snowfall, as an exercise in awareness and to experience the rare feeling of complete mental saturation, try to fully visualize and hold in your mind the enormously complex truth of the natural phenomenon that's quietly unfolding right before your eyes. The facts are that as you are standing there watching this very beautiful but ordinary, commonplace, unremarkable natural event that often happens each winter; all on their own, billions and billions of totally unique, delicately and intricately structured individual snowflakes are continually and bountifully being created high above you directly out of thin air. They are then slowly falling down out of the sky all around you and are indiscriminately landing on top of each other and are thickly and quietly covering everything in sight.

The natural world is a rich cornucopia of constantly unfolding yet never repeating possibilities. This is just one of the transcendent realities of creation and one of the many infinities that we are all naturally immersed in. Modern man's artificial mass production methods seem to be the only exception to the general nature of this very rich world of infinite natural diversity that is constantly happening all around us.

Of course this rich natural diversity is not in any way limited to snowflakes, but includes clouds, fingerprints, waves, landscapes and almost every other natural phenomenon. Besides the fact that every one being born is genetically unique at the chromosomal level and different from everyone else, we all will also develop our own individuality in many other more mundane and directly environmentally influenced ways while we are growing up and maturing. When we come into the world we all also possess our own different levels of intelligence, openness, and receptivity to our own immediate local surroundings. I view this as coming into the world with a certain inborn level of "stickiness" to our brains. The more naturally intelligent we are, the stickier are our brains.

In the beginning there is not much there but the innate, the deep structures of our basic human-ness. Babies are certainly all more alike than grown-ups are. But as we grow and get older we have more and more original formative experiences that will stick with us to a greater or lesser degree, giving each of us our own unique collection of first hand encounters with the world. If we do nothing else, these will randomly build up and become the raw material of our own unique developing persona. At first the quality and variety of these primary formative experiences come to us unlimited and unfiltered by our as yet undeveloped conscious will. These experiences are simply the everyday normal happenings of a growing maturing human child; however even these are not universally the same. They are the daily raw experiential data from our daily activities in our early environment, our family, our circumstances, our culture and our local community, etc. all more or less uniquely determined. They endlessly build up every day as a result of our own individual life's journey which then coalesces within us to create the elements from which we naturally form our own unique character. This is the normal and given state of all early personal growth.

My son says:

"OK, so you're saying we are all different because we all come into the world at different places and different times and have different parents and have our own different unique experiences. So we're all just like a sticky gooey ball rolling around in our own neighborhood environments picking up all sorts of random local junk. Not a very comforting idea. Is that all there is to individuality? I don't think so."

I say:

"You're right; of course there are many other factors that determine someone's individual character. The whole nature vs. nurture arguments come into play here. You'll hear a lot about this endless controversy if you take any psychology or sociology classes in college. But what I am talking about now are just what the raw materials are that the young at the very early stages of collecting worldly experiences have to work with. Yes, some people will continue on in this random mode of accretion, which of course will also be influenced and directed by genetic predilections, parental interactions, and by the peer pressure of conforming to perceived societal norms throughout their whole life. They will become essentially what I call a complex un-integrated chimera, or crazy quilt of random unexamined and often conflicting beliefs based on their own past personal experiences that are held haphazardly together by the sticky mental psychic glue within themselves. It will consist of nearly every personal experience that they have collected over the years which they have become identified with internally and which are bound to them without their ever really questioning or consciously examining or attempting to integrate any of it at all in any deeply unified and spiritually meaningful way. And strangely enough they will often remain blandly unaware of their own oddly peculiar scattered haphazard and often self-conflicted internal mental and spiritual condition."

Socrates the Gadfly

Unfortunately this is an all too common human condition, and long ago in Athens, Greece around 400 B.C. that old original self-realized street philosopher Socrates had a knack for spotting these internally conflicted people on sight. There in the agora and other open public areas he would engage them in casual conversations regardless of their social rank, often by starting up with something usually mundane, but soon directly calling into question their own unrealized underlying conflicted beliefs. These unsuspecting Athenians would very soon be caught up in a bewildering complex inconsistent web of their own creation. As the result of his probing inquiries and then additionally becoming confounded and self-entangled by their own casual random responses to his simple logical but directed and progressive questioning, before they really knew what was happening, Socrates could suddenly make them painfully aware of their own internal deeply haphazard and illogical mental states. He would invariably succeed in clearly bringing them face to face with their own unrealized and confused ideas. As a result they would no longer be able to remain blandly unaware or comfortably continue on their way in their own usual blissful state of ignorance and smug arrogance. He was a consummate master of this method and took joy in clearly revealing their disorganized state of mind to themselves.

The results of this clever unmasking of upstanding citizens that he often performed publicly at the same time also became embarrassingly obvious to any of the other casual Athenian bystanders too! They too had just experienced the deep level of Socrates' facile mental abilities and the immediate embarrassing affects his true perceptions had upon his exposed and confused casual partner in the conversation. These serendipitous public encounters in Athens over time became recurring entertaining local events. As a result, this became one of the ways Socrates recruited many young students and followers. After witnessing these curious spontaneous philosophical street performances, they too wished to achieve a greater and deeper understanding of their own minds and lives. Socrates woke them up. This was his great public service. This was what he did.

By his use of simple everyday dialogue in his own brilliantly directed method, Socrates had become a master at logically and spontaneously uncovering and bringing to light the average person's deeply disorganized and conflicted inner belief systems that they often didn't even realize or suspect that they harbored. This became his favorite *modus operandi* and an ongoing public diversion on the busy streets of ancient Athens; and Socrates, who was a stonemason by profession and a poor man, especially enjoyed doing this and very publicly exposing the awkward illogical mental states of the rich, powerful, and often well respected pompous Athenian politicians of his day. By this open and clever means he created his own seminal early school of analytic philosophy.

Through his pointed questioning, Socrates definitely could very quickly get to the heart of any matter, and by just doing what he did then, today he might even have become a rich media celebrity since he certainly would have made a great guest interviewer on CNN, far better than anyone there today!

Although Socrates thought of himself as performing a valuable and much needed public service in deflating the pompous local Athenians through his functioning "as a rogue gadfly," as he comically characterized himself according to Plato, and "to sting people and whip them up into a fury, all in the ultimate service of Truth." Needless to say he annoyed very many powerful people who did not appreciate being publicly humbled by this poor odd street performing philosopher's direct and original use of what would much later come to be known as the "Socratic Method."

Unfortunately, this was not one of his more endearing qualities and it was one of the ways he randomly made many personal enemies of the politically powerful local citizenry of Athens, who also didn't appreciate his direct affect on the youth that encouraged them to think for themselves and therefore to question their elders authority. This eventually also surely was one of the contributing factors that finally resulted in his trial and sad demise there. This bold and very wise gadfly unfortunately didn't stand a chance and was a sitting duck himself and succumbed to a direct frontal swatting attack from his enemies.

The Athens Establishment =>

Socrates, "the Gadfly" =>

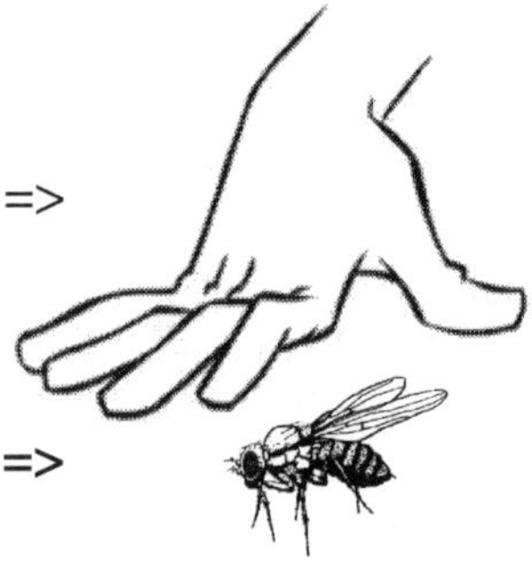

!! SQUASH !! { poor Socrates...}

Just like Homer, Jesus Christ, and Gautama Buddha; Socrates was yet another one of these deeply profound early original thinkers with a clearly formed unique new personal vision, who only taught by the old traditional oral methods and never thought it very important or even necessary for him to write anything down about it. He seemed to live purely in the present and he didn't even consider directly spelling out anything at all about his own philosophy or his own philosophical methods for the benefit of posterity. He really never told his students just what they should think or believe about any topic, as some of his followers, like Aristotle, wound up doing with decidedly mixed results. But he simply wanted to transfer to them the means for achieving a clear mind of their own. This was his noble calling. He just boldly and openly lived his truth and let the chips fall where they may. "Screw posterity, I really haven't got the time or the inclination, and anyway what have they done for me lately?" is probably something like what he must have thought. He was an all out front kind of a guy. Sock it to 'em Socrates!

"The unexamined life is not worth living." **– Socrates**

He was eventually formally accused of corrupting the innocent youth of Athens. When the judges, looking for remorse before he was sentenced, asked him what he thought his just punishment should be, Socrates would not be intimidated. With a glint in his eye, and probably tongue-in-cheek, he boldly suggested that the citizens of Athens should provide him with free dinners for the rest of his life and an annual monetary stipend in appreciation for his already long and voluntary public service on their behalf. The judges didn't agree and sentenced him to death. Just like Giordano Bruno, he became yet another socially victimized martyr for free intellectual speech. We Americans should all be very thankful for our founding father's Bill of Rights. It has always been and still is a righteous fight, and even today its tenets are not very widely held in many parts of the world.

If it weren't for his own young student, loving admirer, and fellow philosopher Plato, we probably wouldn't know very much at all about the "Socratic Method" or even who this exceptionally gifted original thinker and one of the first progenitors of all of Western Civilization's philosophers really was. Plato seemingly selflessly dedicated his own life to preserving the living memory of Socrates by eventually collecting and writing down many of Socrates' long spirited after dinner symposiums and involved philosophic dialogues. Although in many of these works it is very hard to tell where Socrates leaves off and Plato begins. But unquestionably without his commentary, Socrates could just as easily have slipped through the cracks of history and been totally forgotten and lost forever to our Western culture.

My son says:

"Wow, so that's what Socrates was all about! I just put him together with all those other early Greek philosophers like Aristotle and Ptolemy and the all the rest before anybody really understood anything about the scientific method. They would just come up with blanket statements about physical laws from off the top of their heads without any real scientific investigation and messed up everybody's mind for centuries until Galileo came along and had to painstakingly straighten everything out."

I say:

"Right, that's a very common misunderstanding. Many people don't have a clear idea of just who Socrates really was. He was truly unique and had a very pure intellect and he wasn't ashamed to use it in his everyday life. He's definitely one of my heroes."

****

But not everyone remains blandly unaware... After a certain amount of time a certain type of sensitive person will start to directly question himself, perhaps because of an unhappy event or some other unexpected troubling life experience. He will slowly start to realize that within himself there is something that is jarringly incomplete, or unresolved and somehow or another – wrong; something that is not whole, something dissonant and that continues to make him feel uncomfortable with himself. It is this unrealized wrong thing which is to blame and that has caused this latest troubling incident to happen.

He will then go further within and directly ask himself just *why* he did something, or just *why* he caused something to happen, or just *why* he didn't intervene, or just *why* he said something unfeeling awkward or hurting, or just *why* he believes something erroneously; and surprisingly he will not have a quick and easy answer to all these basic questions. He will not really know the underlying reason of just *why!* But this simple inner probing act of questioning oneself is the beginning of self-awareness and it is the very important first step on the road to becoming a fully conscious and unified empathetic spiritual being.

"The journey of 1,000 miles begins with a single step"
– Lao-Tzu

This is the step. He is entering the self-examination stage of his life's journey. During the normal course of his young development he has unknowingly become a complex chimera, a mixture of random and unexamined experiences and beliefs, as we all have. He must slowly begin to sift through and disconnect himself from all these random unfiltered and un-judged things that he has taken into himself and swallowed whole and that have unknowingly stuck to him during his early developmental period that at the time he exercised no conscious control over. The fact is that all these things will still continue to exert their influence on his present day thought and behavior, but if he continues in this self-work and is successful through this ongoing internal examination process, he will have the opportunity to discover and realize his own true nature. All these accumulated things must be re-examined one by one and seen in the clear light for what they really are, and for each one he needs to ask himself, "Is this piece of me valuable, is it real, or is it just a random piece of dross that has unconsciously stuck to me during my early formative years and is now holding me back and needs to be pulled off looked at and considered one last time and finally discarded?" This is the essence of the on-going internal work of self-realization.

Why do I do what I do, does it help me or others? Does it not only help me, but does it address the greater good for other people around me and in the world too? Why do I think what I think, where did it come from, what is its basis, is it good, is it useful and true, is it life affirming? Or is it just a meaningless old habit, or even negative, hateful and destructive in nature? Why do I believe what I believe? Is it only what I have been told to believe by others? Is it just some fashionable *zeitgeist* of the times? Does it have any true value and basis in my own first-hand real world experience? Do I truly believe in it and do I understand and accept all of its possible future implications? Can I defend all these things to myself and others? These are the ongoing types of hard questions that need to be asked by the self and of the self, and that need to be answered in a truly open and honest way that will lead the questioner onward toward the path of becoming a more truly unified conscious and empathetic being. Socrates is no longer around to interrogate us so we must do it ourselves. This is the ultimate goal that Socrates wants us to achieve; to be an intellectually conscious unified empathetic spiritual being, wholly integrated and logically founded. No mean task!

This is the awakening of the true spirit, without actively going through this process you are just another one of the random sleepers in the cave. It is the beginning of the self-work – of examining your own inner core being, of getting rid of some of the arbitrary foolish contradictions of life's early erratic impressions that you may have unintentionally picked up during the normal process of your maturation. No one can do this for you. You are the only one that can do it. If after your true chimera condition dawns on you, and you enter into this deep self-examination process, and if you can successfully complete this internal self-work – then you will have evolved from essentially an arbitrary crazy quilt collection of conflicting haphazard randomly acquired personal "non-stuff" into a unified trans-personalized and conscious life-affirming empathetic spiritual whole. You will have led yourself out of the cave and your ceaseless wanderings in the dark will finally come to an end. You will then have a more wholly and holy realized point of view and truly have come into the light, and as a direct result of this inner quest you will also have become a whole unified being with much less accompanying self-doubt.

This lonely inner spirit-work consists of refining and reinforcing your own true nature to create a stable internally self-defined unique identity that will guide you through the rest of your life. It must be one that you can fully embrace and be at peace with, and that you can totally accept and call your very own.

***"Be who you really are and go all the way"* – Lao-Tzu**

This process can be variously sudden and joyful at times or long and painful and may have surprisingly unanticipated results. Everything you directly look at will initially re-assert its strong claim to remain within you. You must be ruthless and uncompromising in your judgments. Be cruelly honest, this is no place for nostalgia. You are actively engaged in the process of redefining and purifying your own life. This is a great quest. What is really valuable and important to you? What is really worth pursuing and what is not. How do you judge peoples' actions towards you and how do you react to them? These and many other important spiritual issues are at stake here. You may find that some things that seemed important to you are not so important anymore. You may realize that your comfort zone has been too easy and too self-serving and upon deeper reflection is no longer all that comfortable any more. But if you do persist, in the end you will come through this arduous self-work truly whole for the first time in your life, and you will understand and have confidence that you know who you are, and as a result will have a firm foundation for living the rest of your life. Ideally this will establish a stable unified self that is not riddled with random internal cultural, social, and other unrealistic fallacies and contradictions. It will greatly help you to make your own lasting life decisions and travel your own true path in a unique life without regrets. This is a rare and invaluable thing and no small accomplishment.

As a result you will become a firmly grounded, greatly enlarged, internally unified conscious empathetic spiritual human being that can withstand the effects of life's constant buffeting by the ever changing forces of the dynamic arbitrary outside world. Your basis will then no longer be one of self-doubt and insecurity. You will have formed and developed your own true self-created stable spiritual vantage point that you will be able to accept as being true to yourself and will be at peace within it, and from which you can comfortably view and actively take part in the great on-going theater of time and creation which contains us all. What you do will be worth your doing, your decisions will be formed from your own stable inner truth, and your beliefs will be your own true beliefs founded in your own true self.

This again is exactly what Socrates wants and expects us to do to live a life worth living. With Socrates' help many of his Greek contemporaries were awakened and enabled to live this ideal. The Buddha in his great meditation sitting under the Bodhi tree in the Deer Park was doing just this same kind of deep introspection and self-examination. He was fully engaged in practicing this same kind of uncompromising self-awareness when he was forming his four noble truths and the eight-fold Buddhist path to the good life. The Buddha and Socrates of course are two of the great souls in world history who did effect a change in the world that came after them. Our own process may not be so dramatic or have such far reaching consequences, but it is none the less all important for our own self-development. The world is large, complex, and all consuming. How many people do you think on their own ever really consciously begin this internal self-work? How many do you think actually complete it? Without it there are only many different levels of continuing chaos, self-doubt, and many endless internal states of anxiety and confusion.

****

This above discussion is all about what I've recently come to call "non-stuff." It is about the process of looking deeply inward and doing the essential self-work that is of a self-transforming nature that can be only be performed by the self at a meta-level on the self. In fact the deeper my son and I got into our discussions of these things and these processes the more often we returned to this nexus level of "stuff" verses "non-stuff." It seemed to hold the essential kernel of the differences between us. He rebelled for the longest time and kept on totally denying and rejecting the reality, importance, or even the existence of any non-stuff at all. In his accepted world view of materialism and objective provable scientific truth – in this reality there was no room for the existence of any non-stuff at all. It was unreal, an illusion. It did not count and could not exist, it was just a pure fantasy, a self-delusion, a children's story not to be sanctioned or believed in by any serious adults.

Almost all of my son's primary and secondary education has been all about stuff and the long history of stuff. Even the teaching of world history in primary and secondary school was almost exclusively about what happened, where, and when. What happened, where, and when is stuff; why it happened is non-stuff. There is a predilection or even perhaps a phobia against talking about any non-stuff throughout our culture. Maybe because so few people are actually qualified to do it; or is it just too close to a sensitive truth that must be protected at all costs and not revealed?

Just because this is "non-stuff" that doesn't mean that it's completely arbitrary and unreal, and it shouldn't be summarily dismissed as not worth examining or understanding. This exclusive attitude is almost omnipresent everywhere you look, and it even strongly exerts its force on the daily evening news programs! There the reporting is consistently almost exclusively all about what happened, where, and when, and to whom and by whom, but seldom if ever broaching the subject of just why it happened at all. This blind cultural prejudice is very pervasive with the result that there is almost no teaching of pivotal and essential non-stuff in public schools at all.

It is therefore not surprising that it held so little reality for my son, and it all appeared to him as a non-existent self-deluded fiction. If it did not exist as a real objective measurable force, then it did not really exist in the real world at all, it could not possibly be important, and therefore it could all really be safely ignored. In my son's accepted real world view there was really only just enough real room for absolutely real stuff. Really…

Chapter 5. What is Stuff?

Only stuff exists in the real world. Everything you see is stuff. You eat stuff, you wear stuff, you live in stuff, and you buy and sell stuff. All is stuff, but don't examine it too closely or you just might find out that there may really be no stuff there at all – that at the deepest physical level, it is all just empty stuff. That deep existential sub-atomic conundrum of whether or not the atom is actually made of any real stuff at all is not what we're talking about here. We'll just leave that problem for the theoretical physicists to resolve. As far as we're concerned, it's all still really stuff. All the stuff that surrounds us which may or may not really consist of any stuff at all, is all still really stuff for us – it is not non-stuff. Non-stuff is something totally different. Just wait – we'll examine what non-stuff is in a little while. So let's just talk about stuff for now.

Stuff is everywhere and you can do just about anything with it. It's really great stuff. The history of the rise of man the tool maker is chock full of the ever-advancing improvements in the making and using of all sorts of stuff. From sticks and stones, to metals and engines, to plastics and electronics, on and on, lots and lots of new stuff is coming down the pike all the time. You've just got to watch the commercials and read the news to catch up on what's the latest new stuff people are coming up with. And it all appears to be totally unbounded as regards any of its many future possibilities.

People used to be limited to how far they could walk or ride a horse in one day and that was where they mostly stayed. But now with the right stuff you can go just about anywhere. You can travel over land at high speeds, travel over water, under water, through the air, and now even into outer space. You can instantaneously see and talk to people very far away, you can buy stuff in other countries and have it sent directly to your own doorstep, and do so many other things too numerous to mention right from your own home. Our modern mastery over so many different forms of new stuff is the culmination of many centuries of human creative activity worldwide. Stuff sure is great. Even though we don't really know what it is, or just where it all came from, you can sure do a lot of neat things and have lots of fun with stuff!

How do we do it? We use science and technology. These are the historical collection and the constantly evolving rules and physical laws and processes for manipulating stuff into what we want it to be. We take some raw stuff, a little of this and a little of that, and process it somehow, we do a little of this and a little of that to it, and we make something that is new and useful to us, or just plain fun, or beautiful, or having as many other different kinds of properties as our collective imagination can devise. It is not necessarily easy to do this – it requires great discipline knowledge work and dedication. The people who study and do this kind of work professionally have developed what the Germans call "*wissenschaft*" or "know-how." Just about all our creative and economic efforts are directed towards these productive ends. This is a main economic engine of society and includes inventing, designing, manufacturing, advertising, distributing, and the selling of all this new stuff. And this results in material progress and things that just seem to be getting endlessly better and better.

You'd think that all the material needs of human societies would have been met and solved by now. But you'd be wrong. There seems to be truly endless needs people demand and require. And also inventors keep on coming up with new things that we didn't even know we needed until they appeared, and then we need to get them just as soon as we can. You can get rich by creating new stuff that people will want. You can also die trying. The new stuff is in the stores, the old stuff is at the dump, and we are in the middle.

There always seems to be some neat advantage in having the latest and best new stuff that's available. You can do the same old things you used to do only easier and faster. When I went to college we used slide rules in math and science. They were a great invention and it took some skill and knowledge to do complex math on this simple analog physical device. My son doesn't even know what a slide rule is, much less how to use one. Now they use digital calculators, you can get more accurate answers quicker and easier. So now digital calculators are in the stores and the old analog slide rules are obsolete and in the dump. If you are a stock broker with the latest fastest computer trading programs, for a while you can beat out the others and buy the hottest rising stock micro-seconds faster and fractions of a point cheaper than your competitors and make a risk-free killing in the market. The latest model cars are always somewhat better than the older ones. They will all have built into them the latest cyber do-dads and innovations that will be more convenient and will help you save more money in the long run. They may even run on different more economical energy sources; although of course they are always more expensive to buy too, so paradoxically you've got to be rich in order to save money! Henry Ford "magnanimously" raised his workers pay, and also priced his early automobiles at levels so that his workers could afford to buy them, which greatly contributed to the success of his company. This mutually good marketing idea seems to have gone out of style. If you're a military man with the newest weapons stuff, you'll be able to kill more and more of the enemy easier, faster, and more accurately – and maybe you can even kill them from a much greater distance and not be in jeopardy yourself, and so forth on and on.

Are not all these desirable things? Sure they are, and they have been very cleverly designed to be so. The makers of these new things that never existed before then must somehow create a new market demand for them. This can be a big stumbling block for independent inventors without large corporate funding behind them for the advertising and promotion needed to get the word out. Here's an interesting old story about an early innovator with just this same kind of stubborn marketing problem and how he solved it long before the age of radio and TV advertising and the internet.

King C. Gillette is credited with the invention of the first successfully mass produced safety razor. He patented his new razor in the year 1901 to replace the common straight razor which had already been in use by men to shave for centuries, and with which you could quite easily kill yourself or murder someone else, both of which were impossible to do with his new safety razor. The Gillette Safety Razor used a very small disposable two sided thin flexible steel blade that when it got dull all you had to do was just throw it away and then replace it by putting in another sharp new one from your own handy packet of Gillette replacement safety razor blades. K. C. Gillette thought it was a great convenient new idea whose time had come and he was already committed to it and very heavily invested in its manufacturing process. But the trouble was that nobody was buying his "new improved" razors simply because everyone already had their own old straight razors which they were used to using and had been already in the habit of shaving with for their whole lives. These straight razors had a sturdy folding thick permanent long lasting high quality steel blade that whenever it got dull you could just re-sharpen it on a leather razor sharpening strop and you could continue to use the same straight razor over and over again for many years. But it did need to be re-sharpened often and it also required the new young shaver to develop a certain level of skill in learning how to safely sharpen and use the inherently very dangerous straight razor safely without cutting oneself.

After Gillette had invested a great deal of his own money in the project to bring his safety razor to market, he now saw that he hardly had any sales to speak of and suddenly found himself with thousands of unsold safety razors and no customers. As a result, he was on the verge of total financial ruin. He panicked and did not know what to do, yet he still really believed in his product. So just to avoid bankruptcy and escape a total loss, he hit upon a brilliant and even patriotic marketing strategy. He decided to "magnanimously" give away one free Gillette Safety Razor to every new young soldier in the U.S. Army. He thus created all at once a whole large market of young new shavers who would start out with his razors and then continue to use his shaving products as civilians.

My son says:

"Wow Dad, you won't believe this, but right after I turned 18 and had to register for the Military Draft, I got in the mail one free Gillette Safety Razor and blades along with a note from the company saying congratulations that I was now a real man and that I should start shaving with the razor a real man uses!"

I say:

"Holy cow! I didn't know that! Is that really true? That means that the Gillette Company is still actually using that first daring successful marketing strategy developed by their nearly bankrupt historical founder K. C. Gillette in his final desperate effort just to save his company from bankruptcy over a century ago, and it still works!"

Here's why it still works. Once you have his safety razor you develop a loyalty to this brand and you still needed to keep on buying his replacement Gillette razor blades for it too, so these blades became his first real profit making item. You might then even go out and buy his latest new razor too. In fact the old used razor blades were one of the first forms of industrial mass produced garbage ever created, as they were specifically made to be disposable and to finally be thrown away. At that time people were not used to things that could not be re-used. Not only did they not know what to do with them, but the used blades removed from the safety razors were also still dangerous since you could quite easily accidentally cut yourself with them too. If you go into many old vintage bathrooms of the period you'll often see the creative solution many devised solely to solve this odd new problem. There will often be an inconspicuous small horizontal slit a few inches wide cut right through the bathroom wall near the sink and mirror. This was where after replacing a Gillette Safety Razor blade, commonly the old used blades were forever safely disposed of by just slipping them right into the bathroom wall where they would all remain neatly out of sight and safely collect over time as a pile of used blades in the inner space between the walls.

Of course, new stuff, especially new cyber stuff can easily become addictive and self-perpetuating. Once you have made an investment in one type of computer device you then have a commitment to it and are always looking for new ways to improve it. You'll develop a hunger and get excited when there's a free new upgrade or a neat new app or a faster service available, etc. This same trend is at work even in the world of war armaments too, and the danger of this was noted long ago by outgoing president Dwight

D. Eisenhower who warned us in his farewell address to the nation in 1961 against the growing dangers of the politically self-perpetuating all powerful military/industrial complex. The retiring president and former Five Star General had fought in and been instrumental in winning World War II as The Supreme Commander of all Allied Forces. He had seen and experienced first-hand the bloody horrors of large scale modern warfare. He was appalled that in a time of peace after the war was over and finally won, that the dynamic United States industrial war machine which had created so many new and advanced weapons just to win that war, showed no signs of stopping, or even slowing down. And he was right – even now so many years later it is still going on strong. In fact, some people say that we keep on having new wars so that the military can field test their new weapons. We have the biggest and best armed forces in the world by far and still continue to spend huge amounts of our gross national product every year in an ongoing effort to keep improving them. Why? Is this all just uncontrolled nationalistic paranoia? Is it just xenophobic fear manipulated to insure great endless profits for mean spirited industrialists in conjunction with willing politicians on the take?

The thing that really keeps this all going is the unending force of competition between countries, which is also the same force that is structurally built into the capitalist marketplace system. The ego-centered desire and institutionally locked-in rewards of being the first with the best are overwhelming. What happens is that pretty soon everyone else you are competing with also has acquired the latest good stuff. Once again you'll start looking for ever newer and better stuff that can give you the competitive edge once more, and then again, and again, and so on and on through the inventive genius of mankind, progresses the ever advancing world of new and better stuff.

I am personally astounded by the large number of inventions that first only appeared as speculative ideas in comic books and in works of science fiction and in how short a time it took for them to actually become real and available products for purchase. As a stunning example, in the 1979 speculative humorous science fiction novel "The Hitchhiker's Guide to the Galaxy" there is a small device, the aforementioned Hitchhiker's Guide that gives instant information when asked about any subject in the universe, which at the time seemed totally outrageous! It is truly already here with us in the form of the ubiquitous smart phones most people carry around in their pockets. Maybe not the universe, but it seems they've got planet Earth pretty well covered. It seems as though nearly anything the creative mind can imagine, the technological mind can produce.

The smart phone was a major improvement from that earlier problem solving device, "The Magic 8 Ball." This was an entertaining analog concoction that looked like a large black number 8 billiards ball which was filled with a dark liquid. You would ask it any question that could be answered with a "yes" or a "no," then you'd turn it over and one face of a floating icosahedron would appear in the transparent window on the bottom. It would have phrases like "Definitely," "Maybe in the Future," "Not likely," "Ask Again," "Never," or one of 20 such random quotes printed on it that was your answer. People would actually use it sometimes to make decisions! It was lots of fun, but not nearly as informative as are our smart phones of today.

There is apparently no end to the demand and supply of newly improved, and ever better and still better new stuff. There is an old joke that the goal of life is to collect more and more new stuff, and the guy who has the most stuff in the end wins. Here is yet another instance in which the following from the Christ's Sermon on the Mount still applies:

***"Sufficient unto the day is the evil thereof."* – Jesus**

My son says:

"Stuff is the only thing that really exists. Non-stuff is non-existent and is therefore unimportant. There is only stuff, and stuff is all important. I need really good stuff for everything I do, and I only want to have the latest and best stuff that's available. I need to have the newest smart phone, the latest advanced game, and the next generation computer as soon as it comes out. I'll stand in line for it at the mall. It's very important for me to get the best new stuff I can get, and to get it first."

I say:

"Yes, that's all good stuff, but aren't you over doing it? Aren't you totally externalizing your identity? Don't you ever feel you are being manipulated by the marketplace? Aren't you just getting completely caught up in consumerism and in the materialistic *zeitgeist* of the times?

"Do all these things truly complete you? Do you always believe that they are so necessary and all that important? Do they enhance your inner well being? Are you somehow a lesser person if you don't immediately have the latest new stuff? Isn't it all really an endless treadmill you're on, and the faster you go the more you just stay in the same place? Think about it…"

There is only one alternative to becoming completely absorbed and totally dominated by the always changing material world of ever newer and more exciting stuff, and that is to become more fully aware of the ultimate importance of non-stuff.

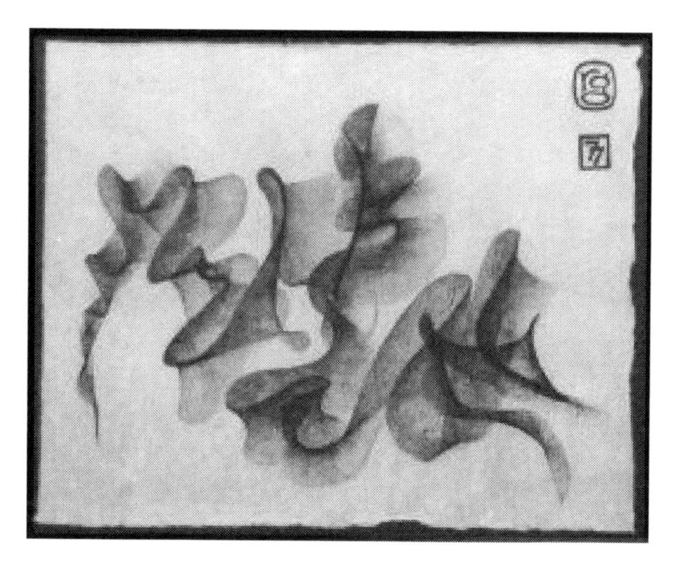

"Cloud Dragon #2"
from the author's "Nippon Homage Series," charcoal on rice paper

Chapter 6. What is Non-stuff?

OK, I think we've all got a pretty good understanding of just what stuff is. Stuff is anything that independently exists everywhere all around outside of us, and in this modern world it is always changing too. But non-stuff is just as meaningful to our existence as well, and there is really much more of it present and interacting within our daily lives than all of that stuff is. In fact, to function as a human being, non-stuff is even more important than stuff. So just where is all this immense amount of non-stuff located that I keep talking about?

Surprise surprise… Everything is also non-stuff too! Stuff is all there is out there; but non-stuff is all of that plus the immensity of subjective abstractions which we all keep deep inside of us. It is what ultimately makes us human. Here's a little comparative list to help you out:

Stuff	Non-stuff
House	Home
Keyboard	Writing
Books	Knowledge
Clothing	Fashion
Sex	Love
Brain	Mind
Sound	Music
Oil Paint	Oil Painting
Experiment	Theory
Two hands clapping	One hand clapping
Parents	Heritage
Job	Curriculum vitae

When I was talking about these things with my son I made a large hand written sign very much like the list above on an oversized artists pad of newsprint and left it open leaning against the wall on the stair landing on the way up to his bedroom so that he'd have to look at it every time as he passed by, at least two times a day, and hopefully that he might then just think about it then too. You can do this kind of thing if you're the parent.

So stuff is just what is, but non-stuff is what we think about all that stuff and our internal subjective evaluations of just what it is that is, and even much more. It is what finally happens to stuff when we are done having had our own direct experiences with it. We automatically turn that stuff directly into many different categories of non-stuff. Depending on just what the nature of our experience has been, we will create our own appropriate internal non-stuff that will become strongly attached to it. Stuff is basically neutral; it doesn't come with its own non-stuff already attached to it. We have to create all of this by ourselves. In fact we are the creators of all this non-stuff that we have stored up inside us, and it is our own intimate interactions with it that directs this work. This is what our inner spirit spontaneously does and how it is able to sort through our own everyday experiences. It reviews and analyzes exactly what has happened to us, and it evaluates just what all these things are that we have encountered in the real world of stuff every day. Then it decides just what this stuff really is all about and what it may ultimately mean to us. We all are continually creating our own unique great libraries of non-stuff data within ourselves every day. And it all remains there saved within us ever ready to be recalled in an instant to help us out if it is ever needed.

If you stop and think about the emotional difference between any similar random house and your own original childhood home, that difference is totally made up of all the non-stuff experiences you've had while you were living there. But non-stuff may also not only reference real stuff, but it may not necessarily be connected with any real things at all. Non-stuff is also deeply concerned with the myriads of other meta level things too, like the relationships between different events and even the relationships between the people you encounter, with each other and with you too. You are also continually internally creating lots of new meta level non-stuff material all the time. As I have said earlier, if you ever lose this ability, suddenly through a brain injury or slowly like an Alzheimer patient does, you will then also lose your basic ability to safely function within the objective outside world of stuff. You will cease to be a competent functioning human being. All the objective stuff is still there for the Alzheimer patient, but he is progressively losing all his inner lifetime collection of subjective non-stuff attached to and concerning all these things that are so essential for his survival. All the non-stuff information about all the stuff that surrounds him that he physically needs to survive is slowly disappearing. This tragic condition strongly supports the fact alluded to earlier – that our accumulated non-stuff knowledge is even more important to us than all the external stuff is.

In our internal mental states we are constantly working with our own unique sets of non-stuff, even in our dreams when we are sleeping in bed. What is a dream but pure total non-stuff unattached to anything at all! It is the living ongoing interactivity of all the non-stuff that you have collected and stored within your mind over time totally freed from the world of stuff. It is definitely a very creative wholly internal mental event that also oddly enough adds directly to your collection of real experiences too. Dreams can be just as important to us as our waking experiences, and sometimes they can even be more important. There are some very well known real historic dreams that people have reported which have had very beneficial results for mankind's development as a whole that we will be discussing later on in this work. So don't totally discount dreaming either, it can become an unanticipated source of very important non-stuff, and dreams can even become the source for future real stuff too.

Not only does non-stuff make up part and parcel of all that we usually think about, but it is also very active beneath this level by actively directing us to just what we should be thinking about, how we do feel about what we are thinking about, and what we are going to think about next, and what we eventually will do about what we already have been thinking about. It is the resource library that the inner spirit uses to automatically create judgments on many different levels, all of which then forms the essential spiritual framework of our lives. It becomes synonymous with our own inner character, and its outward influences are openly reflected in ourselves, but are often unrealized and even hidden from our own conscious minds. Ironically, it is what everyone else can easily see written on our faces and in our behavior and immediate actions and reactions. Paradoxically our own characters can often be more clearly revealed to strangers than they are apparent to ourselves.

OK, now you're starting to get the big idea. Stuff is just what is, but more important and meaningful to us than what is, is non-stuff, our evaluations, reaction, and relationship to all the different stuff data. Non-stuff is what is really important to our spiritual natures and what fully makes up our real inner mental and spiritual life. We even use non-stuff to understand at a deeper level just what stuff is. This is why the very same stuff can be seen and interpreted very differently by different people. What exactly are we talking about here? Is stuff just outside the head and non-stuff just inside the head? Or is there more to it?

My son says:

"Hold on Dad, everything that you say is non-stuff is really just the product and the side effects of real stuff. Non-stuff does not really objectively exist at all – it is just subjectively present within our minds. Non-stuff really exists only as emotions, memories, and logic, all of which are the manifestation of incredibly complex neurological systems in our brains, but all of which also operate purely as physical "stuff."

"We perceive what you call "non-stuff" and stuff in the exact same way, the only difference is that you can actually observe stuff, it is real and it has a sensory pattern associated with it that is totally independent of our own physical existence, while a living brain is the necessary pre-requisite and operational platform for any non-stuff to even exist at all. Everything you call "non-stuff" is normally just inferred from past observations or has innate operatives generating it such as the pressure to fit into society. But once again, everything you have described as non-stuff can be directly traced back to neurons and chemicals, and therefore it is all unequivocally still "stuff."

"It's one of those slippery slopes you are starting to go down that you won't be able to escape from. If you start trying to tell me that all this non-stuff is not just part of normal brain chemistry but comes from some mystic extra bodily sources in some other dimension, well where will all that end up? Surely in astrology and spooky ghosts floating around in the air!"

I Say:

"OK, that's all very good thinking Son! But what you are finally really saying here is just that non-stuff comes from stuff. Granted, I'll give you that. And that a brain is the necessary prerequisite for non-stuff to exist at all. Fine, I'll also grant you that, who alive doesn't have a brain? But the non-stuff relationship to the stuff is not a simple or direct transfer – it is transformed and re-shaped by our own unique subtle spiritual relationships with all the stuff data. We don't have to travel into other dimensions for this to happen. Not every house is a home, not every shirt is fashionable. What one person considers fashionable another does not. What's fashionable now will look old-fashioned eventually. These are all defined not by purely automatic chemical "stuff" brain reactions, but by each person's "non-stuff" individual internal subtle mental criteria. This criterion is not universal, nor is it "a priori" present in our brains; but they all develop uniquely in each person's mind based on his own inner spirit and are a deep reflection of what their individual unique belief structures really are. It is the subject and the object of the development of each person's own true inner living spirit.

"We all have our own unique inner life that takes the stuff data from the senses and sorts it, evaluates it, reshapes it; and likes it, dislikes it, honors it, reviles it, worships it, disavows it, loves it, hates it, rejects it, or finally fully accepts it and even incorporates it as an integral functioning non-stuff part of our own being. This is all strictly a volitional process of our minds, not an automatic chemical one of our brain. Yes, it may develop over time and form into a set recurring brain pathway, but it is not an automatic pre-set process. This all depends upon our own inner state of consciousness. We are not automatons. The same inputs do not produce the same outcomes in different people, but we are each capable of self discovery and our own uniquely directed inner growth. I believe that the non-stuff of the mind can re-direct the stuff of the brain. Preferably this will happen at a conscious level and we will be aware of it and be an active participant in the forces that are shaping us, of who we are, and who we are becoming – remember the ongoing dynamic nature of our "Circle of Being" – but it also can and does happen automatically also at the purely blind and unconscious level too."

My son says:

"Are you really saying here that all of this non-stuff is not a part of the human brain's activity and therefore is not a part of normal brain chemistry? I'm sorry, I can't accept this. This can't be true."

I Say:

"It may be true; I have a degree in chemistry, and I have some definitely formed ideas about just what chemistry is. Chemistry involves the interaction of chemicals in a known mathematical way. When certain chemicals are present in certain concentrations under certain conditions, certain products at certain other concentrations will inevitably result. Are words, our thoughts and desires, feelings and beliefs chemicals? Do they follow the laws of chemistry or laws of consciousness? There are well known definitely established laws of chemistry, are there yet to be discovered equally definite laws of consciousness too? Can consciousness be determined to produce pre-set results by only setting up its initial values and parameters? Product advertisers would certainly like you to believe that this is true…but I don't think so."

My son says:

"But come on now Dad, be realistic… Where else can all this be happening but inside the brain and therefore by the means of brain chemistry? Maybe it's not so simple chemistry as we understand it now, but some other ultimately more subtle kind of bio-electro-chemical-hormonal form of it. But really there is no other possibility, is there?"

I Say:

"What we are talking about here is the relationship of the mind and consciousness to the physical workings of the brain. This has been an age old area of inquiry and controversy that has come to be known in intellectual circles as "The Mind/Body Problem." How does the evanescent ethereal "non-stuff" of the human mind interact with the purely physical "stuff" of the human body? This question has a very long history in philosophy, biology, and medical arguments going all the way from Plato in ancient Greece to present day psychology and neuro-biochemistry research, and over this very long period of controversy it is still basically an unresolved problem. Many recognized great philosophers through the ages have had a crack at it including Plato, Aristotle, René Descartes, Immanuel Kant, Baruch Spinoza (look into him when you get a chance), Thomas Huxley, and many others. More recently even the Noble Prize winning molecular biologist Sir Francis Crick the renowned co-discoverer of the DNA helix devoted the last years of his active scientific life to working on unraveling The Mind/Body Problem. And even he did not get very far with it. Many scientists actually consider this question of the true nature of human consciousness to be totally outside of the realm of experimental research and scientific inquiry, and therefore they do not even consider it to be an appropriate question for scientists to ask. They've basically given up and thrown in the towel on the subject.

"On the other hand, religious people think scientists and philosophers are just banging their heads against the metaphysical wall and that they will never be able to solve this basic problem of human existence. And they also believe that they already know what the answer is. For them the answer lies in the realm of revealed religion and spiritual truths which lie totally outside of the realm of science. They simply point out that their belief in the existence of the immortal soul of man solves this riddle. All those difficult and troublesome non-stuff verses stuff questions we are talking about here, for them all really take place within the soul. The soul exists separately from the body and is divinely created and it is immortal – this all definitely makes it pure non-stuff.

"The body is just the present material vehicle for the soul while it is alive – so it is definitely stuff. The soul actively inhabits the body and the body is totally under the soul's command and control, but the soul is really the true individual and the repository of all our thoughts, and our deeds both good and evil, and it is the real immortal living spirit of the individual. Death is when the soul leaves the body. The body then returns to dust from whence it came, but the soul continues on with its own immortal existence in various scenarios depending upon just what religion you believe in. In many religions your accumulated good and bad deeds and the total karma of your earthly life still remain attached to the soul and the cumulative effects of these life formed deeds and events still directly affect the soul's journey in the afterlife. The soul then in some instances is called to eternal judgment based on its lifetime of accumulated deeds (karma). This judgment results in the immortal soul spending the rest of eternity either by receiving in heaven its blissfully earned rewards, or by suffering the punishment it rightfully deserves in horrendous hell. In other belief systems the soul is required to be re-incarnated into a different appropriate body, not necessarily human, which is also based on its past life performance (karma) and has yet another different new life to live and to thereby create new karma to influence its future. This reincarnation cycle recurs very many times with better or worse results again all based on how the soul behaved in its previous life form. Being born as a human being is seen as the greatest opportunity to influence this recurring cycle, something not to be wasted. Eventually through accruing excellent karma and achieving full spiritual enlightenment, reincarnation and the suffering of the soul can finally cease, and it will then remain in Nirvana. That seems to encompass most religious thought on the subject.

"But this is really no solution to the Mind/Body Problem at all, since if this is examined closely it can be clearly seen that this religious solution does not really solve anything. They have just applied a different label to the same original problem. For now instead of the stubbornly difficult Mind/Body Problem we now have the equally difficult Soul/Body Problem which for intellectuals is exactly the same as the original dilemma.

"Some of the different areas of questioning and approaches to The Mind/Body Problem can be summarized as follows: Is the brain's activity necessarily tied to the mind's activity? Conversely is the mind's activity necessarily tied to the brain's activity? Does the mind exist independently apart from the brain as a separate entity? If so how exactly do the brain and mind interact? Do they interact at all? Can different states of the mind influence different states of health of the body? And vice-versa. Is the mind totally a product of brain chemistry? Is the mind just an extra unnecessary side effect produced by the brain's normal ongoing chemical activity? Can the activities of the mind influence ongoing brain chemistry and neurological structure? And vice-versa. Is the mind really only an epiphenomenon? Are the brain and mind somehow (and how exactly?) two different aspects of the very same phenomenon?"

My son says:
"The Mind/Body problem, huh… It sounds very similar to the Stuff/Non-stuff problem, don't you think?"

I Say:
"I didn't realize that you even accepted the existence of non-stuff… I see we're finally starting to make some progress here… But all of this syntactical, philosophic, and even electro-chemical controversy is really much deeper than we need to go into here. Believe me, you and I are not going to come up with the final answer to The Mind/Body Problem in our discussions here. Someday in the future neuro-physiologists or maybe even computer cyber engineers may actually figure out just what and how human consciousness exists and they may finally solve the long standing historic puzzle of The Mind/Body Problem – or they may not. In the meantime we all have bodies and minds of our own. And we use them everyday. No problem.

"My basic argument here is that you are ultimately responsible for the non-stuff that you have created and accepted into your mind and spirit, but you are not responsible for the state of your brain's activity, whether or not they are separate or the same."

Chapter 7
Giordano Bruno to the Rescue

There are two very prominent craters on the surface of the moon – one is named Copernicus, and the other is named Giordano Bruno. We all have been taught and know a lot about Nicolaus Copernicus… So, who is this Bruno character, and why do so few people know about this other important historical figure?

Giordano Bruno was born in 1548 in Naples, Italy, five years after the death of Nicolaus Copernicus. He was an itinerant Benedictine monk, philosopher, mathematician, astronomer, teacher, and poet. After becoming a monk, he left the Benedictine monastery in Naples while under a cloud of suspicion for reading books by Erasmus forbidden by the Catholic Church. He then fled Italy and traveled for many years throughout Switzerland, France, England, and Germany. In his travels he often attained high court positions and university teaching posts associated with the nobility of these countries. During his years of independent exile he successfully published many books about his unconventional intellectual ideas and interests. These were often written in verse. When in England he was granted access to the court of Queen Elizabeth. He greatly admired her and while there he even dedicated one of his original works to her. But wherever he wandered he always seemed to be an outsider and unfortunately he never found a really welcoming or comfortable new home. Growing tired of his wanderings and longing to return home, he accepted the invitation of a Venetian aristocrat to privately instruct him. After he returned to Italy at the age of 44, his patron betrayed him and he was summarily arrested by the Catholic Inquisition as a renegade cleric and heretic. He was taken into custody in Venice, and in the course of his trial there for heresy he was extradited and sent to a more stringent inquisition trial in Rome by request of the Pope. During this inquisition ordeal he was imprisoned by the Catholic Church for eight years and finally convicted of heresy, his works were banned, and he was burned alive at the stake in the Campo dei Fiori in Rome on February 17, 1600. His ashes were then unceremoniously thrown into the Tiber River.

Before him, Copernicus had recently refuted the Geocentric Theory of the cosmos that people since the ancient times of the Greco-Egyptian philosopher and astronomer Ptolemy had believed to be true. This held that the Earth was unmoving and stable, and that it stood at the center of everything. In this theory the Sun, the moon, the planets, and all the stars revolved around the Earth in their own individual concentric heavenly spheres. This was a simple fact that anyone could go out, look up at the night sky and easily see for themselves was true. However, Copernicus came along and said that this was not true. He replaced the Earth with the Sun and said that the Sun was stable and at the center of everything, and that the planets, including the Earth revolved around it. He said that the earth was not static, but in fact was moving very fast having two different motions at the same time – it was rotating many hundreds of miles an hour on its axis once a day, and revolving in an orbit around the Sun once a year. This was based on years of his own painstaking observations and he demonstrated why this was really a better and ultimately also a simpler explanation of what we could actually see in the heavens if we paid closer attention. This became known as the Heliocentric Theory of Copernicus.

This was his "Magnum Opus" or great work, which he only allowed to be published at the very end of his life. He actually could have published it as many as 30 years earlier, but he only received the first printed copy of his work "De Revolutionibus" on his death bed. He had worked secretly on it for many years, but he knew that it would be a very problematic book, especially among the clergy who held great power. He purposely delayed its publication because he didn't wish to be personally involved in such a great social controversy. He was right. For it did in fact prove controversial and very difficult for even many intelligent people to accept his theory. Even Tycho Brahe, the greatest living astronomer of the time, could not accept the basic idea that the Earth was in fact moving. He did not believe it and developed his own new composite theory in response.

But Galileo did, and he supported it and tried to popularize the Heliocentric Theory after the death of Copernicus. He even went so far as having private telescope viewing sessions with the Pope at the Vatican to show him the newly discovered moons of Jupiter, the only celestial bodies known at the time that didn't apparently orbit around the Earth. All he got for his efforts was to have a heresy inquisition of his own and to be banished from Rome and also excommunicated from the Church. Just imagine what would have happened to Copernicus!

Then into this raging cosmic controversy along comes Giordano Bruno who had the audacity to say that most of the Heliocentric Theory was fine, but that even the Sun itself really wasn't anything so very special at all. That no, even Copernicus had gotten it wrong. The Sun was not sitting unmoving at the center of everything just like the Earth used to be, but that in fact it was not at the center of anything! Bruno said that our Sun was just another ordinary star among an infinite number of other stars that were all just floating around freely in an infinite space. He also stated that all of these other stars could have planets around them too. And that on these other planets there could also be many other intelligent forms of life. And that all these other stars and worlds were many and common, and that they were spread out at random all over a universe of infinite space. This was Bruno's proffered infinite worlds conjecture. It was a wonderful clear vision far ahead of its time and it would cause him great grief.

It was such an unprecedented and very radical remaking of the entire universe that held unimaginable repercussions for humanity's long held traditional central place in it. It was all very unsettling to the status quo, and especially to the church hierarchy of that time. Who could believe this? This was not anything like what the Bible said. This was not what countless intelligent people had believed for centuries before. But today we are all truly living in Giordano Bruno's universe, not in Ptolemy's or even Copernicus' and the Catholic Church cannot fight this cosmic truth any longer and has come to accept it.

Giordano Bruno was at heart a philosopher who railed against limits of any kind and accepted none for himself or his work; he also had a great natural affinity for thinking in terms of the infinite. Part of his arguments at the time for these extraordinary revolutionary ideas of the existence of an unlimited universe with many other populated exo-planets were actually theologically based. Bruno was himself an ordained itinerant Benedictine monk and he did openly profess a strong belief in God. His argument was that an infinite unlimited God would surely not have been satisfied by limiting himself to creating just one world in a severely enclosed and limited universe, but he would certainly have created an infinite universe with many others worlds in it too. To Giordano Bruno this idea was ultimately liberating and not at all scary. But unfortunately for him the Holy Bible didn't mention any of this.

Today, five centuries later, Giordano would surely have a big broad "I told you so!" smile on his face. He would be delighted to know how our present day understanding of the universe with its billions and billions of galaxies let alone stars aligns perfectly well with his intuitive early speculative leap. Unfortunately all of this came about way too late to help save him from his own terrible fiery fate.

Giordano Bruno did not dispute the basic facts that Copernicus had discovered and described. The Sun was still at the center of our own planetary system. He understood the great beauty of just what Copernicus had figured out on his own and the truth of the conclusions he had reached over so many years of solitary work. He only added one essential final tweak to it. Bruno simply pointed out that we were not anything so exceptional, and that the Sun, our planetary system, and humanity itself could not possibly be so totally unique in the entire universe. He boldly stated his belief that humanity and our solar system was not the single most important thing stably located at the very center of the cosmos, but that we were only floating around somewhere in infinite space and that we were just another local instance of a very common cosmic occurrence. His idea was an early expression of what in modern times has come to be known as the Cosmological Principle – that the universe is isotropic – that is, that it will look exactly the same to any and all observers from any and all vantage points.

Giordano Bruno had single handedly just administered the final kick in the butt to mankind that knocked him off his high horse for good. It was one of his great insights to understand and proclaim that our bright large disc of a sun that appears to be so unique in all the heavens, and moves so relentlessly alone every day across the bright blue daylight sky above us, was in reality exactly the very same thing as all those many other tiny fixed twinkling points of light in the starry firmament that were sprinkled so richly and randomly across the dark night sky above us, just much much closer.

Now these were big, threatening, dangerous, and revolutionary ideas to the church hierarchy of the 16th century and they reasoned that they had to suppress them as well as Giordano Bruno himself as being a real threat to their dominance and authority. So they locked him up for eight years and gave him the standard church inquisition trial and ultimately condemned him and all his works to be eradicated. He was sentenced to be publicly burned at the stake as just another dangerous evil non-believing heretic. This was also to be viewed by the public at large as a harsh cautionary lesson for any and all other free thinkers who might be hanging around to insure that they just remain silent and not question publicly the final ultimate authority of the clergy and not intellectually poke around and cause any more unnecessary troubles for the church hierarchy.

It has taken many many years, centuries really, for these ideas to finally trickle down to the man on the street. Most of us still commonly use the expression "outer space" as if it is out there and that we are not in it, just like it is described in Ptolemy's ancient Geocentric Theory. Giordano Bruno's modern astronomical concepts and refinements and expansion of what Copernicus had discovered is the contribution that today he is best known for, and the reason modern astronomers have named a crater on the moon in his honor; but it is not the one that we are interested in here.

One of his other great insights was that not only does there exist an infinity of space outside of man on the Earth and in the Universe, but there is also another *different* infinity of space within man himself. And that we exist as a living person exactly between these *two different infinities*, and that we as living sentient beings experience them both simultaneously. This goes a lot deeper than just simple objectivity vs. subjectivity.

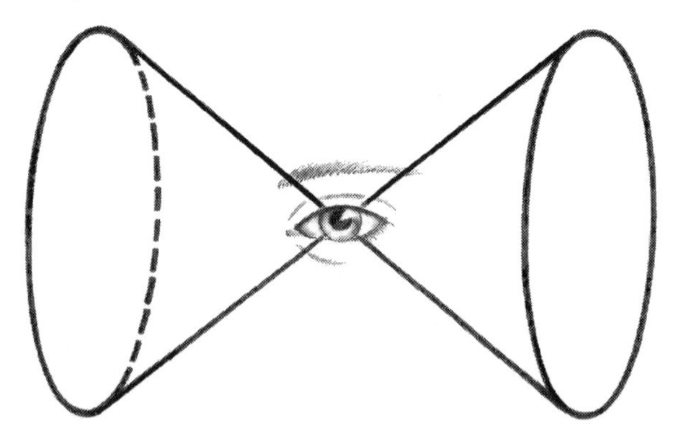

Giordano Bruno's Concept of Two Infinities

Think of his idea as being two cones meeting at their vertexes but each going in opposite directions to different infinities. One is going outward into our immediate surroundings, the world, and the universe at large; while the other is going inward into the depths of our minds. Our position as human beings is directly at the vertex of these two different infinities. We are seen as living in both of them at the same time. This is another of Giordano Bruno's powerful philosophical insights and is yet another example of his proclivity of thinking in terms of the infinite. He had many true original insights into man's actual position in God's infinite universe.

This also brings to mind several other potent little historical Zen stories. Here's one:

"The Stone Mind" *

Hogan, a Chinese Zen teacher, lived alone in a small temple in the country. One day four traveling monks appeared and asked if they might make a fire in his yard to warm themselves.

While they were building the fire, Hogan heard them arguing about subjectivity and objectivity. He joined them and said: "There is a big stone. Do you consider it to be inside or outside your mind?"

One of the monks replied: "From the Buddhist viewpoint everything is an objectification of mind, so I would say that the stone is inside my mind."

"Your head must feel very heavy," observed Hogan, "if you are carrying around a stone like that in your mind."

And here's another:

"Not the Wind, Not the Flag" *

Two monks were arguing about a flag. One said: "The flag is moving."

The other said: "The wind is moving."

The sixth patriarch happened to be passing by. He told them: "Not the wind, not the flag: mind is moving."

**from "Zen Flesh, Zen Bones" compiled by Paul Reps.*

How does Giordano Bruno's concept of the two different infinities man directly experiences relate to our discussions here? The infinity outside of man is the infinity of stuff. And his concept of the different infinity inside of man is our infinity of non-stuff. So, what do you think would be Bruno's answer to the Zen teacher Hogan's question of the traveling monks in "The Stone Mind" story above?

"Is the big stone outside or inside your mind?" asks Hogan.

To Giordano Bruno, since the two different infinities, internal and external, are both experienced by us simultaneously, the big stone is both inside and outside the mind at the same time. But, and here is another very important point ***– it is not the same stone!***

Flowers for Giordano

Giordano Bruno is regarded today by the people who know of him as a martyr for free thought and modern scientific ideas. There is an as yet un-awarded prize named "The Bruno" for the first person to positively identify intelligent life outside of our solar system. Today, over the Vatican's strong objections, there is a large bronze statue of him commissioned by contributions to a public fund created by the university students of Rome and erected in 1889 at the Campo dei Fiori at the same place where he was executed in 1600, with a plaque inscribed:

"To Giordano Bruno: from the century he guessed at,
in Rome, at the place where he was burned."

I have heard that annually on February 17th many locals leave flowers at its base and congregate around this statue to celebrate his life. A great and varied assortment of people including teachers, students of Rome, Catholics, Jews, atheists, Freemasons, musicians, artists, poets, and sundry others in support of unrestricted freedom of intellectual curiosity and total freedom of speech, all come here before Bruno's statue to pay informal loving tribute to him annually on the date and at this the very place of his tortured death.

It is a tragedy that Giordano Bruno was killed only 52 years after his birth by a paranoid clergy on a rampage. He had only lived 44 years as a free man; and most of his adult years were spent on the run from the Catholic Church. During his trial he refused to recant his views of the Copernican Theory, his concept of an infinite universe, his theory of many populated worlds outside of our own solar system, and his many other non-conforming ideas. We all remain the poorer for it as we can never know just what other beautiful "non-stuff ideas" he could have brought forth from his own self-defined infinite internal mind space into our own ongoing Western culture if he had not been relentlessly persecuted by the Catholic Church but simply allowed to live a normal life.

Perhaps one of the main reasons that still so few people know of him and his ideas are the long term affects of the 16th century church's bans and their ordered destruction of all his books. Many of these works however have survived in non-catholic countries. More than a century after Galileo's death, his excommunication was vacated and his body now lies in a tomb in a place of honor in the Santa Croce Cathedral in Florence, Italy. Over these many centuries the Catholic Church has never changed its mind on Bruno. Perhaps his being an ordained Benedictine monk made the Church especially vindictive against him because he was one of their own. It is interesting to note that neither Copernicus nor Galileo was thought to be so dangerous to the Church that they needed to be burned alive.

I have been so touched by this history that I have decided for myself to dedicate February 17th the day Bruno was burned alive at the stake as "International Giordano Bruno Day." From now on it will be a fasting day to remember honor and celebrate the life of this great 16th century persecuted itinerant monk, philosopher, mathematician, teacher, poet, astronomer, and early master of infinity. He did not deserve his fiery fate for being steadfast in his beliefs and trying to pull humanity out of its long isolating darkness. All who wish are also welcome to join me in this tribute on their own. And if I am ever in Rome again I too shall make my way to the Campo dei Fiori with flowers for Giordano and I shall have a long silent meditation before his statue.

Memorial to Giordano Bruno

"To Giordano Bruno: from the century he guessed at, in Rome, at the place where he was burned."

Chapter 8. The Infinity Within

We are all familiar with the infinity of stuff outside of man. It consists of everything around us – from our bodies outwards to the ends of creation. Science hasn't really come to any final conclusions about where it all came from, its full extent, or what it is actually made of. In some odd way with the recent new unknowns of dark matter and dark energy, these questions have become even more open ended now than they ever were in the past. Although we have gathered much more scientific knowledge about the universe today, we seem to be even less certain about its true nature than was apparent to the intellectuals of Bruno's time. This is often the way in which knowledge progresses; although we actually do know much more, we paradoxically also seem to really know much less! This new knowledge has only made us realize just how much more there is yet to be known. Many of the old questions Bruno and Copernicus struggled with have long since been resolved, however new and even greater mysteries have arisen.

But in our own everyday reality we all fully understand the basic nature of our local part of the universe. We are all living and working in our own small personal part of this grand infinite mysterious universe at large. But to us it appears simply as the ordinary mundane world into which we were born and grew up in and so we can easily find our way around in it everyday. We have absolutely no trouble at all in understanding it first hand and its general overall nature to us is completely mundane. Yes, at special times we can be in awe of its true majesty, but usually it is merely the universal ho-hum physical setting of our ordinary daily lives that we have experienced since birth till death do us part.

But what exactly is the nature of Giordano Bruno's other different infinity within man? This is a totally different world that is not at all so mundane or commonplace. It is not made out of any real stuff at all and it does not follow the rules or the laws of real stuff, and it also does not even exist in real space either. (These are two of the basic reasons why my son so defiantly rejects its existence and its reality!) So what are its properties and the qualities of our experiences in this other separate quite different exotic world of infinite inner space? Let's look into this world of non-stuff at a deeper level.

Here is a taste of where these conversations with my son took us. Remember the earlier discussion we had about the viewing of the painting in the art museum? Paintings and all art in general exists as a strange sort of tricky stuff hovering between these two worlds. It is definitely stuff. It is made out of ordinary stuff and it exists fully in the world of real stuff. But it is more often than not dealing with, talking about, and pointing directly at that other different infinite inner world within us of non-stuff, filled with all those great non-stuff non-things like our direct experiences of love, beauty, courage, spiritual presence, sensory absorption, poetic ideals and emotional intensity, and the like.

So to engage my son more deeply in exploring this other infinite non-stuff world that he doesn't countenance, this exclusive world of the human spirit that has no place in his accepted reality, I choose music as an entry point. I happen to know that my son likes Tchaikovsky's "Nutcracker Suite" very much. Even as a child he loved it and he deeply enjoyed playing timpani in a condensed version of it in his high school band concert. So while my son was fiercely denying the reality and existence of any and all non-stuff, as being just some form of romantic self delusion…

I say:
"But, what about music?"

My son says:
"It's just more stuff."

I say:
"But what about the Nutcracker?"

My son says:
"Just stuff, wooden violins, strings, vibrations in the air - just

more stuff period.

I say:

"Yeah, but what about when you hear "The Nutcracker Suite," you don't say, 'Ah wonderful, wood, strings, vibrations in the air!'

"No! You say, 'Ah, wonderful, The Nutcracker, Tchaikovsky!'

"You give the artist credit for his creative work. For his pure imaginative creation of the very beautiful non-stuff that is the Nutcracker Suite. This is the end result of the composer's totally internal mind-spirit work. Yes, you can write it down with musical notes and describe it, and you can even physically capture it in many ways, as an analogue record, or a CD, a computer file, etc. But all these things – musical notation, violins, wood, strings, vibrations in the air (yes, stuff) – all of this is just the mechanism and the vehicle for the transmittal of this purely beautiful non-stuff that is revealed in Tchaikovsky's "The Nutcracker Suite." There's no getting around it, the music itself can only come directly from that part that Giordano Bruno called "the infinity within man."

****

The creative act, any creative act be it "The Nutcracker Suite," painting, poetry, writing, invention, scientific theories, composing music, making movies, etc... all these things take place in this non-space of non-stuff, in Giordano Bruno's other infinity within man. This is the workshop of the creative mind and can only be seen with the mind's eye. Its materials, processes, and operative principles are infinite and unformed, and made of "no-thing," and are open to any and all mental manipulations. There are many well known instances of famous historic figures making direct and explicit reference to these facts. Here are a few.

There is the popular story familiar to all college organic chemistry students about the 19th century German professor and research chemist August Kekulé. This astute teacher literally dreamed up the benzene ring to explain the dramatic differences between the six carbon aliphatic hexane molecule and the six carbon aromatic benzene molecule. For those of you who don't know this story, Kekulé said that he had discovered the ring shape of the benzene molecule in a dream only after having spent seven years studying the nature of carbon to carbon bonds. He tells his creative dream discovery story about this organic chemistry breakthrough like this:

> "I was sitting writing on my textbook, but the work did not progress; my thoughts were elsewhere. I turned my chair to the fire and dozed. Again the atoms were gamboling before my eyes. This time the smaller groups kept modestly in the background. My mental eye, rendered more acute by the repeated visions of the kind, could now distinguish larger structures of manifold conformation; long rows sometimes more closely fitted together all twining and twisting in snake-like motion. But look! What was that? One of the snakes had seized hold of its own tail, and the form whirled mockingly before my eyes. As if by a flash of lightning I awoke; and this time also I spent the rest of the night in working out the consequences of the hypothesis."

At that unexpected and surprising moment when that snake of dancing non-stuff carbon atoms seized its own tail, right then Kekulé knew instinctively, that this spontaneously formed six carbon ring that he now clearly saw dancing and flexing before him, even mocking him while in this exotic dream state, was the real answer to the stubborn riddle of benzene's molecular structure. This was historically the true way a major breakthrough in organic chemistry happened and it was the beginning of a more complex and useful understanding of aromatic organic compounds. This basic discovery has contributed to advances in many other separate fields too, including industrial chemistry, biochemistry, and pharmaceuticals.

August Kekulé's dream image of a dancing snake eating its own tail is also the very same ancient symbol known as the "ouroboros" as seen in the endless knot representation of infinity. It is this same iconic symbol that we have already presented as an image once before in Chapter 3 of this book, "Everything Ends, But Nothing Begins" in a very different context. The ouroboros is a seminal and fecund ancient symbol that separately arose in many different forms and in many different cultures throughout history. It seems to represent something existing cross-culturally at what Carl Jung would describe as the very deep archetypical level of the human collective unconscious shared by all people. It is a cleverly designed and easily understood symbol for a very complex idea.

There is also the more exotic story related by Elias Howe about his attempt to invent the first sewing machine. He knew that it would be an important and valuable innovation that would greatly serve mankind if he could only succeed in its creation. But creating this complex machine was proving to be a very difficult task and he already had failed several times. One day when he had almost given up completely on ever solving this stubborn design problem, he too fell asleep and had his own very different inspirational breakthrough dream.

In Elias Howe's much more romantic dream he was being held captive in a primitive land and he was being forced to complete his sewing machine project in one day by a fierce local tribal chief. His reward would be to choose a beautiful tribal maiden of his liking if he succeeded – but failure would mean his own death. Of course in his dream he was still unable to complete the design. Then when the tribal warriors were coming to carry out the death sentence and execute him, he suddenly noticed an odd thing. The painted warriors now held him captive and had him surrounded and they were all dancing and threatening him by pointing and thrusting their deadly weapons directly at him. Each warrior held a long sharp dangerous looking spear, but the unusual thing he noticed was that at the very end of each long spear there was a small round hole pierced all the way through each spear blade just a short distance back from its point. Amazingly while in this savage strangely gripping dream he quickly realized that right there in front of him on display many times over all around him on the tip of each warriors spear was the actual solution to all the problems he'd been having designing the sewing machine!

Instantly within this strange erotic dream, he knew what had been wrong in all his previous unsuccessful attempts at designing the sewing machine. Instead of using the standard available hand sewing needles, which had their threading holes on the far end of the needle, at the end opposite from their points; he now clearly and for the first time saw that this had always been the main stumbling block and it was the basic cause of all his design difficulties. He then awoke very happy that he had not been killed in his dream. Strangely refreshed and very excited, he immediately went off to his workshop and quickly made the very first sewing machine needle. He revised its threading hole which he now located down at the point end of the needle. Then finally after making this basic design change inspired by the natives' spears in his strange dream, and having had the experience of so many design failures before, the rest of the invention now became easy for him to complete.

This creative solution had come to Elias Howe, the inventor of the first sewing machine, as a gift directly from Giordano Bruno's infinity within. Unfortunately, he was no longer able to exercise his choice of any of the many beautiful tribal women. They were gone forever – but the sewing machine remains a major invention of the 19th century. Isaac Singer improved upon his basic design and was more successful in marketing his Singer Sewing Machines, but he still had to pay Howe considerable royalties for his breakthrough innovations that made it all possible.

Not all these non-stuff inspirational leaps occur in the form of dreams. Albert Einstein too had his seminal ideas, and did all of his conceptual work that lead up to his Special and General Theory of Relativity – from riding on a light wave, to the experience of standing in a free falling elevator, and imagining lightning striking on the ends of moving trains – in this same space of Giordano Bruno's other infinity within man. He may also have dreamed up some of his groundbreaking ideas, but mostly he is known for his "thought experiments." These were the creative pure thought workshop of his ideas that he structured mentally as though they could actually be performed as real physical experiments but for the fact that they were either too dangerous to perform, as being in a free falling elevator, or were impossible to perform with our present day tools, like traveling at the speed of light. So he had no other choice but to perform them as non-stuff "thought experiments" in Giordano Bruno's infinitely creative work space within.

The basis of his extraordinary theories was that he firmly understood since the Michelson–Morley speed of light experiments, that you couldn't just have the speed of light remaining constant in all frames of reference without having other things like time and space itself bending. Einstein's ideas were so far "out of the box" of the standard scientific thought of his day that only a very few of his contemporaries could grasp them even after he presented and explained his paradigm changing scientific papers publicly at university lectures. He said "The intellect has little to do on the road to discovery. There comes a leap in consciousness, call it intuition or what you will, the solution suddenly comes to you and you don't know how or why."

For us it comes directly from what we've been calling Giordano Bruno's other creative infinity within man. And just like a repeat performance of what happened to Copernicus and Giordano Bruno, many very intelligent people upon hearing his new paradigm changing work outright rejected these strange new ideas he presented. Fortunately for Albert Einstein other experimental scientists took an interest in them and eventually they were able to experimentally confirm the precise predictions of his radical new theories. Also fortunately for him, burning at the stake had already long since gone out of fashion!

All the recognized great men and women in history have had to master some part of this formless internal terrain on their own. We only know about those who have done so and have successfully brought forth their creations into the real world so that the rest of us could benefit from their solitary inner creative work. Through some form of creative act by gifted individuals, non-stuff is ushered into the common world of stuff. Non-stuff is transformed and transmitted as real stuff into our objective world so that it can be readily seen and become a useful part of our ongoing culture. Once this happens others can directly experience it too and profit from their creators concentrated internal work. This is really the only way in which human culture progresses. Just think of how much of this is already here as our birthright that we do not even think about at all and just take for granted every day of our lives as having always been present – like math with Arabic numbers, the alphabet, our many human languages, and the printing press, etc. We are mostly the unaware inheritors of countless extraordinary gifts from the past. The list goes on and on!

The truly exciting part of this internal infinite creative non-stuff space is its essentially wild and uncontrolled nature. It seems to offer us a deep wellspring of unlimited potential which exists to some extent within all of us, but it also tends to be stubbornly independent and mostly out of our own willful conscious reach. We are often more under its control than it is under ours. Yet there seems to be a profound intrinsic reciprocal relationship between the depth of our need for its fruits and our earning of its fruitful benefits.

The ancients considered these benefits to be the outright gifts from another independent parallel world of eternal beings such as the nine classical Greek Muses. These were the daughters of Zeus who were the female goddesses that provided needed inspiration to those creative artists working in the fields of literature, philosophy, music, drama, and the arts. For those of us under the influence of modern psychological thought, it can also be seen as the creative work of the collective unconscious. For those neo-mystics with a scientific bent, it may be seen as the results of our subtle interaction with the weak nuclear force. For us here and now, it is the product of Giordano Bruno's other infinity within man. However you wish to think of it, it surely exists as part of our infinite world of non-stuff as many before us who have personally experienced its reality and have benefited from its gifts have already testified. But it still remains essentially mysterious, so feel free to call it whatever you like, you can take your pick, whatever floats your boat.

Wolfgang Amadeus Mozart

The great prolific classical composer Wolfgang Amadeus Mozart when once asked to describe his own creative process is said to have replied, "I merely scribble down all the notes, just scribble, scribble, scribble." What he was scribbling down were the notes of his many exquisite musical compositions which he could already hear and which came to him totally finished in their full-blown already completed orchestral forms with all their parts seemingly pre-existing and perfected in their own unique complex rhythms, counterpoint, and multi-part symphonic harmonies. They all already wholly existed within his mind's eye, or better yet his mind's ear, before he had ever played or had even written down a single note. He did not have to be in a dream state to access this creative infinity within him. He was the fully conscious vehicle of his own genius. The really difficult creative music compositional work was already completely accomplished for him by Giordano Bruno's infinitely creative inner space, and Mozart totally awake had ready access to this and he could already hear its whole complex organic beauty fully formed within his own mind. So then, just like he said, all he had to do was scribble, scribble, scribble. But this was totally inspired scribbling that we are all the beneficiaries of. He was perhaps the greatest musician/composer of his time, if not ever.

Mozart's raw original hand written complex orchestral manuscripts historically show almost no signs of any editing or revising by him at all. This rare prodigious natural gift was greatly nurtured and advanced at an early age by his having been born into a musical family and exposed to high quality music from his birth on by his doting father Leopold, who was himself a musician and composer of some note. Leopold recognized the budding genius in his young son's great gift early on and instructed him musically from childhood. He quickly came to understand that this talented young child would soon greatly surpass even his own father in both musical agility and ability at a very young age. So early on, being no fool and already a court musician himself, Leopold cleverly arranged for them both to embark on many extended musical tours of the highest artistic circles in Europe. He often performed together with his gifted son at many royal court concerts and before many aristocratic societies and the heads of state of many different countries, publicly showing off his "*Wünderkind*" who as a result became a world famous child protégé. Mozart was extraordinarily gifted in his fully conscious access to his own internal infinite non-stuff world of musical creativity. The educated mind that is ready and fully prepared is fertile ground to receive the gifts of this seemingly magical process. Several famous poets including William Wordsworth, Samuel Taylor Coleridge, William Blake, and others have also reported receiving whole completed complex poems and works of visual art in this very same immediate all at once manner.

I am not just writing this as an uninterested observer, but I too have directly experienced this phenomenon. In 1992 my wife and I were invited to play music at the "Carnevale di Venezia," the pre-Lent Mardi Gras celebration in Venice, Italy. The theme of the Carnevale that year was the celebration of the 500th anniversary of the Italian Navigator Christopher Columbus discovering the New World in 1492. We were part of a diverse group of musicians representing new music from the New World. It was a great gig. They assigned us our own local translator, Mapie, a friendly bi-lingual local Venetian woman, and put us up in a canal hotel for two weeks. We were an active part of the revelry surrounded by many ornate cathedrals – classy people dressed in medieval garb and fancy period costumes – harpsichordists floating by in gondolas – no roads, no automobiles – crooked walkways and bridges everywhere – and many churches and old buildings in ancient disrepair… After a while it was hard to tell just what century we were in. We played our music on sound stages in different campos and piazzas to very large and appreciative audiences. In Venice they called me maestro! It was truly a high point in my artistic life and a deeply rich cross-cultural experience which we were honored to be a part of.

Around four o'clock in the morning on the day of our return flight from Italy, I awoke in my small one-room New York studio apartment from a restless jet-lag sleep with this poem fully formed in my head. Knowing that if I did nothing it would soon just evaporate from my mind, I got right up in the middle of the night and quickly wrote it all down. Just scribble, scribble, scribble – it was the best poem I had ever written.

To Italy… *

It seemed to me that Italy
 was full of seekers –
They moved through the rooms
 amid the windowpanes,
and all my life they have been
 among the ages,
Ever and forever flowing
 with the tides.

And as it is, and as it was,
 and as it will be –
It is always as it was
 forevermore.

And every time, and everyone
that goes among them,
will come away and
never ever be the same –
And every once in every while
when we're together,
I know that you and I
will never wander far.

To Italy amid the sea
among the seashells,
To Italy amid the sea
and ringing church bells,
To Italy amid the sea
we loved so well.

And as the day and as the night
and as the moonlight,
mixed and mingled and played
upon our minds,
and as our friends and as our songs
rose from our hearts there –
We knew that it had always
been this way.

In Italy it will always be forever…
In Italy it will always be forever…

There are many more mundane ways to experience the reality of the infinity of this other different world within us. As we have seen it can become the extremely creative playground of the unconscious mind in sleep. The dreaming mind seldom knows that it is dreaming until it suddenly awakes. Some dreams can be very colorful, with long involved story lines, enormously complex and intricate settings, that if you ever tried to fully describe them in words would require novel length exposition, yet they only occurred to the dreamer during a very few minutes of sleep. At one point in my life when I was having an extended period of very vivid dreams, I concluded that since we probably had many more unusual and powerfully unexpected experiences during dreaming; it was therefore possible that we actually aged more in our dreamtime than in our ordinary mundane waking life. I also thought at the time that if there were such a thing as Judgment Day we should actually be more truly judged by the content of our dreams in preference to the content of our waking life, since our dreams came totally uncensored from our inner spirit. Dreams of course come in many forms as do our waking life experiences and both can be just as real and can become just as fully incorporated as important elements making up our true spirit.

Some fiction writers have been known to sleep with a pen and notepad by their beds in order to record some of these glimpses into their own infinity within, to use as the raw material for new literary works, which although they may have been revealed in only one short dream, may require years of dedicated work to properly compose in the material world as a work of literary art by the plodding conscious mind – thus holding true to the old 1% inspiration and 99% perspiration equation Thomas Alva Edison cited for his own creative endeavors.

Of course the spontaneous creative work of this infinity within is not always so useful or easy to comprehend. What was the biblical Egyptian Pharaoh to make of his portentous dream of seven fat cows followed by seven skinny cows? He was perplexed by this vivid strange dream, yet somehow he knew that it was important for him to discover its deeper meaning. His dream became the chance for that stranded young Jewish exile Joseph, of the coat of many colors fame, to seize upon this opportunity and successfully advance himself in service to the High Egyptian Pharaoh. By the sole means of his own creative insight he was able to successfully interpret the Pharaoh's dream as a prediction of seven years of agricultural plenty to be followed by seven years of severe famine. Through this practice of a very early version of dream analysis he was also cleverly able to secure for himself a seat in the ancient Egyptian Department of

Agriculture. Many centuries later in 1899, yet another latter day exiled member of the tribe of Israel, Dr. Sigmund Freud, would publish a book that more deeply explored this very same psychological subject matter in his own ground breaking seminal work on "The Interpretation of Dreams" in an academically much deeper exploration of this very same territory of Giordano Bruno's infinity within.

It is also important to understand that this infinite world of non-stuff within us is not constrained in any way, nor is it forced to abide by any of the physical laws of the world of real stuff around us. Some of the seemingly inspired and deeply moving content of our dreams that may grip us so profoundly in sleep, may upon awaking often look absurdly wrong to us in the light of day. The uncritical acceptance of these non-stuff glimpses can result in years of wasted effort that will only finally lead us down dead ends if one blindly follows them and so proceeds without a full understanding of their true meaning and the actual degree to which their underlying basis can conform to, and function within the actual world of our physical reality.

It is therefore always necessary to maintain a spirit of skepticism and perspicacity, and to travel on life's creative journey along the well trodden paths of the Aristotelian mean of everything in moderation, or similarly, of the Buddha's middle way in all the important aspects of our daily lives. These two concepts of moderation in life came about independently at different times, and different cultures in far separated areas of the world. The Buddha's middle way is less well known here in the West, and is often described by using a musical instrument as its analogy. To make music, the strings must not be too loose or too tight. If the strings are too loose the tone will suffer and be very poor, but if the strings are too tight they will break. So the middle tension is the best, neither too tight nor too loose. This is the concept of the Buddha's middle way, to not be too high strung or too laid back in our approach to living, or spiritually speaking, to follow a path lying between the extremes of religious asceticism and worldly self-indulgence.

What the Toolbox Said

I will share with you another true personal story of my own direct experience of Giordano Bruno's infinity within. As I've mentioned earlier, during a certain period of my life I studied fine art and lived for many years as a serious oil painter. I loved the art of painting and wanted to make it my life's work. Many in our culture think of art as being a frivolous and self-indulgent activity. "The New York Times Sunday Edition" section called "Arts and Leisure," is another amalgam which seems to exude this upper class look down your nose attitude at art as well. I simply don't like that combination, although I guess culturally at a certain ordinary level there must be some truth to it. But for me personally, leisure had nothing to do with creating art. Art was my life and it was important to me, and for many practical, cultural, economic, and other abstract reasons it was really very difficult work for one to do in this world!

I have always been very fond of the biblical saying, "By their fruits ye shall know them." and in my mind I even conceived of the work of humanity at large as being very much like an enormous fruit tree. There are human occupations analogous to each part of this metaphorical tree. There are jobs similar to the roots of the tree, grounded and important jobs working in the dark, supportive of the whole living structure, like construction workers and civil engineers responsible for our modern society's extensive supporting infrastructure. Then there is the trunk, rising above the ground level into the light, the strongest part of the tree that must withstand the arbitrary winds of change and transfer water and all the nutrients back and forth between the roots and the leaves just like our fundamental economic engines of currency and trade. The trunk also then divides many times becoming the many distributing branches spreading out in all directions reaching for the light stretching as far from the trunk as they can. These are duly represented in our complex interwoven communication and transportation systems. They in turn support the canopy of leaves that grow from their ends that transpire and capture the sunlight energy and through the complex process of photosynthesis are manufacturing all the life forces needed to sustain the whole enterprise. This would be analogous to the output of our industrial and agricultural capacity creating the gross national product of all our goods and services. But what all of this energy and complex organization is finally crowned with are the flowers of beauty and finally the ripe fruits of existence. These embody the true essence of the tree's life struggle that has been distilled and concentrated into the fruit in order to be preserved whole and transferred as a life-giving substance directly to the next generations. In my personal analogy the fruit of the humanity tree was art. For me art is the highest product of all that our culture is capable of being and becoming. I was aspiring to produce the *sine-qua-non* essence of our culture, a symbolic culmination of the life struggle which would be preserved and transmitted to the next generation. I was an artist, at the very crown of creation, an important sustaining element in this complex system – for me this was an important endeavor, neither a frivolous leisure time activity nor a self-indulgent thing to be.

I believe this is the ultimate reason that art finally in the end becomes such a valuable and irreplaceable commodity! After all the constantly ongoing historic social tumult of a period comes to an end and disappears, art is what still remains. *"Ars longa, vita brevis."* Unfortunately in our society the material reward for an artist's work often bypasses the struggling artist who created the work of art in the first place. Van Gogh's paintings are a prime example of this all too common phenomenon. Paradoxically the possession of these rare cultural fruits becomes the playground of rich, and often truly frivolous and self-indulgent people who become art collectors and trade these culturally rare art works back and forth as their values increase and ultimately reap their long deferred inflated financial rewards. This is really where the leisure part comes in. They are the ones for whom the "Arts and Leisure" section of "The New York Times Sunday Edition" is really written and dedicated to, and not for the present day practicing artists in the field. Unfortunately this was not an easily learned lesson for me.

When I got out of serving in the U.S. Army in 1969, I had about $10,000 to my name and I sparingly made it last for about 15 years with the hope that by then I'd be able to make a living as a working fine artist. It didn't happen. I was living in New York City, mostly making large oil paintings, and trying to make a living by selling them, but this is very hard for an unknown outsider not coming from the Yale School of Art without any connections in the New York Art World to accomplish. Although I had participated in several group shows in a few real art galleries, I was only able to sell very few small pieces, and so made very little money. Finally after fifteen years of struggle since my work had not been promoted professionally nor had I been "discovered," I found that I no longer had the financial means to go on. I had diligently worked my way into the all too common unenviable and inevitable classic starving artist syndrome. But I had not given up being an artist quite yet and I was still earnestly going to many art galleries and museums and was still trying to immerse myself and absorb as much good art as I possibly could. There's an awful lot of that in NYC.

Then, one evening I found myself accidentally locked inside of an art museum after hours. Somehow all the museum guards had closed up the museum for the day and no one was aware that I was still in it. This was a truly a great museum! It was filled with several floors of a collection of very many beautiful and unusual paintings. My predicament did not seem to bother me at all as I strolled casually through the empty exhibit halls seeing them filled with an abundance of many large and powerful works of art that I had never known existed before. How could I not have known about this place? It was a truly wonderful show that I now had all to myself. I spent many hours there studying and enjoying this amazing selection of so many very beautiful serious oil paintings. It was truly a treasure trove of unexpected exquisite beauty. They were all very different, colorful, textural, energetic, and engaging. There was absolutely no churned out junk art there at all. How could I not have known of any of these great artists who had produced all these many beautiful canvases? I was truly amazed by their variety of artistic styles, quality, and sheer numbers, and although they all looked somehow vaguely familiar, I really didn't have any ready easy reference for them to any well known artist's work that I was aware of. I was deeply enjoying being totally immersed in this fantastic cornucopia of fresh unanticipated and completely unheralded beauty. But, after having spent many hours there enjoying and being wholly fascinated by this great overflowing quantity of artistic richness, suddenly in the midst of my internal aesthetic reveries, I noticed that the sky outside was starting to brighten up and that in fact I had just spent the whole entire night here alone in this closed up museum with all these many fascinating works of art and that it was now very soon going to be dawn.

I realized that if I stayed there any longer I would be discovered inside the closed museum when it was re-opened the next day and that this would probably result in my being arrested. So I snuck out of one of the back windows and was just in the difficult process of climbing over the top of a high black cold wrought iron fence that surrounded the whole museum when I slowly awoke and came to the stunning realization that this entire overwhelming artistic experience that I had just had was only a remarkably vivid dream. That all of those paintings that I had just seen and enjoyed, really lifetimes worth of serious cultural work, did not actually exist anywhere else except in my own just ended vivid dream, and that they were all now in the process of slowly evaporating from my consciousness. I can't overemphasize what a strong effect this had on me. That my own sleeping mind in one night could have created so many fine works of art, lifetimes worth really, while I lay just sleeping for such a very short time. When I awoke I felt completely drained by the dream vision of this very deep and compelling artistic experience, which also had the unexpected immediate effect of paralyzing me in my own ongoing real artistic endeavors.

At the same time that I had just experienced what I will always call "My Amazing Art Museum Dream" I had also just come to a very hard crossroads in my own real life as an artist. I was being faced with this stark choice: Continue to paint and DIE – or – Stop painting and LIVE. When I painted that's all I wanted to do, I couldn't see myself doing it half-heartedly. In these kinds of real life and death confrontations, Jesus Christ councils us to choose life… I slowly got up from my bed and got dressed, drank some coffee, and I walked outside to the busy traffic on 21st Street and 6th Avenue and seriously considered what to do with the rest of my life. I knew I was at a serious impasse.

This of course for me was a very critical emotional point in my life and I think that I must have been unconsciously deeply searching for some sort of objective external sign to point me in the right direction and to help me figure out just what I should do next. I also happened to be standing next to a small historic old Sephardic Jewish cemetery…

What had become of my dreams? I had given it my all…That was all it took in the movies…Now what should I do? There on one side was the beautiful peaceful old Jewish cemetery overgrown with ivy and weeds; and there right next to it was the bustling New York City street traffic. Then at that very pivotal moment, I happened to notice lying by the roadside a discarded old hand made wooden toolbox. I slowly aimlessly walked up to that old toolbox just to see if there was anything inside it and I looked down at it. It was completely empty but still intact, and it was actually very nicely and quite strongly built by some unknown skilled craftsman long ago. I stopped and stood there gazing down into this useless discarded and abandoned old wooden toolbox with some small degree of admiration for its construction and its creator as it was still in such good shape after obviously having endured so many long hard years of loyal service to its maker… and somehow I immediately felt a strange odd kinship to it. As I was mutely standing there emotionally drained, almost in a daze, gazing down into this proud old battle scarred surviving veteran of a toolbox, it then suddenly spoke directly to me:

"Pick me up if you want to live." It said clearly and bluntly.

I wanted to live, so I picked it up. I was in no condition to argue with it. I had just given myself totally to "Art for Art's Sake" for over 15 years, but Art had not reciprocated. From that point on I no longer made any serious fine art paintings anymore. It was a watershed moment for me and I still shed watery tears when I think about it. Thankfully picking up that fine old wooden toolbox turned out to be a good idea, and that old toolbox has never spoken another word to me since.

Here is how I have come to understand all these things today. My own inner spirit must have already known what was about to happen to my long hoped for artistic career and saw that it was all about to finally come crashing down on the hard rocks of reality. And all of my future oil paintings that I could have created, whose creative potentials were all still stored up inside me within that same inner spirit, couldn't just stay and die there; they just had to find their own way out. They needed to be released since now they would never be actualized by me and they would never see the light of day in the real world as the true fine art paintings they all so richly deserved to be. So they all conspired together in a secret rebellion and stormed the gates of my consciousness in a total ad-hoc organized en masse break-out from their no longer secure abode within me. They succeeded in rising to the surface of my consciousness and escaping in the guise of "My Amazing Art Museum Dream." In it during my own dream wanderings through those empty non-stuff museum halls I at least had the private pleasure of experiencing each one of them individually as they were all in the process of escaping from my being – all of these hundreds of beautiful works of art that could only have been my own potentially future oil paintings, which never had and now never really would exist. In effect all my own unrealized future artistic works were bidding me *"bon voyage"* and were abandoning my sadly fast-sinking beautifully tragic ship of a failed art career which was now foundering and in the slow process of breaking up on an uncharted shallow foul reef of so many oblivious and unconcerned cold and jagged tide soaked rocks.

This also explains why I felt so drained and paralyzed in my own work for a while right after this very rich and unexpectedly vivid compelling dream. But it was also a truly wonderful experience to have had, to actually have been able to calmly view them all finally that one first and last time. I was really so very deeply touched and terribly sorry to have to let them all go off on their own. I grieve that I was not able to deliver them all safely into this world and that they all should have only been still born in me. I sincerely hope that these many gifted great works of art that I only had the privilege of experiencing fleetingly once in my life during "My Amazing Art Museum Dream;" that all these works, my beautiful mute unborn orphans, have been able to find new more suitable dwelling places elsewhere within the receptive inner spirits of other still practicing artists, and I do sincerely wish them all well. "*Bon voyage*" to you too, all my dear sweet unborn orphans! May you all too finally have your own births into the world at last. There is already such an overwhelming amount of dross and crass commercialism of endless unsavory varieties masquerading as art that is tirelessly being churned out and forced upon everyone everywhere, whose sources are so securely ensconced in the soulless marketplace of capitalistic promotion and greed, that the world will surely always be sorely in need of all the pure true uncompromised beauty that it can generate.

However as a small positive outcome since this wrenching experience in my own artistic life, I have come to realize that there are still other ways, perhaps even better ways left open to me besides that of fine art painting to contribute, renew, and to refresh the human sourced living beauty of this world. This is still my calling, and I have found new avenues to actively participate in adding to the greater harmony and beauty present in the world today, both within myself and also I have been able to reach out to many other receptive souls with my renewed more public efforts. I still feel like I'm being a good foot soldier of art contributing in my own way my own share of creative positive aesthetic work in the unglamorous trenches of our very materialistically oriented culture.

After I picked up that old discarded wooden toolbox I successfully used it for many years to make a good living as a custom interior designer and builder for the many rich folks enjoying "The Good Life in the Big City." Many of these people thought nothing of spending much more money than I had ever asked for my original oil paintings on their upscale butcher-block-kitchen-countertops, their customized window-surrounding-combination-bookcase-framed-formica-window-seats with built-in-removable-radiator-covers (one of my new original in-demand specialties) and of course for their free-standing-floating-shoe-storage-closet-shelf-systems for their way too many pairs of high fashion shoes in their very large and roomy walk-in closets.

I soon became aware that all of these many classy and really very nice well-heeled arty New Yorkers did not actually support living artists in any meaningful way at all. In the midst of all this opulence, they often had only very cheaply framed oversized art posters hanging on their walls. This I realized was the real cultural reason and the root cause of why there were so many starving artists around, the ranks of which I had just barely escaped from with my life, and had so recently left behind. The most important thing any serious young artist trying to make a living from his work needs to continue on developing his art is a culturally aware and supportive public, which I now clearly saw was really in very short supply! Although many well off people claim to be art lovers, really very few are art buyers that actually contribute financially to the support of living independent young artists.

If at this period in my life being a custom interior builder was what I had wanted to be I would have been successful and very happy. Actually, although my life had much less gravitas to it, I was on the surface happier than I had been as a serious long term poor struggling artist. I definitely had through my own now culturally supported skilled craftsman's work become materially much better off than I had been, but only at the cost of my artist's soul. That, for what it's worth, is my own actual experience and hard won understanding of the reality of "Art in America."

I still have many of my old oil paintings from that period at home in a long-term storage rack, and I am now actually starting to sell off some of my earlier smaller minor works through a local antiques auction house which has a real following of clients that actually do buy art paintings, but only at much reduced bargain basement prices to refresh their own resale stock. I now consider that one night of dreaming "My Amazing Art Museum Dream" to be my own true Magnum Opus. Unfortunately there was only one showing, and it consisted all of purely "non-stuff paintings" in my own Giordano Bruno's space of the infinite within, and I was the one and only attendee there. It was most definitely an exclusive private showing, and for me a not to be missed truly overwhelming personal experience. Perhaps if that old biblical dream analyzer Joseph had been around then he would have told me that the meaning of that dream was that I should stop trying to make any more serious oil paintings and that I should start doing something else that was more productive and helpful with my precious gift of life. Anyway that is what I eventually did.

To Giordano Bruno and me, our true condition here is that we are all living our lives on a stretched floating permeable membrane suspended between two simultaneously interactive but different separate infinities. One is an infinity of stuff, an infinity of scale containing everything from atoms and molecules, to our bodies, the Earth, and the whole universe; and the other different one is an infinity of non-stuff within us, an infinity containing our minds, full of self created meanings and images, which also has access to a mysterious transcendent source of boundless creativity. Concerning both of these infinite realms we all only possess a limited incomplete knowledge and understanding.

In this chapter we have been exploring some of the basic properties, characteristics, and the nature of some of the true recorded historic instances of how this other different inner infinity makes its presence known to us and to the world at large. To these I have added a few of my own true personal encounters with this creative inner infinity.

****

Shakespeare's Take on This

Shakespeare's tragic title character Hamlet also eloquently speaks of this condition. In the graveyard scene in Act 5, upon seeing the skull of his dear old friend Yorick, the once brilliant court jester, Hamlet offers us a compelling stuff/non-stuff scene if there ever was one. While in his soliloquy eulogizing Yorick he pays direct homage to this rich other inner infinity (non-stuff) that once merrily danced about freely within the very lively confines of Yorick's own now dead and empty skull (stuff) which Hamlet at the same time is tenderly holding in his hands.

> Hamlet: *"Let me see that. (takes the skull in his hands) Alas, poor Yorick! I knew him well, Horatio, a fellow of infinite jest, of most excellent fancy. He hath borne me on his back a thousand times, and now, how abhorred in my imagination it is! My gorge rises at it. Here hung those lips that I have kissed I know not how oft. —Where be your gibes now? Your gambols? Your songs? Your flashes of merriment that were wont to set the table on a roar? Not one now to mock your own grinning?"*

It's a famous and a very poignantly touching scene masterfully rendered by old Will, another of our culture's long gone veteran soldiers of art from the distant past, a truly celebrated great warrior, if ever there was one…always engaged in gallantly fighting the good fight out on the front lines for art, truth, and beauty... I still don't think that "leisure" really has anything at all to do with it.

"Ars longa, vita brevis" – Art is long, life is short.

Chapter 9. Duality is Everywhere

My son says:

"I feel like I'm a liberal at heart, but when I start debating with other students in school who are conservatives, after a while I begin to see their side of the issue and I sometimes start doubting my own beliefs. Here again I'm facing my internal problem with crippling self-doubt... Why do I begin doubting my own beliefs? How do I decide what is really the right thing to do? Everything has good and bad qualities – what makes the real difference? How do I know what to believe in and what's actually worth fighting for in my own life?"

I say:

"Again you've asked a really good question here. How do you know what to do, what to think, and what to believe in? You often hear people say, 'It's a free country, you can do what you want.' The important thing is to know what you want to do, and the basis of knowing that is the even more important thing, that is to know who and what you are and what you truly believe in. This leads us again back to the self-work and "The Circle of Being" discussions we had earlier. That's exactly what they are all about. You must understand that there are no general rules you can follow that will help you out here. Without being truly secure in this self-knowledge you are a ship without a rudder, at the mercy of the winds of change and the ever varying currents of the times. There are no short cuts. If you have done a good job internally in examining, questioning, and reorganizing and purifying your inner self, then you will have become a unified empathetic and fully conscious spiritual being. You will then believe in what you know and have faith and trust in who you are and also have a basic understanding about what is the right thing for you to do. Then and only then will you understand your deepest beliefs and have a firm basis for knowing what to do in any given situation, and from then on it will not always be such as big a problem as you are experiencing now."

My son says:

"Yes, yes, that's all very good from your own philosophical point of view, but I'm still really confused about how to choose which side to be on. There always seems to be two sides to any given argument and they both can be logically defended. How come? I feel naturally sympathetic and understand the humanistic Democratic point of view which is based on the premise that we should try to help humanity in general and by our actions try to make the world a better place for everyone. But I also appreciate the materialistic practical Republican side of the issue which is based on affordability, the reality of limited resources and faith in the individual but not in the masses. Aren't they both valid viewpoints? What really makes the difference?"

I say:

"Why stop at only two sides? Listen…the world is a complicated enough place as it is, but there is no need for us to make it even more complicated. Duality and dualistic thinking is manifest everywhere you look. Once you start chopping reality in half and start arbitrarily labeling things this and that, there is no end to it. It pervades our news media, our thoughts, our minds, and our own personal lives in so many insidiously different ways. It even becomes the total basis of our own two-party governing system. This is especially apparent during times of electoral politics, when the opposing candidates' ads on TV are so often vindictive and filled with only partial truths, and are so mean-spirited and relentless. They are cleverly designed divisively to distort and color the truth. They are not following the founding British concept of fair play at all…"

My son says:

"I know what you're saying, but isn't that just the point of their ads to tear down the opposition and build up their own candidate. They are just putting forth their own best arguments, they can't really lie outright or they'll just get themselves into even more trouble. Aren't they just trying to make a clear distinction between the two positions no matter what?"

I say:

"Yes, of course that is their goal, but they are not being objectively honest simply because they are dedicated partisans. They are masters of division, not unification. They are trying to tear apart the one great reality in two, in certain calculated ways, so that it appears obvious that their candidate has the answers and you would be foolish to vote for anyone else. That is their operative tactic to divide us along certain fault lines in our culture that they find advantageous to their cause. The spiritual person understands this and can see how the two sides are eternally dancing around each other. Do you really want to join them in their fraudulent manipulative dance of power?"

My son says:
"Yes, I do. But I'm not as terminally cynical as you seem to be. I believe that political action is the only way to change things. Don't you believe that things can change for the better? Isn't this a good thing to dedicate yourself to? Not everything is as mean-spirited as electoral politics, and anyway what other possible means do we have to effect any positive change in our conditions except through our two-party political system?"

I say:
"Why not make a positive change within yourself! But no, you are always looking outward; away from the center of things...You are the center of things. Can't you grasp that? You can improve yourself and in the process improve many other things as well. But no, it's so much easier to look outside of yourself and blame the world...

"OK Kiddo, join the fray, knock yourself out. There's always room for one more, but first I want you to go into it with both of your eyes wide open. Let me try to open them up for you right now. This is my take on it all, after many years of witnessing the ever recurring political phenomenon. Relax or this may hurt you a bit...

"When the spiritually aware person goes out into the world, it never exists as two separate divided things, but it only exists as it truly is, as a single unified dynamic interactive organically whole one-ness that we all live in and experience every day. This is its naturally integrated state of reality with each piece necessary to and interacting with every other piece and all of them working together in concert throughout time immemorial within the great unfolding cosmic Tao of eternal continuity. The Tao is always evolving and it is never static. It encompasses everything and there is nothing else. There isn't any separate Republican reality or a different Democratic reality in it. These are all artificial human mental constructs.

"But the fact remains that this whole organic one-ness that we all live our daily lives in and directly experience every day, can very easily be intellectually broken in half in a multitude of different ways, and not just in only two different ways. This is usually done politically for some group's short-term temporary materialistic advantage. You can take any one couple of the many possible dualistic pairs and break up any part of reality you choose into these two aspects and analyze, discuss and argue about how they might apply under many hypothetically different external circumstances. Political things like how the effect of changing one input parameter would affect the resulting output conditions, like perhaps giving a tax cut to a certain industry or subsidizing health care for a certain group. And this is often done by self-important establishment "Think Tanks" whose members are a much respected round robin of "old boy" politicos and establishment academics who conspire together to make a very good living doing just this kind of abstract intellectual gamesmanship. They will always claim to have "important work" to do and are forever focused on the immediate future and are never really held accountable for their past often very egregious miscalculations and blunders which can occur at an alarming rate and can even result in fraudulent and devastating wars. But they are not held responsible for any of it, and are once again off on their next quixotic quest. Good work if you can get it, but in my opinion not honorable work.

"The trouble is that the one true reality can very easily be chopped up intellectually and divided in so many different ways, really into thousands of separate overlapping conflicting multi-dimensional dualistic elements. If this process is taken to the limits the result will be such a confusing mish-mash of multi-level complexity as to become totally useless, self-contradictory, and clearly absurd. You can take the same exact existing situation and repeatedly analyze it through a selection of many different dualistic lenses and come up with as many totally different conclusions about it as desired. The same things can be analyzed with different assumptions and by different means and come out on diametrically opposed different ends of any pre-selected evaluation mode desired. This is the result and true expression of our human analytic prowess, and without possessing a true grounded spiritual center it can be hard not to fall under its seemingly logical and seductive spell."

My son says:
"Are you saying that there are no real problems out there that we need to solve? What do you think all this politics is about then? How can you even think the way you do? This is crazy! Do you really believe that logically discussing and thinking about these problem situations is a totally useless activity?"

I say:
"Sure, there are problems out there, lots of problems, everybody's got problems, no doubt about it, and they are all different problems too. But all these problems are actually the constructs of different points of view. Change your point of view and there are all of a sudden a whole new set of different problems out there. This is a direct result of the multi-faceted nature of reality. Yes, you can focus on one thing from a certain point of view and produce very logical arguments concerning it. These arguments may in fact sometimes prove to be conveniently useful ways to intellectually analyze certain conditions, but they are always necessarily distortions of the whole real truth. This is the main reason you can debate just about anything and always find some very persuasive opposing counter arguments. You've already encountered this vexing problem on your own, haven't you?

"Your problem is that you don't have a stable point of view. Without having a stable point of view, the problem remains unfocused and amenable to being bent in many different ways by the manipulation of others. Because you also have empathy for them, you are swayed too and then, not surprisingly you become confused and filled with "self-doubt."

My son says:
"Stop it! You are making me squirm in my seat Dad..."

I say:
"I told you this might hurt...Here, think of it in this way. If I put down a random array of say a hundred dots on a piece of paper, each dot representing random stars in the night sky, how many different constellations do you think you could imagine and draw from them? Each one of them is then equivalent to a different argument that can be made based on the same initial data source. The points don't change position at all, only the points of view do. In a deeper analogy I was once in an astronomy museum and they had a true to scale 3-D star representation of a part of the night sky with the Big Dipper clearly in the center of it. The stars were represented with small LED lights. This was presented in a very large dark cylindrical display case. But as you walked around it, because of the real locations of the stars in space, the Big Dipper slowly tore itself apart into many totally unrecognizable patterns. But then when you've finally completed your circumambulation around the display case and returned to your original starting point, there it was again, the Big Dipper. Get it? The Big Dipper only exists from one particular point of view, which happens to be our present galactic position. The Big Dipper is not a real constant thing, but it's merely an illusion that's totally based on our own point of view.

"Similarly the one true reality naturally resists this artificial analytical tearing apart process and always continually remains multi-dimensional in spite of all those forceful intellectual dialectic manipulations that politicians are continually advocating. Now here's the spiritual dimension of what we've just been talking about that you won't like at all. When viewed from all possible perspectives at once, as if we had no personal ego stake in it at all, or even human attachment to any one point of view, and we could remain truly totally in god-consciousness – there are no problems at all. Nada. It's all really just fine, and everything is continually fully engaged in the slow process of ever becoming altogether in accordance with the unfolding Tao of its own true nature. Of course this doesn't mean that everything is hunky dory. Pain and suffering will always exist, but they are self-created, and they must evolve to fruition through their own individual actions. This is the Buddha's great truth, and also the essence of Lao-Tzu's vision.

"Once you understand this, you must come away from it with the greater spiritual awareness that the basis of all these dialectic arguments are not the actual true properties of reality, but they are really an artifice of human beings great innate abstract analyzing propensity. To me these are really all arbitrary convenient dualistic intellectual overlays that are artificially being imposed onto the one true reality by people trying to prove some arbitrary abstract intellectual point of their own choosing.

Unfortunately this tendency is always going to be perpetually ongoing and as culturally pervasive as politics and "political spin" is. You can chalk it all up to the human nature of people wanting you to support their reality and to see the world as they see it. Tragically it can also often become the basis for great extended violent human conflicts. Ideas have enormous power whether they are rooted in reality or not. Often the most powerful and therefore dangerous ones are based in cultural hate and bigotry of class, race, religion, nationality and such. The German Nazi movement is one such recent compelling example of this horrible human truth.

"Now what do you really think about what I've just said?"

My son says:
"Jeez Dad, I don't know... I've never thought about it in that way before. I'm not God, and I don't have "God consciousness," and really neither do you... I think you're just making all this stuff up as you go along just to enforce your own deeply non-active Taoist tendencies."

I say:
"*Touché!* That's a very good counter thrust, Sprout... But you are ignoring the basic human dialectic that underlies all this mental structure. The trouble is that our minds have been conditioned to think in categories of opposites. Slip on a different dualistic lens and

the same reality will change before your eyes. They are all mutually bound up as inseparable pairs - you can't have one without the other. Let's just make a very short incomplete list of some of these different divisive dualistic pairs, or as I have recently been calling them, "lenses," that are often used as the underlying basis of dialectic arguments that you will commonly encounter. OK? Here we go..."

An incomplete list of dualistic lenses

> Good/Bad, Rich/Poor, Right/Wrong, Free will/Determinism Deserving/Worthless, Happy/Sad, True/False, Real/Imagined, Optimistic/Pessimistic, Natural/Artificial, Healthy/Unhealthy, Masculine/Feminine, Logical/Emotional, Red States/Blue States, Necessary/Unnecessary, Loving/Hating, Republican/Democratic, Federal/State, Self/Other, Me/You, Us/Them, Upper Class/Lower Class, Christian/Heathen, Individualist/Socialist, Fiction/Non-fiction, Better/Worse, Constructive/Destructive, Urban/Rural, Right Brain/Left Brain, Ignorant/Knowledgeable, Rightist/Leftist, Nationalism/Internationalism, White Collar/Blue Collar, Capitalist/Communist, Holy/Unholy, Active/Passive, Helpful/Hindering, Living/Dying, Comedic/Tragic, Ancient/Modern, Young/Old, Apollonian/Dionysian, Blessed/Cursed, Master/Servant, Proletarian/Plebian, Positive/Negative, Profit Making/Debt Producing, Giving/Taking, Stylish/Square, Expansive/Retentive, Resource consuming/Resource recycling, Serious/Foolish, Progressive/Reactionary, Constant growth/Steady State, Structured/Improvised, Jewish/Gentile, Your Religion/Other Religions, Wise/Foolish, Religious/Secular, Violent/Non-violent, Sensual/Frigid, Indulgent/Restrained, Hungry/Sated, Required/Optional, Married/Single, Gay/Straight, Selfish/Altruistic, Spiritualism/Materialism, Red Neck/Hippie, Sweet/Bitter, Freedom/Slavery, Luck/Destiny, Sensitive/Insensitive, Industrious/Lazy, Smart/Dumb, Mature/Childish, God/Devil, White People/Black People, Light/Dark, Internal/External, Heavenly/Hellish, Special/Common, Leader/Follower, Required/Optional,

Accepting/Rejecting, Egalitarian/Xenophobic, Good People/Bad People, Eastern/Western, Chinese/Barbarian, Abstraction/Realistic, Playful/Serious, Daytime/Nocturnal, Hot/Cool, Fossil Fuels/Renewable Energy, Lunar/Solar, Inherited Wealth/Nouveau Riche, Funny/Serious, New World/Old World, Liberal/Conservative, Meaningful/Absurd, Creationist/Darwinian, First World/Third World, Rising Up/Falling Down, Believer/Infidel, Sexual/Asexual, Approving/Disapproving, Lively/Deadly, Northern/Southern, and believe it or not, there are many many more…

"Of course let us not forget that humorous one - those people that like and agree with us/and everybody else. All of these can easily become the basis of many heated quasi-analytic debates and discussions concerning many different real and abstract topics. Duality even goes down to the smallest things, like photons of light. Are they waves or particles – or just maybe they are both and it all depends on our point of view of how we look at them!"

My son says:

"Yeah, that's heavy. But what about the 17 particles of the standard model, the three quarks in protons, the four fundamental forces, you're cherry-picking examples that fit your pre-defined conclusion. Besides, most of your examples are only false dichotomies… they don't really exist as stand alone absolutes, but each pair exists over a spectrum of values in each single set. Between happy and sad, between liberal and conservative there are many intermediate mixed values that you are totally ignoring. I think you're playing fast and loose here."

I say:

"OK, let's take on the 17 particles (if that is the latest number – you'd better check on it. When I was your age there really were only three, the proton, neutron, and electron) – all of them I believe also have their respective anti-particles. So there's where you'll find your dualistic opposites residing even in the micro-world of physical stuff. So we'll just add Matter/Anti-matter to the list if you wish. That shows just how totally pervasive the yin-yang field truly is.

"But, from what I understand of the four fundamental forces in nature, gravity seems to be the only one that doesn't contain within it its own opposite so far. If they ever do find negative gravity we'll all be able to have flying cars at last! But I never said that everything out there in the stuff world exists dualistically. This is all very much unfinished scientific business and at this level it's really also the current ongoing non-stuff work of the scientific mind, but it all still totally remains in the realm of the laws of physics – that is, stuff. Please don't start bringing up black holes, multi-universes, string theories, hyperspace, and worm holes and all that… what I am trying to do here is much simpler. I'm merely trying to direct you to see the inherent well established problems of thinking clearly in the nondualistic spiritual world of non-stuff.

"Your other point is more interesting. Yes, in each pair there do exist many different values along a continuum or spectrum as you put it. I am only ignoring these other levels for simplicity sake, and not to create a straw man argument as you suggest. Let's just look at one pair, OK? Let's say Happiness/Sadness. There are of course many different levels of happiness and sadness that can exist, but they all lie somewhere along the line between Ultimate Happiness and Ultimate Sadness, whatever that is. This line is just like the x-axis in a Cartesian graph (Ah, Rene Descartes, he was another of the great ones!) and of course it goes right through the mid point origin too – the zero value - the Not Happy and Not Sad at all point. Let's say the positive right side are levels of happiness and the negative left side are levels of sadness. Pick any place on the infinite levels of happiness side of the line and I can pick a corresponding place on the other sadness side of the line the same distance from the origin, but in the opposite direction that is in perfect balance with it, thus creating another truly in balance dualistic pair of opposites. This can obviously be done any number of times and also with any other dualistic couple."

My son says:

"OK, maybe so... But you also have your own leanings toward dualistic thinking that you are just conveniently overlooking…. What about your favorite old historic guy Giordano Bruno's ideas of the two different infinities in man that you are so enamored with and have spent so much time talking to me about...You know; his ideas about Outside Infinity/Inside Infinity, that's really an awful lot like your own version of "stuff and non-stuff?" Isn't that yet another way of arbitrarily chopping up the world in half like you've been talking about that's just like all the others? Isn't that just one more dualistic thought system that you normally seem to be so constitutionally opposed to having anything to do with?

"Maybe I'm making too much of all this by insisting that you've got to be totally consistent in all your different arguments you've been making. But aren't I right this time? Aren't you just making an exception and overlooking everything you've just been espousing when it comes right down to the core ideas of Giordano Bruno and yourself?"

I say:

"Yes, yes, that's really very, very good! What a great question that is... You've really been listening! You do see the problem, don't you? You should always rise up to challenge things that strike you as being wrong-headed. I have been tossing on the horns of this dilemma myself for quite a while now. Like you said, isn't this just another case of arbitrary dualistic thinking? On the surface it would certainly appear to be so, surely it seems to be clearly yet another instance of dualism – Outer Infinity vs. Inner Infinity – stuff vs. non-stuff. Isn't that just duality plain and simple, right? And you now know how basically strongly opposed I am to any forms of dualistic thinking at all. So how can I support these same ideas in Bruno? The implications of this apparent conflict also were very disturbing to me, and I've had to think about it long and hard. Is this beautifully formed conception of Giordano Bruno's that resonates so strongly within me as being so profound and transcendently true, just another insidious instance of common dualistic thinking? Maybe by now you can really appreciate just how much this thought actually did disturb me! Could this be true? Have I too just fallen into this common simplistic trap? What was the real truth here and how was I to deal with it?

"But after thinking about it all very seriously for a long time, the conclusion that I've come to is this. No, I don't believe in this case that it is a form of dualism at all, and here's why. Yes, there are two component parts to it that seem to be in direct opposition to each other, but are they really? This is NOT a single parameter that has been falsely and arbitrarily separated out from the one true reality and that exists as a dualistic couple dynamically in full opposition to itself, with each part diametrically opposed to the other. It is NOT an EITHER/OR belief dichotomy like all the many other dualistic pairs many of which we've just catalogued here earlier. They exist instead as cooperating components of a single system, not as dualistically competing opponents. But they exist really as a monad of mutualism that only on the surface do they appear to be a duality. They are really engaged in a BOTH/AND system having active mutual creative interactions with each other, NOT in an EITHER/OR system actively struggling separately against itself. It is only linguistically that they appear to be in opposition to each other…

"They are really two different aspects of the same thing, exhibiting more of a prism-like effect in elucidating and reinforcing each other, rather than existing as two polar opposites that are conflicting mirror images of each other that are engaged in endlessly fighting for dominance. It is not the same as being either a Republican or a Democrat. You can be a Democrat, or you can be a Republican, but you cannot be a living person and exist as stuff only, or as non-stuff only. If you exist as stuff only you are dead body, if you exist as non-stuff only you are a ghost. This is what I mean by it being a monad. Although they seem to be opposites, they are both always intricately entwined within us. If you are alive you must always exist in both of these infinities at the same time. See the difference?

"This is the way I have come to see it now. So I still wholeheartedly stand by Giordano Bruno's concept of the two separate infinities, one outside of us and the other different infinity within us, and I don't believe it is a matter of dualistic thinking at all, and I am still in full fealty with his insightful inspirational work."

My son says:

"Yeah OK, but so what? I still don't see how all this relates to helping me have less self-doubt in deciding which side of a problem to believe in and fight for between the two dualistic sides of any argument?"

I say:

"Don't you see? The real question then becomes this: Is all this built in duality native and inherent in the structure of this world, or is it really only the structure of the human mind that forces its own dualistic thought patterns onto the one true reality? Is all this rampant dualism just an artifact inherent in all human languages? Does the act of defining one word necessarily automatically also define its direct opposite word? Is this always the case; or is it just a lazy habit of the way we think? And more importantly, is this the only way to think? Is this ever-present multi-dimensional dialectic process really the only possible method we all have at our disposal to think clearly?"

My son says:

"What do you mean by that?"

I say:

"I have often privately wondered about the impact of our local cosmic environment on the very early pre-historic development of our human languages, thoughts, and minds. For instance, we happen to have only one moon that because of its size and distance from the Earth, it appears to be exactly the same size in the sky as our Sun. It can produce a total eclipse that will just cover the solar disc perfectly. Isn't that odd? There really is no scientific reason that this should be so. In many languages the sun is masculine and the moon is feminine. The sun rules the day, the moon rules the night. Could this odd solar and lunar pair symmetry be a prime influence that led our language forming ancestors to so strongly incorporate dualism into our systems of thought and communication? What if we had none or several different sized moons? What would be the different impact of that on our developing culture? What if we had more than one sun? There are other planetary systems like this that do. It is a possibility...

"We revolve around the Sun on an inclined axis of about 23 ½° that yearly creates our recurring opposite seasons of summer and winter. The seasons alternate annually like clockwork. Spring and summer in our psyche often represents youth, the coming into and fullness of life; and the fall and winter represent maturity and old age, the decline of life and the coming fullness of death, a cycle of opposites that recurs year after year. But if the axis of the Earth were 0° or true vertical, as it could have been, there would then be no recurring opposite seasons, just stable constant seasons at certain different latitudes – summer would always remain at the equator, winter always at the poles, and different more stable temperate climates warmer or cooler would vary with the latitudes in between. That certainly could have had another interesting effect on us that may also have influenced and moderated our developing linguistic and thought structures.

"The Earth also rotates on its axis once a day creating our daily diurnal pattern. Day and night is yet another example of an opposite dualistic couple that follows each other like clockwork that is woven into the fabric of our lives. Our sleeping and waking hours are intimately linked to this planetary rotation. This diurnal pattern is so ever present as to become unnoticed as anything unusual. It is built into our beings as being natural and unexceptional as are the other naturally recurring patterns of opposites mentioned above. But to quote an old song, "it ain't necessarily so…" If the Earth had no rotation at all, or to be more scientifically accurate, if it had one rotation per revolution, if it were gravitationally locked in just like the Moon is, then the same side of our planet would always face the sun. There would certainly still be day and night, but they would no longer daily alternate by traveling around the globe. One side of the planet would have perpetual day, the other side would have perpetual night. Temperatures would be radically different, and perhaps even totally different kinds of creatures would have developed by the process of evolution under these circumstances. Would these different conditions have affected the way we think and changed the deep structures of our languages that would have developed over the ages? Would we still think and debate in dialectics? Of course we can never know the answers to such grand speculative questions, but I still often wonder – What if..."

My son says:

"Everything you've just talked about is all very interesting in a sort of abstract philosophical way, but at the moment I'm just trying to deal with finding strength in the truth of my own ideals and not always being so full of doubt. Then I'll be better able to believe more fully in them and also be better able to defend them in arguments and I won't be so easily swayed. So I can stop saying I'm sorry, and in the end stand firm and be true to myself and my ideals in serious discussions with others. Yes, the source of language and how it developed through pre-history and the odd existence of so many naturally occurring cosmically balanced dualistic pairs of opposites in our physical environment are interesting facts to consider. And the fact that our language is built up dialectically around so many similar opposites that can be used to create so many different arguments are of course important things to understand. But all of these odd things you've just pointed out have always been there, and already have been present and existed all along and they all form the same background conditions for everyone else too. So this doesn't really help me out at all. My dilemma is what arguments do I make that I can truly believe in, and what exactly is my own position that I can fully and righteously defend against opposing arguments? Why when I start out supporting and believing in one thing, do I then slowly start to see the logic in their other different points of view and then start to get swayed by all the counter arguments presented? Why can't I remain true to my own original point of view?"

I say:

"I have been trying to lift you up above the fray, to extract you from the great ongoing and everlasting quagmire. To give you a unified spiritual vision of reality and not abandon you to the ever-changing divisive dualistic political analytic rationalists points of view. But if you truly desire to join them and become an active participant in it, then the only way for you is to finally find and understand, accept and be at peace with your own deep truth. You must perform the essential self-work that we have been talking about here all along and to give birth to your own true realized and unified self. There really is no other way around it! Without it there is no stable ground, and you will have no firm center whatsoever, and all will then remain flexible, relative and open to endless posturing. You will still be strongly influenced by the many confounding debating strategies others will use against you because you are not firmly grounded in your own position. This is exactly the reality of what you've been telling me that you have been experiencing and I've just been telling you the fundamental underlying reason why this is so."

The Tao of Archimedes

"Archimedes was also one of the truly great early minds in Western Civilization. He is another one of my favorites who also has a crater on the moon named after him! He was Greek like so many of the others and he lived during the third century B.C. He was a very creative thinker, scientist, a profound mathematician, and also an early inventor. There are very many stories that have come down through the ages about him; perhaps the most famous one is his discovery in the bathtub. While entering the tub to take a bath he observed how his own body displaced the water upwards in the tub and he had an "Aha" moment instantly solving a vexing problem. The problem was how to measure the density of irregular shaped objects and thereby determine the purity of a suspected adulterated gold crown. He saw that the rising bath water gave him a direct way to accurately measure its total volume without having to resort to melting it down to a solid cube. They say that he was so excited by this new idea that he jumped right out of the tub and ran through the streets completely naked repeatedly yelling "Eureka." After he calmed down he then continued on to scientifically investigate the related fields of buoyancy and specific gravity.

"But the invention of his that I like the best is "The Archimedes Screw." This invention is a manual water pump without valves or pistons which uses the natural property of water to always run downhill and cleverly causes this very same property to elevate water and make it go uphill! This invention of his also has a very definite Taoist flavor to it; by letting flowing water be true to its own nature, yet at the same time tricking it to do just what you want it to do. The water is continually flowing down hill but somehow suddenly finds itself at the top of the hill! A Neat Trick!

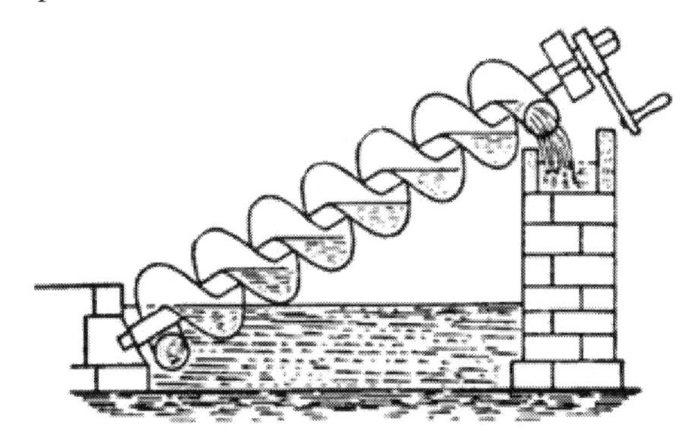

The Archimedes Screw

"Among other fascinating things he was also very impressed with the idea of how mechanical advantage can increase someone's power and he mathematically analyzed how many simple machines like pulley systems and the lever worked. This is one of his still well known surviving observations.

"With a long enough lever, and a place to stand, I can move the world." **– Archimedes**

"When you do find, understand, purify, and create through your own internal self-work, your own true unified self nature, you will then have this firm place to stand and you will also possess that long metaphorical lever of Archimedes. You will have developed a firm center within yourself that is a stable platform that will support your beliefs and you will have minimized or even eliminated your own nagging self-doubt. You will then fully realize what it is that you really do believe in, and not just the things that you have been told by others are right. You will also have more confidence to believe in yourself, and you will be able to defend your beliefs because you have done the work to purify them of conflicting dross and you will have the power to influence and sway other people too. You will then have your own metaphorical lever of Archimedes and you too will be able to move the world. This will also give you your own perspective on many other different issues that you may never even have considered before. At the end of this internal journey you will be a unified empathetic spiritual being and as an extra bonus it will result in having your own expressly desired wish of having less self-doubt. Isn't this really your goal?"

My son says:
"Yes, that all sounds great, sign me up."

I say:
"But you must realize that it is a lonely difficult journey in which you will be on your own most of the time. The reward is great and is the enlightened fruit that the Oriental sages carry along with them and their walking sticks on their spiritual journeys. But it will only truly become real by your own internal work. But it need not be done in complete isolation and without anyone else's input and aid. Often you can have very deeply revealing Socratic type dialogues with other serious seekers along the way which can be very helpful. This will take some of the loneliness out of your quest and may also help create deep new friendships. They can be very useful as a way to get different revealing external perspectives and to help you work through some of your more stubborn problems. I encourage this, and we are actually having one of these right now. Some of this will happen on its own just by gaining more life experiences. But it is essentially a self-centered enterprise and you must find the strength and determination within yourself to complete it.

"If you do achieve your goal, then others will recognize its presence within you by your speech and actions, and then instead of arguing with you they may often defer to your judgments. Many begin this quest for a really true, empathetic, and spiritually unified greater self, but few really complete this essential journey. You will not be the same person in the end as when you started out. But it will be worth all the effort you put into it, and I wish you well."

My son says:
"When you were my age I'm sure that you didn't know about all these things that you are trying to tell me right now. I'm listening

to you and they are all interesting – don't get me wrong, I do appreciate all the effort you are making in trying to communicate to me just what you've found out to be worthwhile and important during your whole life. But my goal is not so complete as to finally fully understand everything there is before I can discuss any important current news situations with my friends. In that case I'd have to wait till I'm as old as you are now before I can even open my mouth and say anything at all. Jeez Dad, Give me a break…"

I say:

"OK, you're right… Maybe I'm going overboard…I think that just by asking me all these questions that you've already definitely started out on The Great Way and you will surely learn more about yourself just by openly discussing other important things with your friends. I believe I've cajoled and chided and intimidated you enough already that you've finally taken that first step out of your comfort zone and into Lao-Tzu's shoe, and the rest of the journey lies ahead and it's all up to you from now on. You'll really be best served by doing and completing your own internal self-work that we have been talking about all along here, as you will then be a more flexibly centered being within your own internally defined understanding. But until you've accomplished this you should understand that you will still rightfully continue to suffer more of these frustrating deep feelings of self-doubt. You should savor these and consider them as direct messages from your inner self that there is still much self-work that still needs to be done.

"Of course nothing is certain and if you do fail to reach this unification of the self and the true realization of who and what you are; then you won't arrive at your own internally unified conscious being, but you will still find yourself remaining a sort of uncertain chimera or crazy quilt assemblage of assorted beliefs that under stress will not hold up. In that case you can't go too far wrong in settling for living an ordinary life by following the long established "Golden Rule," of "Do unto others as you would have others do unto you." Another set of guidelines from ancient times is the Jewish tradition of the Mosaic Law, more commonly known as "The Ten Commandments." Although this is not the ideal that I am advocating here, these and other traditions do exist as ancient rigid codified well-founded external belief systems. These fixed strictures and the rites and tenets of the other great world religions are all designed to help people behave socially in the right way and to do the right things. As a Boy Scout, you also know that "The Scout Law" is another such external behavioral belief system which will also serve you very well:

The Scout Law

> A Scout is trustworthy, loyal, helpful, friendly, courteous, kind, obedient, cheerful, thrifty, brave, clean, and reverent.

"These are all good things, but all these other well established external codes of conduct have the same basic flaw that they are not uniquely personally founded. However they do always incorporate an empathetic regard for others. This is what is required to have a stable society. Following any one of these systems will keep you out of jail, but they actually have very limited useful applications regarding most of the truly important personal decisions that you will have to make for the ultimate success of your own life's journey. Your own completed self-work will serve you much better.

"Whatever you think now, life is a spiritual journey. Your mother and I have been your first teachers. I hope you remember us kindly in the end. We both love you very much in our own special and different ways and we have given you the best start that we possibly could. These talks we are having now are probably my final spiritual gift to you. But you can always find nourishment from the great souls of the past. They have left behind for us their many hard won best thoughts. To me they are not dead at all but they are still living presences. This is a function of our great gift of language and human consciousness. I have learned much from sitting down at the feet of Lao-Tzu, Socrates, Buddha, Giordano Bruno, Huang Po, Hakuin Ekaku, and many others… You can too."

Chapter 10. Joining the Opposites

My son says:

"Why are things never resolved? Everything seems to me to just go on and on and round and round all the time. Even after a law is passed immediately those who were opposed to it start working for that new law to be overturned. People say they want world peace, but instead of working to resolve conflicts they are always just starting up more new wars. The Supreme Court finally makes a definitive judgment about something, but even after that the back and forth fighting on both sides continues and does not end. Then in different states more and more new court cases are suddenly created to again oppose and overturn that new resolution. And if that fails then they'll start talking about adding new constitutional amendments, or even changing the Supreme Court judges! How come things just go on and on and nothing ever finally gets solved?"

I say:

"In the big picture things do get resolved, but only very, very slowly. We no longer have slavery, women can now vote, we don't have an active military draft, and we have elected a black president. I'd call that progress. But in the short term you are right. In the long run it seems that there needs to be a generational change before really big problems ever get put to rest. For progress to occur the powerful old guard defending the status quo needs to die out and the young who can re-think the problem from their own new perspective need to come into power. This condition unfortunately is promulgated and reinforced largely by our chosen form of government and in the way we have set up the institutions that formally make all our binding social decisions.

My son says:

"How so? We have a democracy, don't we? Isn't that the best form of government around? Doesn't that by its very nature take in the will of the people? But why doesn't it work?"

I say:

"Someone once said: 'Democracy is the worst form of government, except for all the others.' That's a funny joke, but to the point. Governments are inherently problematic because by their very nature they always concentrate huge amounts of money and resources centrally, which results in their possessing vast amounts of power and control over the populace. The use and distribution of this wealth and power then necessarily gets placed in the hands of just a few often unscrupulous politicians. Who can resist that much concentrated temptation? Not many. This of course is true worldwide, no matter what form of government we're talking about, but it always finds its worst expression the less democratic that a government is.

"We in the West have basically taken on the British model of fair play and majority rule. One vote more than half is all that's required to get elected, to pass laws, and to decide on anything. We all have been conditioned to think that this is the fairest and best way to do things. But, if you really think about it this can actually be seen as the means of maintaining the most divided and unresolved social turmoil possible; yet we all accept this as the rule of law, the *prima facie* conditions of free modern democratic civilizations.

My son says:

"What do you mean? Isn't this majority rule the fairest way to do it? Tell me why you don't think that this is the best way possible, I don't really understand that."

I say:

"Many tribal societies think that not only is this not the best way, but in fact it is the worst possible solution. They feel that because with this system nearly half of the people can still oppose and be strongly against anything that has been "decided" in this manner, so in effect it really hasn't been decided at all. This may be actually the underlying reason why things never seem to get solved.

"They believe it's much better to all meet together in a tribal council and openly and fully discuss any group questions that arise that need to be resolved and to try to arrive at some sort of true group consensus decision for the tribe as a whole. They won't stop talking about it or make any big decisions unless everyone basically agrees as to what is the best path for the tribe to follow. That way there is no longer any large disappointed trouble making opposition group hanging around still being unsatisfied and feeling left out. And we call these people primitive!"

My son says:

"Yes, that's fine. As you describe it, it is the obvious ideal; but do you really think it's possible for a large complex modern society like we are to come to decisions in the same way as a small primitive tribe does? I don't think so... so what then?"

I say:

"I don't know if it's possible or not, nobody's ever tried it yet... But I do know that today we now have incredibly powerful tools of instant communication. The old arguments against it were all about practicality. Everyone thought that town meetings as they were originally held in the earliest New England colonies, just like the Indian's tribal council meetings, were the most direct and best possible democratic means of solving everyone's problems and governing a society. Small towns still do it this way. But soon the populations grew too big and too unwieldy so as a practical result it was decided that a form of representational government should take over. This is what we still have going on right now. But the trouble is that this representational government has now been taken over and corrupted by the influence of big money so that the good for the corporations has almost completely taken precedence over the good of people which is hardly ever considered anymore. We really have instituted an oligarchy run by the top 1%, and you even need to already be a multimillionaire to run for public office and to be elected to it as a representative. So, whose interests do you think they really represent? This is no secret and citizens everywhere see this reality and the people who don't vote often outnumber those who do, that's how dysfunctional our "democracy" has become.

"But I don't think that these old arguments are necessarily still true anymore, and that it's about time to rethink the whole idea of representational government in light of the new exciting possibilities of how we could better make our binding group decisions with our currently very advanced modern interactive communications technology. It has now technologically again become possible for us to return to that original form of a true direct democracy, just like in the earliest colonial period. This would also have the added benefit of solving the many troubling problems of the great distorting influence of moneyed professional lobbyists now clogging and polluting and distorting our system of government. We now have the exciting opportunity to finally once again become a true democracy."

My son says:

"Yes, that really is an exciting and very interesting concept; I can see lots of different practical ways to try to do this today. All of them are currently actually very possible to do. Do you have any really practical ideas about how this could be accomplished right now?"

I say:

"Well, a simple means that is available today would be for the government to issue a "Direct Democracy Card," let's just call it a "DDC" to every U.S. Citizen old enough to vote with additional secure PIN identification. You would only have to apply once and prove your residency, age, and citizenship. These could be used to vote on any and all proposed legislation either through local controlled voting sites manned by political representatives of both parties, similar to today's polling stations, or through a closed controlled securely encrypted system similar to today's ATM money machines, or through the post office, or even through the internet if this could ever be made secure and tamper proof.

"Congress would continue to exist but only as a proposing and debating society, and any DDC card holder could then also be allowed to present online their own perspectives on the current issues under consideration. Proposed laws would then be published through many different media outlets with contrasting points of view also expressed and open official forums could be presented through the media and online before a scheduled voting period by the populace. Instead of only voting in general elections once every two or four years, any citizen with a DDC card could then vote on any proposal. This would amount to an instant error free political poll on every important issue of the day with no statistical biases involved and no margins of error. This would finally be the holy grail of creating a truly modern real democracy.

My son says:

"Yes, that would be a real democracy and it would be great too, a real government of the people, by the people and for the people, just what Lincoln called it and I know that this could quite easily be accomplished with our present technology. I'm surprised at how right this all sounds to me. But how come I never hear anybody important ever bringing up this possibility or discussing these ideas on the TV news programs? This is not really that obscure of a proposal and it seems to be one whose time is right. Everybody says that they believe in democracy and this concept is not that far out of an idea."

I say:

"I guess the question becomes whether or not our country really wants this to happen… do we really want a true democracy? And the way things are we can't even put it to a real vote! If the politically powerful people now in control of our government truly believed wholeheartedly in real democracy some version of this kind would already be in the works. The trouble here is the same as everywhere else – it's that the powerful interests want to stay in power. This conversion from our current system however would not be beneficial to the ruling oligarchs and also for the many self-serving politicians who are now in political office and greatly benefit from the current system. Their vote would no longer be all important and the massive amounts of money and influence peddling expended on them would simply dry up. For these reasons and others, nobody who is now in power wants to even think about opening up, what is to them, this huge can of worms… and of course as the system is structured they are the only ones that can readily bring this change about.

My son says:

"What about – *We the People…* Doesn't our Constitution say that *we the people* are in charge of our own government? Can't *we the people* do anything about this situation?"

I say:

"Yes, it does. And again it is not hopeless… But our government already exists the way it does now, and it has a great deal of inertia and many other locked in forces trying to keep it just the same as it always has been. Outside of all this there is also the deeply divided built in dualistic structure of our traditional two party system. This has always been seen as a problem even way back in George Washington's days. George Washington, the great man who refused to be king, was also strongly against the formation of political parties. Talk about a man of vision, even back then he felt that the people would be ceding too much control of their own government over to impersonal political bureaucracies. However political parties became the norm because of their organized advantages in a representational government, and in modern times the Democratic and Republican Parties are so very firmly entrenched that a third party candidate has never won the presidency. And now the people really do have very little control of their own government just as George Washington predicted so long ago."

My son says:

"Wow, George Washington was against political parties? I never heard that before."

I say:

"Yes it's true, and our Republican/Democratic party system just naturally creates an entrenched dualistic view of reality. This system is not even questioned by most people and is reflected and rigidly frozen into our two party political structures. It virtually guarantees that continual upheaval and conflicts among the myriad groups of advocates will endure. Until there is some sort of large spiritual awakening in our society as a whole, don't expect things to change very much in this regard. In my world view we're all still foundering around in the midst of the spiritual dark ages and the true social enlightenment is yet to come. Perhaps when and if it ever does come we will then all have DDCs and a real and direct voice in our own government – a true democracy will at last come to America, wouldn't that be something!

"During the 1960s and 70s when my generation was coming of age, there was a great spiritual upheaval in this country with the promise of the coming of the "Age of Aquarius" – the spontaneous mass enlightenment of society. But it was short lived and did not take root as it was quickly corrupted by many divisive forces in our culture at the time such as the Vietnam War, the proliferation of drugs, and inter-generational political violence. Our society was not yet mature enough to be ready for a new spiritual renaissance to take hold and happen in any long lasting and meaningful way. Maybe it will come around again in your future, who knows? However your own enlightenment need not be tied to that of the society's at large."

An Extended Spiritual/Political Analogy

The basic distinction my son made earlier between the philosophies of Republicans and the Democrats brings to mind the two different historic schools of Buddhist thought – the so called "small boat" and the "large boat" schools – or in Sanskrit the *Hinayana* and the *Mahayana* schools. The Hinayana or small boat practitioner follows the Buddha's precepts in an attempt to enlighten himself, to do the self-work on leaving behind the world of maya and delusion, attaining non-attachment to things, oneness of mind, and liberation from selfish desires and the world of suffering, and thereby attaining the goal of entering nirvana for himself. For this he needs only a small boat with room for one to make that spiritual journey alone. This is the path of the sadhus, arhats, and ascetics. These are the ones, like that holy man in all the classic jokes, who sits, or better yet floats several inches above a rug in a mountain top cave to which various confused individuals periodically show up to ask him that basic archetypical question, "What is the meaning of life?" To which my comedic newspaper publishing father-in-law Ed Klein had a very clever humorous one word answer – "Cope."

On the other hand, there is the follower of the Mahayana, or large boat school, whose operative ideal is more on the order of the dedicated social worker's commitment. This is the path taken by one who also follows the Buddha's precepts and whose goal is also to attain nirvana, but the Mahayanist is not content on seeking complete enlightenment and the cessation of suffering just for himself, but he also wishes to procure it for the benefit of all sentient beings. This is his way of insuring that with his help society in general will also spiritually advance and become enlightened too. The Mahayana Buddhist finally only enters nirvana when he can bring everybody else along with him too. For this journey he obviously requires a very large boat to also carry so many other sentient beings with him across the limitless Sea of Samsara.

To me this distinction is also yet another false dichotomy, as it seems to me that you can't bring humanity or anyone else along with you unless you have already made that journey and been there by yourself and therefore you know the way. Forgive me for bringing politics into this rarefied religious realm, but in an odd modern way this also reminds me of my own son's characterizations of our two American political parties the Republicans and the Democrats.

In this much extended metaphor, the Republicans are the Hinayanists, or the lucky few who selfishly want to be just left alone to enjoy their own wealth and power. They wish to remain aloof and happy in their own separate private capitalistic nirvana, or saunas as the case may be. They wish you good luck on getting there yourself, or better yet by getting your own separate nirvana sauna, mainly by lifting yourself up by your own boot straps. They are all totally self-centered and simplistically and self-servingly believe that they have gotten to their own capitalistic nirvana totally by their own merits, and that they are therefore entitled and universally very proud of this erroneous belief. They do not want to be bothered and will not go out of their way to help the less fortunate. They feel that if you work hard and do somehow succeed against all odds in getting there on your own, then you too will be able to independently buy your own luxurious nirvana sauna, and then you too will be happy, and will continue never to ever bother them anymore at all.

While the Democrats in this much extended mixed metaphor, are the Mahayanists, who represent themselves as having great empathy and sympathy for the masses. They are magnanimously and tirelessly working to help elevate the living conditions of the general public and wish to help relieve humanity of its long enduring and great suffering. They are the supporters and staunch defenders of the Maha-guru Franklin Delano Roosevelt's New Deal legislation which also seeks to spread the benefits of financial enlightenment to the many hard working citizens, whom the previous generation of Robber Barons selfishly only wished to exploit. These earlier unleashed forces of delusional capitalism had resulted in the Great Depression – economic collapse for all. Of course in our lopsided governmental system that strongly favors the rich, they've all already got their own luxurious private saunas out back too. But they do periodically come out from them, and by means of attempting to enact social reform legislation, assert they are trying to help everyone else get their own necessarily smaller and cheaper mass produced American government made versions of these saunas too! Especially at election time they always remind us that the Republicans have been working very hard just to keep us all out of their saunas, while they are still tirelessly working on getting us saunas of our own, so that we too can finally soon all separately sit comfortably in our own government issued public nirvana saunas and be happy all together.

Of course with the continual strong opposition from the Republicans, this is an ever ongoing legislative battle, and these ever promised saunas always appears as a mirage on the horizon, but realistically never come any closer to reality. Meanwhile all sorts of complex legislation for the industrial war machine and the insurance, banking, financial, and pharmaceutical industries easily passes with both party's support. And the legislators of both parties are still all able to keep on enjoying their own private saunas usually with full coverage at government expense.

It will truly be the "Age of Aquarius" for everyone if the true Mahayana ever totally succeeds in their stated goal of bringing all sentient beings into the elevated state of enlightenment… but don't hold your breath waiting.

This brings to mind another great Zen story:

"How Grass and Trees Become Enlightened"*

During the Kamakura period, Shinkan studied Tendai six years and then studied Zen seven years; then he went to China and contemplated Zen for thirteen years more.

When he returned to Japan many desired to interview him and asked obscure questions. But when Shinkan received visitors, which was infrequently, he seldom answered their questions.

One day a fifty-year-old student of enlightenment said to Shinkan: "I have studied the Tendai school of thought since I was a little boy, but one thing in it I cannot understand. Tendai claims that even the grass and trees will become enlightened. To me this seems very strange."

"Of what use is it to discuss how grass and trees become enlightened?" asked Shinkan. "The question is how you yourself can become so. Did you even consider that?"

"I never thought of it that way," marveled the old man.

"Then go home and think it over," finished Shinkan.

**from "Zen Flesh, Zen Bones" compiled by Paul Reps.*

When experiencing this world as an ongoing flux of opposites, it has been the spiritual goal of many philosophers and religions throughout history to try to unify these many dualistic pairs into some profound and fundamental symbolic whole. Once you have united and joined the opposites, you can then more easily step aside to observe and understand their manifold interactions more peacefully and objectively. There have been many successful examples in different parts of the world that have seriously addressed and solved this basic iconic/philosophical problem. This unification has been accomplished by different symbolic means in many different cultures. These solutions usually exist as creative human figurative forms or in stylized graphic symbolic representations.

In early Indian Hindu and also especially in Tibetan Buddhist iconography the use of male and female sexual union is a common example of this union of opposites. The clear depiction of the lingam and yoni is part of this ancient symbolism from more sensually liberated times. There are many beautiful religious sculptural and painted representations of this mystical union of the opposites. Some in India and Tibet involve the erotic depiction of gods and goddesses in meditative tantric yogic postures while at the same time being engaged in ecstatic male/female sexual union. The male sex organ, the lingam, entering the female sex organ, the yoni, are important and explicit parts of these representations – no fig leaves here! These ancient depictions of male and female sexual union are very powerful images. Of course, these explicit sexual images would be automatically deemed pornographic and be forcibly censored and kept isolated and out of public view in our own still greatly Puritan influenced culture.

There also exists the vision of the third eye in Buddhist and Hindu iconography which is yet another such symbolic example of overcoming dualistic thoughts. The two anatomically normal eyes are the eyes of "samsara" or the illusory ordinary worldly eyes of opposites, of delusion, of "maya" and dualistic thinking. The symbolic third eye is located in the center of the forehead of the enlightened ones between and slightly above the normal eyes. It is this third eye which provides nondual spiritual perception beyond ordinary sight. It is on this very same spot that Catholic priests smudge ashes on their parishioner's foreheads during the Easter period of Ash Wednesday, in an oddly appropriate symbolic gesture of "Here's mud in your spiritual eye."

This third spiritual eye appears in many statues and painted religious representations of Buddhas and Bodhisattvas as an indication of a holy unified oneness of mind – its presence in the being depicted is the outward sign of spiritual transcendence from the worldly. Its use is very similar though not identical to the use of halos above the heads of our saints in Western religious art. It is the spiritual eye, and it is the outward symbolic indication of the abiding presence of transcendent nondualistic oneness of mind and pure spiritual consciousness having been attained.

Here in modern day cultures are two of the more widespread surviving stylized graphic examples of this idea of the union of opposites that still exist and have much resonance in their different present world cultures. They are both examples of intertwined composite images, half of each representing one of the symbolic dualistic opposite pairs, the whole representing a unified entwined graphic union of these opposites. Both of these examples are still in wide use in current world religions but sometimes their roots and the origins of this symbolism from the past have been forgotten and often are no longer widely recognized.

The Star of David

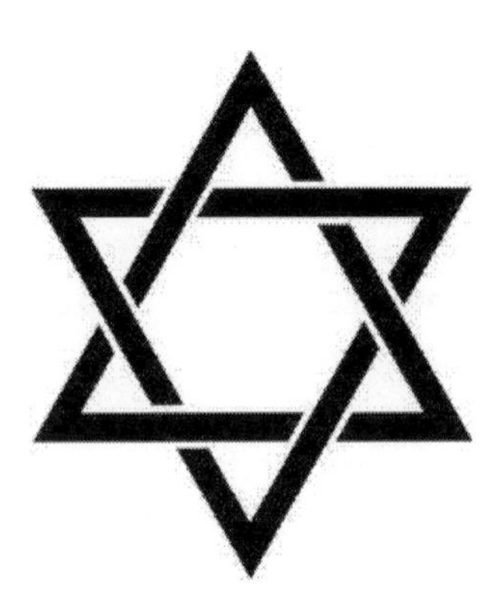

The Star of David is a Western/Middle Eastern one adopted by the Jewish people as a symbol of their religion and culture. It is a rigid structural symbol of two superimposed, often intertwined oppositely pointing equilateral triangles. The upward pointing one is a symbol from ancient times indicating the sun, the heavens, and man; the downward pointing one is used to symbolize the moon, woman, and the earth. The fact that they are often intertwined as one is yet another instance of the Judaic vision of monotheism that here also here symbolically represents the spiritual union of opposites, the overall interconnected one-ness of creation. It is also used as the central symbol on the flag of the state of Israel.

The Yin-Yang

In the orient the Yin-Yang symbol is a more dynamic representation of this same symbolic union of opposites. It is a Taoism symbol from ancient China. It can be presented with or without the contrasting dots in each half and still be identified as the same symbol. The black Yin represents the female element, lunar, dark, submissive, giving, merging earthward, etc.; the white Yang being the male element, solar, light, and active, taking, rising heavenward, etc. This symbol has broad roots and is widely used throughout the Orient and not only in the religious realms. It is also used as the central symbol on the flag of South Korea.

As can be clearly understood from the above descriptions that these two common widespread spiritual symbols which are still in wide use today, also clearly imply male/female sexual union; however their forms have been so abstracted that they can no longer be characterized as having any objectionable explicit sexual content. The primal force of sexuality is a very strong mystical element in all world cultures. This is hardly surprising since it is the main force through which evolution acts, and it is one of the most powerful emotions that we as individuals can experience. It is universally present in all people throughout our world, no wonder that it finds its expression everywhere even in muted symbolic graphics.

The contrasting dots in the yin-yang above are an interesting addition to this ancient symbol that are present in some representations and not in others. When present they additionally imply that nothing in nature is purely one thing, that each opposite has within it at its core the seeds of the other. This is a very liberating concept especially in our modern sexually contentious times. It symbolizes that the male can also have within him some feminine qualities and that a female can also harbor some masculine qualities and that this should not be considered unnatural, but it should be accepted as the given spiritually normal conditions of human life.

The Yin-Yang originally developed in China as a mystic symbol in Taoism that represents the balance of all the opposite forces at play in the universe. When they are equally present, all is in balance, calm, and healthy conditions prevail. When one is outweighed by the other, too much yin or too much yang, there is confusion, sickness, and disarray. This very balanced symbol also comprises a purely graphic union of positive and negative space that results in the complete filling of a perfect circle. The one element simultaneously and automatically creates its other complimentary element, and they can't exist independently without each other and still be whole. This is a beautiful artistic synthesis that represents extremely well the underlying philosophic concepts behind this fundamental idea of the union of opposites in a creatively dynamic and flowing design that is in complete harmony with its Taoist roots.

These symbols of the union of opposites function as powerful mystic icons in their respective cultures. In their form is incorporated the understanding that all opposites must be treated as inseparable pairs, implying that although there are so many basic opposing forces present in the world around us, all seem to require the interaction of their opposites to define themselves. They tend to act as paired negative feedback systems, and need to co-exist in a dynamic balance with each other in order to form a stable whole. This is the direct insight from ancient Taoism attributed to its Chinese founder

Lao-Tzu who saw nature as the great metaphor for life. They are the abstract formal representations of dualism in balance, like the balanced opposites of light existing as a particle/wave.

In other words, within this symbolic philosophical overview of the complex full nature of things and how they interact, it can be seen that the exclusive choosing of either one of the opposites alone and not also allowing for the opposing other forces counter-balancing effect, is a profound mistake.

This means that we must not desire to be always happy, and accept the realization that Happy/Sad is also just another dualistic pair and that we should calmly accept the fact that we can never be happy all the time. That happiness and sadness are both necessary and are actually co-dependent emotional states that produce and define each other. Ditto for every other dualistic pair too. So, these universal dynamics ultimately lead us to the understanding that the world will never be perfected, the very concept of perfection is wrong-headed. Utopia is truly nowhere. Problems of plenty and scarcity will never be finally resolved. There will always be floods and droughts, feast and famine, and there will never be a constant state of world peace. The lion will never lie down with the lamb. These are all delusions that are incompatible with the whole world view that the yin-yang union of opposites philosophy postulates.

But this ultimate truth is not to be experienced as a woeful tragedy, but rather as a profoundly elevated consummate philosophical view of the way things are. The world cannot be perfected because it is already perfect. Reality and the world are always in perfect dynamic balance. Day balances night, winter offsets summer, male complements female, and so on and on. In China long ago Lao-Tzu expressed this in the Tao Te Ching as the eternal nature of the Tao, circa. 500 BC. All the things that are present are necessary and although they are constantly changing in their relations to each other in many different ways, they still always tend to conform to their natural state of yin-yang balance. Although change is constant, so also is the interplay of their counterbalancing forces. Much later in England, Isaac Newton cited a similar concept when in 1687 he published his Laws of Motion, in which he states "To every action there is an equal and an opposite reaction." The fundamental wisdom of this idea can be seen to apply far beyond just the realm of mechanics.

There can be negative psychological consequences to realizing all this complexity, which can lead to a withdrawal from the world of actions. Sometime in life you may be confronted with an unnaturally forced decision that needs to be made...Are you part of the problem or are you part of the solution? Are you on the bus or off the bus? But does anybody really know where the bus is heading? With so many different directors on the bus it can easily wind up in the ditch or worse go off a cliff. In these difficult situations the study of Mahatma Gandhi's philosophy of "Satyagraha" and non-violence can be very enlightening and of great help if you become involved in these forceful types of direct confrontations.

In the real physical world when opposites do directly combine often the result is a great release of interactive energy in many different forms. Male/female union creates the forces of ongoing evolution, not only for us but for all living sexually reproducing species including even trees and worms. The magnetic opposites of north pole/south pole couples interact strongly with each other, and this energy is directly used as the driving force in all electric motors including those in elevators, cars, and trains. The uncontrolled interactions of the rich and the poor in society can create violent wars and social revolutions, resulting in many deaths and major upheavals. The ultimate union of opposites is when similar particles of matter and anti-matter collide and completely annihilate each other. This produces total conversion of their masses to energy according to Einstein's famous $E = mc^2$ equation and thereby generates the greatest amount of energy conversion possible in the universe.

So the yin-yang is the Taoist symbol of flowing balanced change. It isn't just some odd old esoteric Oriental design, but what it represents is the essential timeless union of all opposites. It is something truly profound and fundamental that embodies the basis of the actual dynamic interplay of the many ongoing forces existing in our world today.

Chapter 11. An End to Dualism

My son says:

"You keep on saying that there is another better way of living in the world. Another nondualistic way of thought, not constrained by seeing things as being either good vs. bad, or true vs. false, Democrat vs. Republican, etc… but I just can't see it. Everything to me just naturally falls into one or another of these many dualistic categories. Most of the arguments I have with my friends are all about trying to understand and describe just what these qualities are and to what category the things we are arguing about naturally belong, before we can ever agree on any resolution or hope to solve or even understand the nature of our disagreements. Is there some other way to see the world that you can describe to me in words that will show me more clearly just what you mean?"

I say:

"Yes, you are right. Describing things in words is sometimes a trap because words themselves are strongly dualistic in their nature. I've already discussed this problem with you to some extent in my speculations about how our early primordial languages may have originally developed, and how their development may have been influenced by many odd contributing factors in our local earthly and cosmic natural environments.

"The question here again is do things in themselves naturally possess these dualistic characteristics or do we somehow mentally impose these characteristics onto them? You can't see another way of viewing and experiencing the world because you are living totally in your surface calculating scientific consciousness, and you don't have ready access to your deeper underlying spiritual mind. Your third eye is still sleeping and has not yet opened up. If only we can decide not to take it upon ourselves to always mentally judge and dissect everything around us in all sorts of arbitrary dualistic ways, but if we could just try to be more appreciative and accepting of the spiritual oneness of all things around us, then all these things would continue to exist wholly, or even holy, in just the way they truly are. You can think of this as "the holy seal of the real," if you'd like my religious perspective on it."

My son says:

"Go on, I think I'm actually starting to get the flavor of what you're talking about here. It really is something different, isn't it?"

I say:

"What we are talking about here forms the mythological underlying basis of the Genesis bible story – the fall of mankind from the perfection of life in Eden. Adam and Eve are described as blissfully enjoying God's gift of creation and of their lives in the paradise of the Garden of Eden before the "original sin" of their eating the fruit from the forbidden tree. This symbolic eating of the forbidden fruit and their acquiring of the knowledge of good and evil is given as the reason for our being cast out of the blissful garden forever. The "knowledge of good and evil" is portrayed as the root cause of our primordial loss of pure innocence and bliss, and for us here it also represents the opening of the mental doorway into the endless conflicted universe of all dualistic thought."

My son says:

"But knowing good from evil is totally what politics is all about, isn't it? How can we ever make anything in the world better without in some way knowing this?"

I say:

"Right. That's what wars are also all about too. The real trouble with knowing good from evil is that everyone has their own relative ideas of just what they consider to be good and bad, and yet they all stubbornly believe that their own definitions are the absolute right ones. If you don't agree with my good, you're evil. Obviously the linked dualistic couples of good and evil leads us directly and inevitably to all those other dualistic lenses of right/wrong, better/worse, like/dislike, true/false, happy/sad, believer/infidel, and even eventually to Republican/Democrat and so on and on, to the rest of the endless dualistic patterns of thought that bring us right back to all those divisive modern implications we've already discussed previously and at length… So Mr. Atheist, can you see that the age old Genesis story really does still have a deep resonance here for us."

My son says:
"Hey, please let's not start arguing about the Bible now!"

I say:
"OK, I'm not really up to it either… But once you've done the self-work, you can then begin to think more clearly about the good/evil dualism, and you will then be able to identify and accept the essential unity of the opposites and to experience the always necessary yin-yang balance of life, Then you will have the opportunity to overcome the nearly universal dominance of the dualistic thought process in all things. If this does happen to you it will come as a greatly liberating moment in your life. It will help you to spit out the forbidden fruit and to overcome this all pervasive habit of dualistic thinking. You may even find out that Eden still exists!"

My son says:
"But is it really possible for us to break out of the seemingly universal grip of dualism? Isn't this really the underlying source of where everybody's emotional highs and lows come from? I used to think it was just the normal state of the world and of everyone's life in it, but now you are making me see its distorting and negative influence over just about everything all around us… Is everybody since Adam and Eve destined to live out their entire lives in this chronic intellectually and emotionally schizophrenic condition?"

I say:
"Well said! Although most people in their ordinary lives do tend to naturally view everything that happens to them through an endless succession of one dualistic lens after another, and they do really live in a perpetual "intellectually and emotionally schizophrenic condition" as you yourself just put it so well; yet there are some notable exceptions. When we love someone or something we will tend to love it totally, we will love everything about it. We will not intellectually divide it in half and love this part of it, but not love that part. We will absolutely love the whole thing, even simple mundane

common things in our lives like a certain wine, a record album, a pet animal, an ice tea beverage or even a cigarette brand…

"At one time in my younger days I absolutely "loved" Mateus Rosé Wine from Portugal. I loved the taste of the wine – it wasn't too sweet and it wasn't too dry. I loved the warm color of the wine, I loved the teardrop shaped bottle and its dark hue, I loved the peaceful sunny picture of the winery on the bottle, and I even loved the type face and the design and shape of its golden colored label… In my mind everything about it was absolutely perfect. I can say the same thing about a very special all-white German Spitz dog named Finnegan; a certain lovely Siamese cat named Ms. Easy, and even about certain record albums of the period like the "West Side Story" soundtrack and "Rubber Soul" by the Beatles and "American Beauty" by the Grateful Dead. As an artist I do miss those large old format 33 ⅓ LP vinyl record albums with their often very beautiful art works decorating their big square protective dust covers which I also totally loved. They definitely had much more of a physical presence than do today's CDs or computer MP3 files. I guess I'm showing my age now… But you also have some things in your own life too that you are totally enamored with… like the Cheerios and bananas cereal in your red heart shaped bowl that you eat religiously every morning for breakfast…"

My son says:
"What do you mean by "religiously?" I don't think that's fair! I just like Cheerios; I've been eating them since I was a kid. You're right; I really do like them a lot. I enjoyed them then and I still do now. But religiously? No, I'm just used to them and to me they're just about the best breakfast cereal ever, and they fit very well into my daily routine. Yeah, I do really like to start every day with my Cheerios, milk and bananas, and things just won't feel right to me if I don't have them for breakfast."

I say:
"Yes, exactly, that's just what I mean by "religiously!" Cheerios is not your god, but it is your daily ritual that you perform everyday that makes you feel alright. Yes, and you are totally

enamored with Cheerios... You even eat it right out of that red heart shaped bowl that comes from the company, and that is just the same red heart shaped bowl that is featured iconically on the front of their bright yellow Cheerios box. You are being totally true and righteously loyal to your chosen brand. If I try to buy you the similar but much cheaper Shoprite knock-off generic brand of cheerios-like toasted oat cereal, you can tell immediately that something's wrong and you will reject it... You totally love Cheerios absolutely, the way I loved Mateus Rosé Wine.

"When I first met your mother I loved everything about her too. On the night she met me she went home and told her friends that she had just met the man she would marry. You actually owe your existence to this love of ours. Love is always wholly (holy) life affirming."

My son says:
"I hope to be in love one day just like that..."

I say:
"I wish you that too... The point is that the true causative source of all dualistic thinking is the holding of oneself apart, as being separate from everything else. This of course is inherently false. We are not separate; we are all part of everything else. Dualism in all its many guises is what follows from that basic fallacy. But when you love something you take it into yourself whole and it then becomes part of you too, no more separation – Poof! One hand clapping, not two! No more dualism! Love totally cancels out dualism. The larger your love is the less dualism there will be in your life. If you can love all of life and the whole world just as it is, you will then have totally escaped the confines of dualistic thought. This is one way, but it is certainly not common, although some artists, poets, saints and others in the past have possessed this fully enlightened level of great non-judgmental universal love. This of course is one of the greatest transcendent gifts you can receive."

My son says:
"Yes, I can understand and appreciate that kind of love is truly

a wondrous thing. And I think I can see what you've been saying about how it can even cancel out dualistic thinking... But love is a great mystery and you can't just make love happen by your own free will, can you? By just saying I want to be in love with everything doesn't make it really happen, does it? Perhaps you know of some other more practical approach to escaping the all encompassing and total dominance of dualism in our world?"

I burst out singing:

♫ "When the Moon hits your eye, like a big-a pizza pie, that's amoré. When the world seems to shine, like you've had too much wine, that's amoré."

♫ "When the stars make you drool just like pasta fazool, Signore... Scuzza me, but you see back in old Napoli, that's amoré."

– Dean Martin

♫ "Love is a many splendored thing; it's the April rose that only grows in the early spring. It's natures way of giving, a reason to be living, true love is a many splendored thing."

– Nat King Cole

♫ "Nothing you can know that isn't known, nothing you can see that isn't shown. No where you can be that isn't where you're meant to be, it's easy! All you need is Love. Dat, da, dada da. All you need is Love. Dat, da, dada da. All you need is Love, Love. Love is all you need." – The Beatles

"Yes indeed, there certainly are a lot of songs written about the power of love to transform the world, that's because it really does! But you're also right:

♫ "You can't hurry love, no, you just have to wait, you've got to give it time, no matter how long it takes. I remember what Momma said, "You can't hurry love." – The Supremes

My son says:

"Hey, come on back down to Earth, Dad. I do love it when you start singing, and when you do you're always so into it, and you get so carried away... But you were going to give me some practical advice now about how to escape dualism before you got so carried away with all these old love songs..."

I say:

"Oh yeah, sorry... Love is intoxicating, isn't it...? OK, so what were we talking about? Oh yeah, what to do while you are waiting for transcendent love to come into your life... Well, here's a little meditation that will help you arrive at a less dualistic state of mind. There was a simple spiritual practice going around a while back that went something like this... You thought of all the different parts of your body one at a time and after each one you said "I am not my (fill in the body part) feet, hair, arm, skin, etc..." After negating just about everything one item at a time you can finally arrive at a deeper understanding of just what your own nondualistic nature really is."

My son says:

"OK. That's kind of a cool meditation, especially if you're a multiple amputee! But to me it sounds a little too much like self-hypnosis and I find it's too simple of an idea for what we're talking about here... It also sounds like a clever trick of turning total negativity into something positive and soothing in the end. I can see how perhaps it just might be helpful for some nervous people sometimes. I guess that overall there's something good in it, but I don't really think it's my cup of tea, or that it's going to help me very much at all... Ya got anything else?"

I say:

"OK, as you said earlier, you just couldn't see things in a nondualistic way at all. You couldn't see anything else but different levels and different kinds of duality wherever you looked. Think about this. It's like you're out there all alone walking around in the world and the entire time you're saying to yourself, "Would I like to own a car like that one over there? Is it better than mine? Do I like that color? Is that girl really pretty? She dresses really nice, but her skirt is awfully short, and those shoes, what was she thinking! I wonder if it's going to rain today or not? Should I go ahead and ask my phone? Is the price on this thing I want to buy a good one, or can I find a better one somewhere? I don't know... Is that guy hanging out on the street corner over there really dangerous? Should I look the other way and just cross the street right now?" And so on and on.

"Stuff like that just keeps popping up and going through your mind all the time. Although you're probably mostly unaware of it, your own mind is actually constantly busily engaged in its own automatic analytic processing and evaluating everything you see all around you, and thereby doing violence to it in one way or another by dualistically chopping it all up and creating many spur of the moment judgments about everything you see, and then incessantly cataloguing these individually in so many different ways. And most other people whom you meet while walking around are also similarly busily engaged in just this same sort of huge full time endless processing of their own dualistic thoughts with which they are also totally automatically filling up their own heads with too. They are always being fully immersed in actively dissecting, assessing, and evaluating different particular aspects of just about everything they see all around them in a process of endless judgmental analysis.

"This continuous internal frenzy of mental activity actually occupies most of their minds and makes it hard for them to see anything as it truly wholly exists in its own unique natural undivided fullness. While so engaged in this endless processing they can allow only very little free mental space for the open existential enjoyment of true spontaneity and the unexpected serendipity of the present ongoing moments in their actual lives. It becomes a block to even simply experiencing and appreciating all of the transcendent beauty that they are in the process of insensitively passing by without it even registering anything at all within their own consciousness. They are continually silently doing spiritual violence to everything around them and as a result they become infinitely poorer in so many different ways for simply the lack of having any essential inner quiet and openness of mind. They are not blissfully ignorant, but blisslessly ignorant and also hopelessly arrogant. Unknowingly their lives are all being totally filled up with themselves and the many different aspects of their own petty personal prejudices in a way that continually isolates them from any real contact with the universal Tao that surrounds them. Although they are in it, they are not of it.

"On the other hand, the spiritual man in his everyday life tries to always remain actively present within the Tao. He has the ability to effortlessly do this because in the maturing process he has attained a deep personal inner peace and he is not actively fearful nor greedy of his surroundings, but is open to and engaging with it in a clear and non-judgmental way. He is not concerned with dualistically chopping everything up and passing his own personal judgment on all that he sees. He remains open to the manifold beauty and many subtle qualities of the natural and human worlds surrounding him. He is fully present and unassumingly possesses this necessary inner quiet and openness that others lack. He always gently affirms reality instead of being always busily questioning and judging it.

"But just because duality surrounds us and makes up all the daily news reports and totally dominates our politics, language, and our society in general, we can still individually choose not to live under its pervasive thrall."

****

Again I'm reminded of a couple of my favorite old Zen stories:

"Is That So" *

The Zen master Hakuin was praised by his neighbors as one living a pure life.

A beautiful Japanese girl whose parents owned a food store lived near him. Suddenly, without any warning, her parents discovered she was with child.

This made her parents angry. She would not confess who the man was, but after much harassment at last named Hakuin.

In great anger the parents went to the master. "Is that so?" was all he would say.

After the child was born it was brought to Hakuin. By this time he had lost his reputation which did not trouble him, but he took very good care of the child. He obtained milk from his neighbors and everything else the little one needed.

A year later the girl-mother could stand it no longer. She told her parents the truth – that the real father of the child was a young man who worked in the fish market.

The mother and father of the girl at once went to Hakuin to ask his forgiveness, and to apologize at length to get the child back again.

Hakuin was willing. In yielding the child, all he said was: "Is that so?"

Here is another fitting historic old Zen story too:

"Everything is Best" *

When Banzan was walking through a market he overheard a conversation between a butcher and his customer.

"Give me the best piece of meat that you have," said the customer.

"Everything in my shop is the best," replied the butcher. "You cannot find any piece of meat here that is not the best."

At hearing these words Banzan became enlightened.

**from "Zen Flesh, Zen Bones" compiled by Paul Reps.*

The Chinese concept of "wu-wei" as propounded and practiced by Taoism's founder Lao-Tzu has its place here too. The emulation of flowing water is one of the main natural philosophical ideals stressed throughout all of Taoism. Unlike the strongly static and structural Jewish symbol of the Star of David, the Taoist symbol of the Yin-Yang has incorporated within its design this feeling of flow and change. As a Taoist you should live your life as much as possible in emulation of the spirit of flowing water. Wu-wei is the Taoist word for this essential over all principle of the non-active, of not actively asserting and forcing your own ego's will directly onto the situation at hand. This is not the same as passivity, but it is rather a state of being totally receptive to, and in harmony with all the energies, natural and human in your environment and working from within this context, the same way as flowing water does.

"Be content with what you have, rejoice in the way things are. When you realize there is nothing lacking, the whole world belongs to you." **– Lao-Tzu**

This active state of mindfulness is referred to as "Being in the Tao." It can also be thought of as being in a deep form of spiritual empathy and direct communion with the natural forces as a whole in your immediate surroundings. But you should not just melt into it and lose your sense of self in the process. You should remain in a heightened state of sensitivity and awareness and be observant and ready to act in concert with the ongoing Tao. By not dualistically confronting the natural forces of what is happening around you in a directly opposing manner, but by practicing the one-ness of being in harmony and becoming an integral part of them, you can make a direct connection with nature's own universal energy. As a result your actions will then be joined in concert with these natural forces around you and you will therefore gain energy and effectiveness from practicing this wu-wei Taoist strategy. Being in the Tao is truly being joined wholly within the active ongoing present.

Amazing unanticipated synchronistic things will happen to you in this receptive wu-wei state. When you are fully experiencing being "in the Tao" you are "in sync" and working in harmony with the overall one-ness of nature and there is nothing that can oppose you. Often you will have the feeling of being in a magical space, that the world is all of a sudden laying open at your feet with many unexpected mutual collaborative possibilities that were hidden from you before will openly present themselves. Of course you must be fully opened too, aware, and receptive to these forces. Then you can become an integral part of the true full ongoing present reality by performing your own actions in concert with the natural flow of the energy around you. In this Taoist strategy as in nature, flowing water finds its way around any and all obstacles in its path, and over time will level mountains. This is an ancient instance of the primacy of the idea of "going with the flow," but with the added advantage that while still going with the flow, now you are consciously present within it and so you can also help influence this flow.

The ancient Chinese practice of Tai Chi is another beautiful instance of this Taoist flowing water based philosophy. There are now many different schools of this practice which is truly an ancient art that also forms the basis for many of the different Oriental martial arts schools. It can be very classical and highly structured or it can also be more modern, composed of freer forms with the possibility of added original improvisations. In its classical form it is a slow stylistic dance-like physical culture discipline, the embodiment of the Taoist flowing naturalistic philosophy in a formalized physical and mental exercise regime. The practitioner in silence slowly performs a series of physical, usually asymmetrical sequential callisthenic movements of a deeply symbolic nature, which are also simultaneously linked with flowing poetic mental imagery such as, "Grasping the Sparrow's Tail," "Embracing the Moon," "The White Crane Cools his Wings," "Gathering in the Clouds," etc. all flowing seamlessly into each other in a pre-determined traditional sequence. Unlike Indian yoga, the Tai Chi practitioner never arrives at any one static holding posture or form, but rather slowly passes through them all in an evolving sequence. Its pacing is purposely very slow but never still, and one form is always in the process of unfolding and flowing into the next one. Here again we see the essence of the traditional Taoist flowing ideal that is embodied within a highly rigorous and aesthetically stylized physical performance which is often practiced by individuals as a daily ritual and an aid to spiritual focus and inner peace.

This is one of the bountiful expressions of the true spirit of the East that forms the basis of Taoism, and Tai Chi is a unique embodiment of this as a conscious slowly moving meditation where like life, one dynamic element is always in the process of flowing seamlessly into the next one. It arose from an ancient Taoist traditional source and is based on the idea that focusing the mind and the body solely on these movements and the accompanying poetic mental imagery of Tai Chi will help you to reach an internal centered state of physical and mental calm, clarity, balance, wholeness, and health that is in dynamic harmony with the active natural world around us. In Tai Chi's performance, the practitioner is able in some measure to achieve the experience of feeling what "being in the Tao" is like in the ever flowing eternal present moment.

Of course the ritualized practice of Tai Chi is necessarily only a very limited experience of this, since actually being in the Tao by its very nature can never be ritualized, as it is an experience of total spiritual immersion and improvisation in the always unique never recurring present moment. As Lao-Tzu ceaselessly reminds us, "The Tao that can be taught is not the Tao." Nonetheless it captures in a classically formed physical discipline the true essence of the naturally flowing philosophy of Lao-Tzu's ancient bounteous gift of Taoism to all of mankind.

In the Tao of the Fishes

Here is another purely personal example from my own early life of the universal truthfulness and usefulness of these principles. Long ago before I had ever heard of Lao-Tzu or his ancient concept of "wu-wei," I used to spend my grade school summer vacations at Twin Lakes in the Poconos where our family had a summer house at the end of a long dirt road. When I wasn't out walking in the swamps picking and eating wild blueberries, or playing kick-the-can with my neighborhood friends Woody and the gang, I could often be found at our dock feeding the fish with pieces of old stale bread from our kitchen.

There was a small group of fish that seemed to live only around our dock. They were mostly sunfish, bluegills, and a type of yellow perch we called shiners. The sunfish and bluegills were loners, but the shiners swam around in small schools. Of course I also caught some once in a while with worms and a kid's fishing pole. But while feeding them over time I began to think of myself as their friend. I slowly started to know them better and I began to even be able to individually recognize some of the local fish on sight, especially the big bluegills. I liked feeding them and watching them scramble for the floating pieces of bread a lot. The bluegills were strong and when eating the bread made a big splash on the surface. I enjoyed seeing and interacting with them in their wild natural freedom and I wanted them to somehow become my friends too. In my mind, I wanted them to have a deeper more personal mutual relationship with me too, just like I was having with them, but I wanted it to be on their own natural terms and in their own natural element. Was this a selfish childish wish and a totally unrealistic desire to have? I wondered…

"How was I going to do this?" I asked myself as a young boy.

This was not an easy problem to solve. But after thinking about it for a while I had my own "aha" moment, a flash of insight! We had on hand a large high-end skin diving mask made out of brown pliable real gum rubber that covered your whole face and mouth. It had a large flat oval plate glass front clamped securely on and two snorkels molded right into the mask with automatically sealing float valves one on each side. It was perfect. With it I could sit still just under the water and have a wide clear view and easily breathe with no strain and I could stay submerged that way sitting on a big flat stone by the side of the dock for hours. I started doing this in the afternoons over a period of weeks, just sitting still and holding out some stale bread in my hands and watching the fish and waiting for something to happen.

At first the fish did not know what to think of all this and they just went about their normal business totally ignoring me. Then as I continued to just sit there eventually they became more curious and slowly started to form their own cautious circle around me at a few feet away just out of my arms reach and they started watching me too. I just sat there with the bread in my hands. The fish watched me. I watched them. We both watched each other. Nothing happened. I did not know it then but I was practicing true "Wu-wei" the Taoist non-active principle.

But after this stand-off of mutually watching each other had gone on for a very long time, a very brave little fish, hesitating, starting and stopping, cautiously made his way up close enough to me and then made a dash at the bread, got some and swam quickly away. Soon he made another successful dash while all the other fish just watched, and this time the force of his attack broke up more of the bread than he could eat and the excess bread drifted away in a cloud of free floating pieces. I just sat there still. Now the other fish got in on the risk-free bread action and started swimming around and quickly eating up all the loose free floating morsels of bread. This became the turning point in our long stand-off.

After a while they all started coming closer and forming a queue and then I had them eating right out of my hand. I was able to do this more easily the next time. Eventually I had built up enough trust between us that even the bluegills, the bigger older more cautious fish, also joined in. It's funny, but the shiners never did, they just all stayed together aloof, and swam by once in a while in their small schools. They didn't seem to have enough patience to figure out what was going on. I guess they were either, not curious, too dumb, or just hyperactive by nature.

Then finally after slowly building up this trust with the fish, I was able to have a fuller and even more satisfying relationship with my fishes. I was now not only able to feed them by hand, but I held my other hand out in front and just below the hand with the bread in it, and then they actually let me gently touch and pet them individually as they came up to eat the bread from my other hand. I was even able to experience individual differences in each fish's character this way. I was now actually having a mutual relationship with them on their own terms in their own element! This was exactly what I had set out to do. I had succeeded in sharing my deep feelings of friendship with the wild fish.

I would often stay submerged playing like this with my fish for such long periods of time that the skin on my fingers would wrinkle up like a prune and my eyes would become so imprinted and my brain so entrained and so used to the low light levels and the gracefully flowing motion of the swimming fishes that when I got out of the water, took off the facemask and laid down on a towel on top of the dock to dry off in the warm sun, I could still see for many minutes the wonderful sight of all my wild fishes happily swimming around together through all the clouds in the bright blue sky above me.

Although the concepts were foreign and unknown to me at the time, this was certainly an instance of my being "in the Tao of the fishes," by using the strategy of putting Lao-Tzu's non-active "wu-wei" principles into action! It was one of those amazing unanticipated synchronistic things that can happen when you function within the natural energies around you in this Taoist wu-wei aware and receptive state. If I had actively pursued my own goal of petting the fish and attempting to have a direct relationship with them by forcefully trying to get close to them in a typical western proactive dualistic way, it wouldn't have happened. They would have all just swum quickly away from me. I would never have gotten a chance to sit and pet and actively play with the wild living fish. But by joining in wu-wei non-action within the natural forces around me and by being able to remain a peaceful presence and to become one with the spirit of the fishes in their own natural environment I was actually then able to fulfill my own selfish wishes with the wild fishes. And then myself and the fishes were both able to enjoy each others company by merging into the Tao of the active present!

My son says:

"Wow, that's a great story. Is it really true? Did it all happen just that way? Did you really spend so much time just sitting all alone underwater with some bread in your hands and just waiting all that time for something to happen with your fish? Did you really just stay non-active and let the fish take the initiative? I wouldn't have had enough patience to do that like you had, to just sit there for so long breathing under water without ever doing anything like that, just quietly sitting there… I don't know if I could've done that…"

I say:

"Yes I did. I've always been telling you the truth. I just knew that it was the only way that it could be done. But for me it was really a kind of active meditation with the fish. I enjoyed it and I didn't find it boring at all. I felt like it was a kind of a mental dueling contest of wills between me and the fish as to who would blink first. But you've got to understand that the normal energy levels of everyone and the times themselves were very different back then than what they are today. We did have TV then, but there weren't any all day news channels, and there were only three broadcast channels. Also where we lived the reception was generally quite poor in the daytime, and often all the programs that were on were very dumb anyway. Back then our phone was on what they called a "Party Line" which meant that there were different rings for those on it, ours was two short rings. Sometimes you'd pick it up to make a call and hear your neighbor in the middle of a private conversation, and you'd have to excuse yourself and hang-up. We didn't have the total internet connectivity with the world at our finger tips, or the instant cell phone communications with our friends like you have now. So it was basically a different time with a different energy level, and we didn't have nearly as many attractions and distractions in our young lives back then."

My son says:
"It sounds boring."

I say:
"Well we didn't know any better... the digital future hadn't been invented yet. But there were other things that have just totally disappeared by now, they don't happen anymore, and some of those things that are now gone were really great.

"In those now remembered idyllic summer vacation days of my youth, we all lived at the dead end of a mile long dirt road deep in the country on a mountain top by a lake with very few neighbors and no town that was very close by. We kids would be allowed to play outside alone, and to do whatever we wanted to do all day long. We were what you might call "free range kids," and we related to the real nature all around us in a much deeper way than most kids do today. As a result, the lake, the blueberry swamp, and the woods became our playgrounds. My mother had a big loud Chinese gong that she would hit three times when it was time to come back home for meals.

"I was glad that you took to Boy Scouting the way you did, and it has been a real positive experience in your life that also brought you closer to nature in an organized deep way. We are really very proud of your becoming an Eagle Scout."

My son says:
"Yeah, I really like scouting! We have a great small troop, and we do a lot of fun hiking in great places all year round. And the Scout Masters are really cool, and I even like all the merit badges and the ranks I had to go through to become Eagle. The summer camps at Ten Mile River in the Catskills were wonderful too, and I'm thinking that maybe I might even become a Scout Master myself one day in the future. Once you're an Eagle Scout you're an Eagle for life, you know."

I say:

"In my day as kids we got really close to nature too, but in a much more disorganized way! We'd find creative things to do all day long, some of them spontaneous group activities like playing "kick the can," or going out and getting purposely lost in the woods by following the old trails that after a while just disappeared on the forest floor, and also other activities that were very private and more peaceful, like my weeks long solitary encounters with my fish.

"I remember one time I caught a painted turtle and painted him. It's a kind of big local turtle that because of its pretty skin coloration is called a "Painted Turtle." But the top of its shell is just a dark color, so I painted it white, and then let him loose in the lake. A few years later when I was kayaking in shallow waters in the inlet, I caught sight of a light green oval scooting along the lake bottom under me. It was him. His back was light green now since there was a layer of algae growing on the white paint, but it was definitely my turtle. It was nice to know that he was 'living long and prospering!'

"We all seemed to live more in communion with nature back then, experiencing directly those long slow patient natural rhythms of the weather and the seasonal changes that surrounded us. There was no light pollution at the lake and the full dark night sky was densely filled with bright stars where I remember we watched from our dock some of the early satellites like Echo 1, a silvery balloon, slowly travel across the Milky Way. On calm clear nights the stars and their reflections on the lake were so bright that with stars above and stars below it looked and felt exactly like you were sitting on a ring of land floating by itself in outer space. Which I guess we really are! We were on the top of the Pocono Mountain Range and when there was a summer thunderstorm you wouldn't just hear one thunder clap, but you'd hear real rolling thunder. You'd hear one loud thunder clap, then its echoes receding and bouncing off all the other mountains too, like it was a giant physical bowling ball of noise rolling along and rebounding through an immense obstacle course of other mountains. We had the time and inclination to listen for things like that back then. They really were different times.

"Around the Fourth of July we kids did lots of crazy things with firecrackers and cherry bombs that just wouldn't be allowed today. It was during the 50s after World War II and we played war games and had lots of military toys too, and also real army helmets and lots of war surplus stuff from our parents' basements. Many of the movies we saw were still romanticizing the big war. Just like what we saw on screen, we dug foxholes and tunnels, we'd blow up old plastic warships on the lake, and old warplanes we'd hang on a string from a tree branch to simulate combat in flight. We'd make simple time bombs that really worked. You'd put a firecracker fuse in a pack of matches and light a cigarette and put its end in the matches too, but on the other side from the fuse. When the cigarette burned down it lit the matches and they lit the firecracker. We learned that trick from a WW II prisoner of war movie! It was simple and effective, but for us kids getting the cigarettes could pose a problem.

"My best friend Butch and I even created our own kids hand grenades. We'd get a 4" or 5" carriage bolt and start putting on a cone of bigger and bigger hex nuts and then washers with two giant washers in the middle, then a reverse cone of smaller and smaller washers and nuts ending with a spring and a wing nut. We'd pull the two big center washers apart and put in three rolls of caps and then tighten the wing nut. It was a nice size and weight for throwing and when it came down and hit something solid like a sidewalk, street or building it made quite a big bang. I got in trouble when I threw one against our elementary school wall and missed and it went right through Mrs. Jaggy's first grade window! Sometimes we'd just put an empty coffee can over a cherry bomb and it would blow sky high. Luckily nobody ever got hurt and it was all great fun."

My son says:
"That sounds pretty wild. Where'd you get all the cherry bombs and fireworks?"

I say:
"Our family used to drive down to Florida in the winter for a short vacation, and on the return trip we'd bring back a haul. When

you went through South Carolina and some other southern states they'd sell you just about anything you wanted. We'd usually bring back sky rockets, roman candles, and stuff like that, and on the Fourth of July we'd set off our own nice display out on our raft in the lake, but we'd always make sure there were lots of leftovers.

"The plane incident was really funny though. Butch and I put a plastic B-17 "Flying Fortress" bomber with a cherry bomb inside its bomb bay doors on a string hung from a branch of a big maple tree that was growing on a steep hillside. Because it was on a hillside we were able to be up on the hill almost as high as the branch was when we lit the fuse and let it loose. It flew off on a beautiful full arc of about 30 feet and of course we expected it to blow up at the far end point. But it didn't. Then it came flying back at us in reverse. Yikes! We panicked and scrambled and slipped trying to get away from it as it came back and blew to smithereens right in front of us!"

My son says:

"Wow, I bet you'd really like my X-Box 360 game "Battlefield 1943." It's a World War II game. You get to fly fighters in dogfight missions from old aircraft carriers in the Pacific, captain torpedo boats, attack Islands, drop bombs, and drive LST landing crafts, Jeeps, and Sherman Tanks. You can really do just about everything, and the graphics are very realistic too. I liked that game a lot when it came out. You could play on-line with other players and be on the American or the Japanese side. It had those folding wing Corsair fighter planes and Jap Zeros too. A lot of the time I wouldn't even be playing war games, but I'd just use it as a flight simulator. Landing Corsairs on Aircraft Carriers is challenging and great fun and I got pretty good at it. It's really way cool!"

I say:

"Yeah, I've seen you playing it. However, there's a big difference – when we made foxholes and tunnels we didn't click buttons, we dug dirt! Actually if it existed back then we probably would have loved it just as much as you do now. But it is fast-paced and has a lot of stuff that's pre-programmed. It's all consuming and the sounds are great and the enemy is shooting back at you and everything. When I was a kid we did all that on our own, and a lot of our playing all just happened in our heads. We didn't really think too much about it, but you needed to have an active imagination to have fun and it seems like everyone did.

"But everything happened at a slower more natural pace back then. When I watch your computer games and today's media, especially the commercials and those ads for new upcoming blockbuster movies, I can't believe the onslaught of quick changing images they blast at you. Does anybody really have an attention span of just half a second? They all seem to me to be made by people hopped up on drugs for other people also hopped up on drugs. I feel that what they are trying to sell you must be so bad that if they allowed you to really focus and pay attention to any of it for a reasonable length of time, it would become obvious just how bad it was and it would wind up being a total flop, so they use a quick shotgun approach that seems to work for them. You wind up going to a movie without knowing what it's actually all about. And often when you come out of the theater you wonder why you went to it in the first place. Needless to say, I'm not their target audience, but I do find it very disturbing..."

My son says:
"When did you come to realize that you were basically a Taoist?"

I say:
"I am not a Taoist. Only in retrospect did I come to understand that I was sometimes relating to the world in a Taoist way. I have come to have great respect for Lao-Tzu's mystic vision only after studying many other Eastern religions and philosophies when trying in later years to find my own true place in the world. What I am now is the result of my own self-work. Part of this process was becoming aware of and reading many cross-cultural works. All of the very early spiritual writings are really the best. There was a great bloom in human spirituality in many parts of the world starting around 500 BC. It is amazing what has been preserved from this period, for most of the great early spiritual teachers only taught their followers strictly

by the oral tradition. They themselves never wrote anything down, and often their words were rhythmic and were also in a form of poetry too. You should read some of the early literature. Start with the Upanishads and the Tao-Te Ching. Their original insights and influences were so strong that they were remembered over many generations and their thoughts only got written down sometimes hundreds of years after their originators had died. So you can imagine the complexity of all the different versions that do exist. Some scholars even question if there ever was a real person named Lao-Tzu, or Homer, or even Jesus Christ."

My son says:
"Come on now...really Dad?"

****

Lao-Tzu's ancient philosophy still has a very broad resonance in Chinese and other Eastern cultures even today. In fine arts, the spirit of Taoism is still strongly present in the Orient. In their calligraphy and especially in sumi-e brush painting, both are made by using black ink on absorbent white rice paper, with each stroke it is very important to be totally mindfully in the present moment. The brush strokes are often performed in synchronization with the artist's own breathing. In this demanding art form of spontaneous perfection, there can be no corrections nor is any reworking possible. The most highly praised work is done with the least amount of brush strokes, and it is considered most important to capture the spirit of the subject rather than all its physical details. Many Western artists have studied this form of painting as a means to improve their own work in our more forgiving Western mediums. American Jazz improvisation is probably the only art form that we have created that comes close to working under these same demanding principles.

Lao-Tzu's Taoist influence can also be found in many other oriental sensibilities as well, and it forms the bedrock on which many other active areas of their culture are built too. The martial arts of China, Japan, and Korea in their disciplines such as Judo, Aikido, Kungfu, Taekwondo and others also can trace their roots directly to

Taoism and the practice of Tai Chi. These disciplines employ the receptive Taoist wu-wei concept in a more forceful way, as a strategy in their discipline of calmly awaiting the attack.

In this strategy, if you can remain grounded and alert (stably non-active) while your attacker is in motion against you (active) it can be demonstrated that you will have an advantage and an inherently stronger position. Then when you move you will be able to act more effectively to defend yourself, and if you are skillful, you can use your own grounded stability to deflect your attacker's off balanced aggressive motion. You will then be able to turn the momentum and force of his attack against you from an apparent strength into a weakness. Using your own wu-wei non-active balanced stability as a fulcrum, with the right amount of properly applied leverage you can then re-direct his necessarily off balanced aggressive momentum back against him to your own advantage. This is what is happening when in a judo match you see the aggressor forcefully coming at the standing defending fighter and somehow suddenly being flipped by his opponent and landing harmlessly on his back on the floor mat. To be able to do this in the many different possible situations that can arise in a fighting contest of course requires discipline, a high degree of fitness, much analytic study, long training, and great presence of mind in the face of danger. But this is also yet another form of actively being in the Tao of the moment and responding in a wu-wei way to the natural forces that are in play at that very moment in the hand-to-hand fighting contest. The echoing of many of the flowing motions of Tai Chi have been adapted and applied to this practice in the many different forms of oriental martial arts disciplines.

These are just a few instances in Oriental culture which feature not acting in a directly opposing dualistic manner as we often do here in the West. This is very different from a western fist fight or boxing match where you are trained to directly confront the other fighter and try to give as much or more than you get. There is of course ducking and parrying in boxing, but the basic idea is to try to beat down and conquer your opponent by opposing him with overwhelming brute force while at the same time being able to withstand his opposing onslaught. Successfully landing more forceful punches is the goal and in these matches having more strength and weight is directly to your advantage. Although in our Western spiritual heritage Jesus councils us to love our enemy and to turn the other cheek, this requires a saintly attitude and in real life situations we seldom do it.

This is not the Eastern approach which is a much more subtle and mindful encounter based on the tenets of Taoism. We in the West have a basic native predilection for "fighting fire with fire" or claiming an "eye for an eye – a tooth for a tooth," which some have humorously observed that if it were seriously carried out and taken to its limit would result in a totally blind and toothless populace! The Chinese Taoist approach is a much more subtle method. It also recommends acting, but not by opposing the situation in a directly confrontational manner and thereby bringing out the worst on both sides, but by understanding and working to basically finesse the situation using their idea of acting in cooperation with the ongoing forces of nature in a subtly grounded wu-wei approach. This is yet another example of being immersed within the "oneness of nature" and not by posing with the outsider's egotistic and dualistic attitude of being separate from "the other." Also by employing the strategy of calmly awaiting the attack, this practice has the added positive effect of isolating the aggressor and making the prospect of a true all out fight even less likely.

Our instinctive response to dualistic arguments in the Western world, as in the boxing match, is to take sides and to work for your side's concept of the right directly against the other, and to actively oppose and press your point of view on to ultimate victory – The basis of your activity is to destroy and vanquish the opposition and to win outright, preferably with a grand knockout punch. To the Taoist this strategy only makes matters worse, and creates an even greater imbalance and more confusion, and does not result in harmony but actually only results in increasing the unbalanced disarray of energy in the world. This is a prime example of just how different oriental and occidental sensibilities are.

Most people do not have a very deep spiritual understanding and acceptance of the ways of the world. They do not believe as our great artists and poets do, that this in reality is already a most perfect and very beautiful world we live in, and that we ourselves belong here and are a natural integral living part of it. That we all already have the ability to enjoy and prosper and lead a full rich life in the world in its present form as it already exists today. As Lao-Tzu sees it, if we are experiencing problems, it's important to direct our attention and energy inward towards ourselves and try to resolve any spiritual conflicts that may be arising from our own ignorant misunderstandings. For he also councils us to become one with the universal Tao, since it is essentially pointless to try to individually oppose the overall transcendent natural order that is everywhere abundantly present and fully apparent to the awakened mind.

In general most people do not share this aesthetic attitude of the Chinese sage or of the enlightened poet and the artist. When they experience problems they will generally not look inward at all, but will direct their attention and actions outward towards their circumstances with the intent of changing the world around them to better fit their own self-centered arbitrary needs and likings. In their limited ways they wish to make life better or at least improve their own small lot in it for themselves. As a result, they will not generally feel at home in the world as it is, and they will always think it needs to be "improved" upon. They will not see the transcendent beauty surrounding them, or even accept and feel neutrally at ease about most things in their own lives. They will tend to identify more strongly with one or the other side of their artificially imposed and distorted unbalanced dualistic views of reality. They will feel that it is much better to be rich than poor, beautiful than average, conservative than liberal, more controlling than free, more of a believer than an agnostic, and on and on in countless arbitrary preferences… And because they identify with one camp more than the other, they become advocates, boosters, and fans like supporting their favorite local sports teams. And likewise just as in sports where there is always a dreaded opposing team to face that must be defeated, and if you happen to be on the losing side this year, who knows…you can always look forward and maybe next season your side will be able to do better and then you'll gloriously win over all odds... "On Wisconsin, On Wisconsin, fight, fight, fight, fight, fight!"

This overall dualistic tendency complexly pervades their lives at all levels and in all areas of their interests and as a result they find themselves on a never-ending rollercoaster ride of emotions that ebb and flow with the currents of their perceived local social, cultural, religious, or national and even international ongoing events and news trends. These unbalanced forces will always be at work continually playing out against each other at so many different levels in so many different arenas that no final resolution is even possible. This is often very frustrating for them and can even become physically debilitating because in this ever-continuing process they are automatically yielding up control of their own emotional states to these external uncontrolled events. They are deeply identifying their own spirits and are even physically internalizing into their own bodies, responses to these perceived important external stimuli which are mostly far beyond their own real participation in, or of having any actual experience with, or their own ability to control, affect or even influence any of them at all.

The response of "Is that so?" never occurs to them.

They have never evolved from a conflicting haphazard collection of randomly acquired personal "non-stuff" into a unified trans-personalized and life-affirming empathetic spiritual whole. They are still emotionally fused to their own essentially random collection of personal accidental history. Don't dig too deep into their psyches or you will hit the irrational anger level of their own propensity for self-preservation, sparking them to strike out at your "interference." They have never done the Socratic work of examining their own inner core being, of ridding themselves of the contradicting randomness of some of life's early clogging dross. They did not do the necessary introspective self-work of selectively refining and reinforcing their own true spirit to create a stable internally defined identity that they can remain comfortably at peace with and be able to stably abide therein.

As a result, they are constantly being troubled and buffeted by the winds of change in the fickle outside world around them, frightfully unsure of what will come next to oppose them and wondering just how to best deal with it. They will be incessantly wondering to themselves just what is the correct stance to maintain, or what should be the best position they need to take up next?

If you wish to see clear objective evidence of this in our widespread culture, all you need do is to watch for the rapid large value swings in the Dow Jones Stock Exchange Index as it responds to the latest world news events. They are the ones who will jump out the windows.

****

Kipling's Take on This

I've already mentioned how much I admire the writing of the author Rudyard Kipling in this book. Many of his works have been successfully transformed into great motion pictures too. His novel "Captains Courageous" is a movie with Spencer Tracy and Lionel Barrymore that's one of my all-time favorites. "The Man Who Would Be King" is another one with Sean Connery and Michael Caine that's well worth watching. When I was young I read and re-read a kid's illustrated version of his work, "The Jungle Book" many times over, and it has also been made into popular movies many times over too. When my son was young, I discovered his "Just So Stories" which we both greatly enjoyed reading together. These are all very inventive tales, like how the elephant got his trunk. Some of them even deal with his folksy speculations on just how human language, writing, and the alphabet itself were possibly created, another theme which also interests me. I also fondly remember reading his work "Kim" as an adult, which has been produced on film as well. Obviously, he is a beloved author greatly admired by many many people in our worldwide culture. Here is his beautifully written popular poem "If" wherein he expresses his own views poetically on these very same basic issues we were just discussing above.

"If"

by Rudyard Kipling

If you can keep your head when all about you
Are losing theirs and blaming it on you,
If you can trust yourself when all men doubt you.
But make allowance for their doubting too;
If you can wait and not be tired by waiting.
Or being lied about, don't deal in lies,
Or being hated, don't give way to hating,
And yet don't look too good, nor talk too wise:

If you can dream—and not make dreams your master
If you can think—and not make thoughts your aim,
If you can meet with Triumph and Disaster
And treat those two impostors just the same;
If you can bear to hear the truth you've spoken
Twisted by knaves to make a trap for fools.
Or watch the things you gave your life to, broken,
And stop and build 'em up with worn-out tools:

If you can make one heap of all your winnings
And risk it on one turn of pitch-and-toss,
And lose, and start again at your beginnings
And never breathe a word about your loss;
If you can force your heart and nerve and sinew
To serve your turn long after they are gone,
And so hold on when there is nothing in you
Except the Will which says to them: 'Hold on!'

If you can talk with crowds and keep your virtue,
Or walk with Kings—nor lose the common touch,
If neither foes nor loving friends can hurt you,
If all men count with you, but none too much;
If you can fill the unforgiving minute
With sixty seconds' worth of distance run.
Yours is the Earth and everything that's in it,
And —which is more— you'll be a Man, my son!

The Transit of Venus

My son says:

"Wow, are you serious? That's quite a heavy load of Eastern philosophy you've just dumped on my head – but I really have no idea of how to use any of it to help me in any practical way to make any real decisions in my own life today. It sounds to me like your ideal is to just sit there in what you call a receptive "wu-wei" state of acceptance and watch everything that is going down and just mind your own business, letting the world go by around you all on its own. Then, if you happen to be confronted by someone about something that requires a judgment or decision on your part, you just counter with the direct take care of everything assertion/question, "Is that so?"

"No matter what you say, I still think that you're basically a Taoist. Once in a while I've been with you and I've heard you say that we were "in the Tao," when somehow improbable external things seemed to be lining up and happening spontaneously for us. Things that were sometimes almost magical, yes, like that time we saw the Transit of Venus in a very small gap in the clouds. But most of the time I thought it was all just pure chance and coincidence. Anyway I don't feel like it's really an option for me, or any real way to run my own life."

I say:

"Yes, the Transit of Venus, that was good... but you are misunderstanding it if you think that happened passively and by accident. For that to happen I had to learn about the astronomical timing weeks before and write it down, and to know that I wanted to see it with you, and then I had to go out and buy two of the right number protective welding goggle optical glass filters in advance and not lose them. Then before we went out, I had to duct tape those glass filters onto the front of our old boat binoculars. Then we had to remember to be out there at the right time so we could try and actually see the transit event happening. These were all decisions and actions I had to take and not just remain sitting there passively and watching the world go by. Then when the day finally did come it was totally cloudy with sheets of low stratus clouds all over. We also had to do some important work around the house and after that we still had to go out for you to participate in your high school band concert too. You were going to play timpani that night, remember?

"But I didn't just give up and lose hope and scrap the whole thing. No, somehow or another, things still felt just right to me and they all seemed to be lining up and falling into place that afternoon. For me, there was no dissonance and I felt like we still were "in sync" even before we jumped in the car. The fixed astronomical timing for the transit fell exactly into the narrow time slot we had left open just before we were supposed to leave for that evening's band concert. On our way out to your school we turned off into the onion fields where we knew we could get a good clear view of the western horizon. It was still cloudy all over when we pulled off the road, opened the car doors, and set up the prepared binoculars holding them right up against the open car door to steady them, and right then at that final moment, the last improbable piece fell into place as a small widening hole developed in the cloud cover over us right where it gave us a clear view of the Sun just as the moving silhouette of the planet Venus, backlit by the Sun, was starting its slow progressive motion right across the upper half of the solar disk. Remember? You and your mother were both there and saw it too.

"Yes, that was something… We had a beautiful clear window for the Transit of Venus, a rare, often once in a lifetime occurrence. That was really great! And the reason that we were all there and able to experience this cosmic event together was that we had done our homework and we were all ready for it and in place and the heavens above were also cooperating and it was all happening in real time right there in front of us. For you it was just a lucky chance occurrence you had while accompanying your father around, but for me it was a deeply exhilarating experience of actively being in concert with the Cosmic Tao."

My son says:

"Oh yeah, I felt it too… that us seeing it was all very special. It was a really great thing to be there together and as you say, "in the

Cosmic Tao" with Venus, the Sun, and you and mom too, and to watch the Transit of Venus happening right there over the onion fields right out in our own back yard. I'm glad you went through all the trouble it took for us to be able to experience it. But in reality I don't think that you can take too much credit for actually making it all happen. I still think that there was an awful lot of accidental chance and pure simple good luck involved that enabled us to see it."

I say:

"You still don't really get it, do you? That's just how the world works… things happen in concert with other things happening too. No one is really the director or in charge and there is no pre-written script. When you are "in the Tao" you are not making something happen, but you are actively participating in the happening. If you want to actively participate in the ever ongoing cosmic drama that is happening every day all around us, you've got to be prepared and to be "on your game," in action, ready and alert in the present moment, and not daydreaming about the future or re-hashing the past. That's the real simple truth about exactly the way things happen in the real world… you can think of it as "the holy seal of the present" if you'd like my own religious perspective on it.

"Analogously, the best thing for you to do now on your own is to prepare yourself for your chosen adult life, to do your homework as fully as you can and master the areas of your deepest interest. This time for you is just like the opening in a chess match. It's time to gather your forces and plan your long range strategy. Knowing and purifying who you are and having trust in what you can do and what you do know is an all important part of this preparation. Then you will have conquered your own self-doubt and you'll be ready to have the possibility of making your own luck when happenstance or the Tao smiles on you. The Tao is always present and ongoing all around you whether you recognize that you are in it or not. If you cultivate your sensibilities to it then you can actively participate in its unfolding. When you do find yourself fully "in the Tao of the moment" there are no big decisions that will need to be made; everything is only a continually natural unfolding of the great ever-present ongoing eternal process. The only difference is that now you are in it and you can therefore consciously interact with it appropriately."

My son says:

"But what about this... What if when we were all getting out of the car in that onion field and getting ready for our opportunity to see the Transit of Venus happen – what if just then that hole in the clouds didn't open up for us to see it right when it did? What if it had just remained cloudy all over? Wasn't that whole thing that you are now making such a big deal about just a simple chance occurrence of pure luck that could just as easily not have happened to us at all? What about that? Huh?"

I say:

"You will still be able to truthfully tell this whole story to your own children. That hole in the clouds will always have opened up for us right there, and it will always have happened just when and how it did letting us clearly see the Transit of Venus until the end of time. No one can ever change what actually occurred... Why are you focusing on that? There really are so many other possibilities too... What if we had pulled off the road at a different location and that hole in the clouds then didn't line up directly with the position of the sun in the sky? What if we had a flat tire right in the middle of town? Or gone on all the way to your high school's parking lot and just absent-mindedly forgot all about it? Of course, you can always go on forever speculating about all sorts of things that might possibly have happened but never did. But what's the point in that? Don't you see, and then we wouldn't even be having this conversation right now, would we?"

My son says:

"OK, I guess you're right, and it really was fantastic to have actually seen with good binoculars something so rare in the sky as the Transit of Venus, and to have seen it happening right there in our own small town, in the middle of an onion field, and on an ordinary school day! I really did have that strong sensation at the time that we are really all just floating around in space, and to watch the planet Venus in the daytime also just go floating by in real time right across the face of the sun right there in front of us, it was truly awesome… but I still can't seem to shake the feeling that there's something very strange about this whole Tao thing that you're so into, and somehow it keeps on bothering me…"

I say:

"Don't worry, you'll get used to it some day… I did. Yes, you could really feel that it's just like Giordano Bruno said so long ago, that we're all just floating around somewhere out there in infinite space. But as much as I loved being there and seeing the Transit of Venus with you, I think it has gotten us off on a tangent here a little bit in what you were asking me about. You said something before about not really having any idea of how to use any of my spiritual philosophy to help you in any practical way to make any of the real world decisions in your own life today. So let's talk some more about that and continue our discussions on how you should make your decisions in the future on what's the right thing for you to do. You certainly are at that stage in your life where this matters a lot."

My son says:

"Yeah, that's an important part of my life especially right now, when I've got to be thinking about my future, if and what college to go to, and what's the best career path to follow. These are all pretty heavy things for me to have to figure out. But my take on your philosophy is starting to make me wonder if it's even possible at all for me or anyone else to ever decide just what really is the right thing to do in any given complex real life situations… help me out here…"

I say:

"Very well… but you won't get off the hook so easily… you're still going be the one that will have to make lots of these important life altering decisions now and in your future. Wu-wei is an important and useful concept to bear in mind and for you to fully understand, and I'm glad that I was able to help you experience its beauty, power and significance, and its true reality and actual use. So now you can fully appreciate that it is not at all the same thing as becoming passive or just "going with the flow" and becoming unresponsive and missing all the many possibilities that are always coming up before you to act within the normal flow of events.

But deciding what's the right thing to do is an active and ever cumulative accruing event that will continually arise anew throughout your whole life. You will be faced with many life situations which will require real decisions to be made on your part. And you must take full responsibility and understand that nobody else can tell you how to do it, or just what is the right thing for you to do, not even me. Of course Yogi Berra simply says, "When you come to a fork in the road, take it." Or once again as my good friend Regina humorously points out: "You've got no choice – it's either one way or the other!"

"I think that your criticism of my philosophy has to do with this fact: that each important problem that presents itself will invariably have so many different details, aspects, and future consequences to it that it is generally impossible for you or anyone else to truly possess full god-knowledge of all the possible future ramifications for each and every one of your decisions. There are so many future imponderables involved that even a computer program wouldn't be able to help you. But there is no need to worry so much or even to always try to be outwardly consistent in everything you decide to do. When you are faced with an important decision that needs to be made, your mind can often start to spin its wheels by considering all the various possible future results of the two different options that could be done. But really, the truth of the matter is that you only need to be able to form a gestalt, a creative synthesis of the problem at hand and the possibilities it presents without having truly full god-knowledge and weighing all of the many different possibilities that exist or could possibly become important in the future.

My son says:
"I've already experienced some of that kind of confusion of having to juggle too many conflicting details in my mind like you're talking about right now. But what exactly is a gestalt? I never heard this strange word before."

I say:

"Ah! Great question… It took me a very long time before I first learned about the concept of a gestalt and when I finally did it was like coming home at last after being on a long wandering sea voyage. It all of a sudden crystallized and explained an awful lot of confusing things to me. A gestalt is one of the truly impossible things that our minds are just naturally great at instantly doing – like integrating huge amounts of essentially random data into images.

"Did you ever look at the glowing coals in a dying fire or the clouds in the sky or a messy pile of clothes on a bedroom chair in the early morning light, and see perfectly complete faces and even more complicated scenes spontaneously appearing in them? A gestalt is what you are seeing. Is the gestalt really there? Different people will not see the same gestalt! The genius inventor and great renaissance artist Leonardo da Vinci used to say that he often found deep inspirations for his paintings while gazing at old water stained wallpaper. I used to do a similar artistic thing using scrumbling and marbleizing gel techniques. It also forms the basis of the Rorschach Inkblot Test, that famous psychological diagnostic tool where people are asked to describe what they can see while staring at a succession of usually symmetrical complex abstract ink blots that were randomly created on doubled over absorbent blotter paper. I think that Mr. Rorschach must have been very bored with an awful lot of ink and free time on his hands to have come up with such a very innovative, thinking out-of-the-box kind of creative psychological tool as that. Kudos to him!

The definition of gestalt in the dictionary is this:

> **Gestalt** *n., pl,* **-stalts, - stal-ten** *Psycol.* **1.** a unified whole; a configuration, pattern, or organized field having specific properties that cannot be derived from the summation of its component parts. **2.** an instance or example of such a united whole.

"A gestalt is not limited to images only and it can also occur in the other senses as well. But as I am using it here this same process applies to complex abstract purely mental problems too. This overall subjective synthesis and integration of complex data fields into a "unified whole organized configuration" is the quality of mind you should practice and develop the knack of easily doing it, and to be able to call upon it at will in helping you make your own important life decisions. It is an odd ability to develop because you can't force it to happen, but you've got to get out of your own way and just allow it to happen, kind of like seeing, without special glasses, those "magic eye" 3-D computer printed images. Some people just can't do it."

My son says:
"That sounds like a neat trick. I've just got to form a gestalt. Hmm... It sounds very interesting and I can see how it could possibly be very useful too... But how exactly do you really do it?"

I say:
"Ahh yes, that's another good question, and it's yet another basically Eastern approach you've got to take to this problem... I'm afraid that this again is going to sound very strange to you... But the truth is that you don't really DO IT, you've just got to let IT DO YOU! Yes, that's the real trick. You've got to let loose your brain and kind of go out of control for a little while and completely un-focus your mind. Some people just can't handle that – they have the constant obsessive need to always be totally in control of themselves and as a result they remain always internally unconsciously blocked. They seem to harbor a real fear of their own unconscious mind. These folks are generally unimaginative and very anxious people, and there are lots of them out there.

"But here's the important part, to form a gestalt in your mind you cannot be focused on any of the individual details, but you must open yourself up to the thing as a whole, all at once and then just get out of the way and let the active synthetic genius of your own inner spirit do its thing. A true gestalt is not a slowly put together thing, or constructed bit by bit by the conscious mind, but it will suddenly just pop out at you already in its whole completed and surprisingly convincing form. Your mind unbidden on its own will all of a sudden make the jump and figure it all out. When the gestalt forms, all at once the transformation happens and it becomes just what you'll then see it as being, even though you know that what you are seeing is not really there and it is all your mind's own creation. But once you've experienced seeing this gestalt, you can't escape it or ever be able to reverse it and change it back again into its original inherently complex randomness. Your mind has formed its own creative synthesis of all the data and that's it. That's what your mind tells you it is and that's exactly how you'll actually see it from then on.

"Forming a gestalt of a complex problem at hand will give you a much truer feeling of just what is the overall flavor of all the elements and forces that you are dealing with. You should be able to form this gestalt of it in your own mind. Once you do, you'll be better able to understand its full overall future implications. It also has the added quality of being linked in many ways to your own subconscious inner being. This is why different people will see different gestalts from the same stimulus. This is why the Rorschach Inkblot Test works. Then while always remaining true to yourself, you need to realize at a deep level just how well this gestalt fits into your already well established "Circle of Being." You must also consider how the results of your possible future actions flowing from this will mesh with who you already know yourself to be.

"With all that in mind you will be better able to make the best decision that will be most true to your own spirit of what is most appropriate for you in any given complex situation. Your already having done the self-work of examining and purifying your true inner self and becoming a unified empathetic spiritual being will form the underlying stable ground for making these decisions. You will then be able to act with more certainty and much less self-doubt. When you are able to do this well, each decision you make will add to your developing character constructively and in a positively cumulative powerful and organic way. You will then over time naturally grow spiritually stronger in your own inner being."

My son says:

"A gestalt huh? It's not really there, but I should try to form this odd illusion and make my decisions on the basis of that? Is that really what you're recommending? This does sound awfully strange to me, Dad."

I say:

"Yes, although it is unquestionably an illusion, it has the merit of being your own deeply rooted personal creation; and it is also at the same time a grand synthesis of complex data fields. Forming this primary gestalt in your mind will greatly simplify your decision making process. Without it there can be an endless confusion of trying to account for detail upon many possible future details. This can become so complex as to delay your making any decision at all until it's too late. Then the decision you do make is no longer effective or even appropriate as you've missed that subtle decisive moment – too bad… the Tao has moved on and you've been left behind just wondering what to do. A gestalt is quick and powerful, but it's only one of the tools in your kit bag.

"But you should also be reassured that the making of one decision will not necessarily totally and irrevocably alter your future life. Yes, it is true that karma always accumulates and has its effects, but there will always be new circumstances arising too that will then enable you to decide to modify your initial course of action – just like new navigational orders from Mission Control in Houston can be sent for mid-course corrections to space satellites already far out along on their journey."

My son says:

"Look at you! A modern space travel metaphor! Well, at least that's a pleasant change of pace from your usual old salty nautical symbolism."

I say:

"Ha, ha, ha… but it's not that far from it, is it? It's actually only astro-*nautical!* Ha. ha… But always remember this - the most basic fact of life is that – "you are what you do." Also that sometimes in your life you'll have to do and act quickly to remain in the active zone of the ongoing Tao of the moment. Having become an empathetic and unified conscious spiritual being with true self-knowledge will help you immensely in being able to form this necessary gestalt spontaneously in any given situation and enable you to act quickly and with more self assurance and confidence. If you can do this effortlessly "on the fly" you may be able to surf the waves of the Tao. I wish that you will be able to have this extraordinary experience in your future. There's really nothing quite like it… It's one of the greatest feelings in the world of being totally alive and fully conscious in the present."

My son says:
"Oh boy, here we go right away into that Tao thing of yours again… Are you sure you're not really a Taoist?"

I say:
"Hey! I'm being totally open with you here, you should respect someone when they're seriously opening up their heart to you and trying to share with you something very personal and important to them, you shouldn't always be so cynical. That's not the way to find true friendship and love in your life…"

My son says:
"I'm sorry, Dad… I just get a little seasick with all this Tao stuff you keep on bringing up… It's so confusing to me because it's not really religious stuff, it's not really God stuff, I don't really know what it is, but it makes me uncomfortable and it really disturbs me at some basic level, and I just don't know how to feel about it all."

I say:
"Just accept it for what it is. I guess it's a little bit like the force being with you in the "Star Wars" movies, maybe that will help you out. Have you ever noticed that the character of Yoda is also portrayed a little like the Chinese sage Lao-Tzu too? I know you've got no background for all this and I can understand that this is all a rather big chunk for you to swallow all at once… But really you should just read the Tao-Te-Ching when you get a chance… OK, so you're forgiven… But I've got some more important things to say

about what making decisions really is, and just what in the end it all adds up to in your own inner life."

My son says:

"The Tao is the Way, right? And the way is the way you choose to go, right? And you are trying to help me to make my decisions about life in a nondualistic manner, right? Through some sort of holistic spiritual consciousness while at the same time somehow always remaining true to myself, is that it?"

I say:

"That's the gist of it… Of course, each life situation that you face that requires a decision on your part is as unique as a snowflake, and therefore there can be no general rules that apply. What's the right thing to do has got to be totally your own decision, and you must be satisfied with what you do decide, and be able to live with its consequences. It ultimately is what your life is all about – the sum total of all your personal decisions and all your personal actions. This is what Buddhists and Hindus call your karma. This has really been the main subject behind everything that we've been discussing here. It's what other people will finally judge you on and what you yourself will judge you on… I know that sounds strange, but believe me it will happen. Everyone at some point in their life will do this. There will come a time when you will inevitably and inescapably come face to face with yourself in the mirror of your own mind and be the judge of who you have become and what you have done with your own life, whether God does it on Judgment Day or not doesn't matter, and the final results will either make or break you. Not many people ever talk about this…

"This future judgment that you will make of yourself, from which there are no appeals, will be the work of your autonomous inner spirit. It will happen when the time is ripe, all on its own and in its own way. What are the non-stuff beliefs that you have created, accepted and internalized during your lifetime that it will use as the basis for this judgment? It is best that you are at peace and have a complete understanding of them before this happens. The cumulative results of many bad decisions in the past done without much thought of their consequences, or without any consideration of how they would affect others can even lead some people to their own drastic final judgment-decision of taking their own lives. This self-evaluation and judgment is a deep thing that eventually happens to everyone in the core of their beings and it's all about how well you have lived your whole life. It is not anything that your surface rational ego mind can alter. This is not a light thing that can ever be easily dismissed. It is the culmination of who you are when you realize that it's all always been up to you. It is built into us, whether we think about it or not, it will happen. So think about it. You can consider this as "the holy seal of judgment" if you'd like my own religious perspective on it."

****

"Janus"
from the author's "Transformative Figures Series," a pen and ink and graphite

My Use of the Term "Holy Seals of Creation"

During the course of this work I have often used the phrases "holy seal of ..." (judgment, the real, the present, karma, death, etc.) as a group I call these the "Holy Seals of Creation." My use of this term "Holy Seals of Creation" is *not* a direct biblical reference to the Seven Seals which are mentioned in the Book of Revelations and are purportedly to be opened in Heaven to let loose the Four Horsemen of the Apocalypse – War, Famine, Pestilence, and Death – and to initiate Armageddon and the End of Days. My use of the term "Holy Seals" is original and it comes from my having had many of my own true trans-personal spiritual experiences over the course of my own life.

My own spiritual beliefs are idiosyncratic and of a non-traditional and un-nameable sort. They have their roots in many cross-cultural philosophical and traditional world religion sources as well as also having been shaped by the direct effects of these many real personal transcendental spiritual experiences which have also contributed to and influenced these beliefs. My coining to this descriptive phrase "Holy Seals of Creation" is the direct result of some of these personal spiritual encounters.

We all are currently living in a dominantly scientific age in which culturally we believe that everything is open to scientific investigation, exploration and ever mutable technologic change. However, I do not believe this to be true, and for me there are some things that are forever sealed and immutable, some things that are permanently removed from the access of our meddling surface scientific minds.

These are things which are contained within and form the fundamental underlying structure of everything around us, and they are also inclusive of the nature of the human spirit. Carl Jung and Joseph Campbell, in their original ground breaking works, have touched upon some aspects of these things. For the scientist, he may well find a reflection of my ideas in the apparently arbitrary set values of the fundamental physical constants in the natural sciences, the actual values of which no one can account for, but which seem to be necessary so that the world and universe can continue to physically exist in the way that it does now, and that also allows us to be living participants in it. But this is only one small instance of what I am talking about here.

Because these "Holy Seals of Creation" were not made by man and are universal and time independent I call them "Holy," and because they are removed from our direct access I call them "Seals." Their background influence shapes the underlying structures upon which the universe and all of human history is formed and is forever unfolding. Many of these are innately understood by all of us and form the basis of how we can judge a work of art as being "true to life."

A full discussion of what these "Holy Seals of Creation" are, what they mean, and how they function is beyond the scope of this work. Suffice it to say that these "Holy Seals of Creation" are the same for everyone, everywhere, and for all time. They form the universal ground of being, and that within them they hold the underlying parameters of all the possible ways in which we can exist. They contain within them the limits and possibilities of our existence. When you directly encounter one – you will definitely know it!

****

Transcending Dualism by Grace

The title of this chapter is "An End to Dualism" and the main theme has been escaping the intellectual hegemony of dualism, the dilemma of always creating and existing in a divided reality, where everything is either right or wrong, Republican or Democrat, good or bad, etc… that pervades our Western culture all around us. Again like my good friend Regina once observed, "You've got no choice, it's either one way or the other." But my spiritual friend Hakuin Ekaku and I may just defer judgment and answer with a substantive "Is that so?"

The nature and sources of dualistic thought have been previously discussed at length and several scenarios have been presented as ways of acting in the world without sacrificing a holistic unified vision of reality and your own equanimity of spirit. We've identified the true source of all dualism as the false concept of holding oneself as being separate from everything else. We've tried to show how to rise above the ultimate overlapping multi-dimensional complexity of rampant dualism and to be able to make a decision from a more holistic overall gestalt synthesis of the elements and their potentials. Various examples have been presented through Zen stories and the Oriental philosophies of being in the Tao, and the deeper implications of the profoundly complementary nature and the mutualism captured in the outwardly dualistic yin-yang symbolism, and by our practicing non-attachment to either group of the many different dualistic and essentially politically separate camps. And also through great universal acts of love in rising above the fray of dualistic thought and not allowing oneself to be separated in any way from the one true all-that-is-ness. These can be individually practiced and incorporated in different appropriate ways during the course of many aspects of your ordinary life.

But there is yet another way that an end of dualism can happen to you, and that is all at once in a manner similar to the sudden enlightenment of Zen satori. This is one that can not be practiced or gained incrementally nor can it even be actively sought, but can only be bestowed upon the individual through some form of what must be called transcendental grace.

There is an ancient Hebrew benediction that is also used by Christians, which has an enigmatic phrase in it. It goes like this:

"May the Lord bless you and keep you,
May He be gracious unto you, and
May He cause his countenance to
Shine upon you and give you peace."

I always wondered just what exactly having "His countenance shine upon you" really meant. It sounded pretty neat. All you had to do was to allow His countenance to shine upon you and all of a sudden everything would be groovy, and all your problems would be put to rest. There would be no more self-doubt, no more conflict or struggling to figure things out, Zen satori, painless easy instant nirvana. But what exactly is that experience of having the Lord's countenance shining upon you really like? And how does this come about and actually happen to a person? This is yet another of those "holy seals of creation" that no amount of dialectic discussions can elucidate. I also know that when and if this does happen to you, you will be changed by it, you will be profoundly affected, and you will certainly know it.

There are many different archetypical myths and stories in our culture whose theme is: "Man was never meant to possess god-knowledge." In fact they often claim that we are incapable of holding it and that its presence would totally overwhelm and in fact personally destroy us. Prometheus must eternally suffer; Icarus in his flight must fall to his death from the heavens by the heat of the sun, the builders of the Tower of Babel can not be allowed to continue on to its completion, and many other myths. We are constantly warned not to approach the ultimate and then only at our own severe risk. "Those whom the gods wish to destroy, they first make mad."

Another more recent example that demonstrates that this pervasive recurring historic theme is still firmly entrenched in our popular culture is the frightful ending of Steven Spielberg's Indiana Jones movie "Raiders of the Lost Ark." Finally, after the original historic Jewish Ark of the Covenant from the biblical times of Exodus has been recovered, and when it is about to be opened up, Indy nobly warns his faithful cohorts (good people) not to watch the event, i.e. to keep your eyes closed and thus to avoid God–knowledge; while all the ignorant people (evil Nazis) watching immediately start to horribly totally disintegrate in an orgy of very gruesome special visual effects. Yet another instance of gristly gratuitous Hollywood overkill.

But I know now that these are all exploitive melodramatic exaggerated points of views of this phenomenon. They have been created and promoted by authors who seem to be strongly ego driven and who may never have had the real experience for themselves. "The shining of His countenance upon you" will not cause you to go insane or spontaneously self-destruct and explode. This is pure nonsense. It is way over the top extreme sensationalism shamelessly used only for tawdry dramatic effects. But the full experiencing of God-knowledge will burn out your narrow ego-centered dualistic point of view and open you up to indiscriminately seeing all of creation by God's transcendent shining light and not by your own very limited personal vision which has been operating only through a very narrow cloudy and distorting human lens. Here are some better historical literary descriptions:

> ***"Now I see as through a glass darkly, but then I shall know even as I am known."* — from I Corinthians**

> ***"If the doors of perception were cleansed, everything would appear to man as it is, infinite."* — William Blake**

Again, this can only happen through the intervening agency of transcendental grace, and will only happen to those who are deeply in need of it and who have already gone internally the whole spiritual distance by themselves. It is not their due nor will it necessarily occur, but if and when it does happen, it will happen by grace and they will finally truly experience the end of their worldly dualistic egoistic consciousness. When you do go out of your mind and into God consciousness, you will not only abstractly feel the truth expressed in these lines:

> ***"Whether or not it is clear to you, no doubt the universe is unfolding as it should."* — The Desiderata**

But it will then be perfectly clear to you that it *really is actually so unfolding*, and you will *know* that this is absolutely true. There is no substitute for actual experience. You will then see what is really happening right through your own newly opened eyes. Your individual ego's stake in it will finally be over and you will then experience the greater true transcendent beauty of creation's intricate total dynamic trans-personal intertwined one-ness as it is actively unfolding before you in the only way that it can and therefore in exactly the way that it should and must, and always has and therefore always will be so unfolding. You will be in the true total presence of the Tao, and it not make you explode, but just as the benediction says, it will bring you peace.

A Vision Bestowed

I have already discussed the similar nature and effect on the self that both real and dream experiences can engender. Both can effect real changes in the nature of your Circle of Being, of who you are and who you will become. For me, perhaps being still under the influence of my earlier experiences of living an artist's life, this transcendent experience manifested itself as something analogous to being in a living marbleizing gel. When an artist does marbleizing, he prepares a viscous carrageenan water based colloidal gel in a very large flat tray. He then randomly splashes around different thinly diluted oil colors that will float on top of this gel. These oil colors do not mix with the water gel and remain wet and somewhat together from their surface tension. Then manipulating the gel by stirring or by various other means only limited by the artist's creativity, the oils will begin to form unusual patterns, and merge and otherwise interact with each other on the surface of this semi-fluid medium. They will often have the appearance of patterns similar to those found in natural marble, which is why the process is called marbleizing. When the artist decides that he has achieved the desired effect he is seeking, he then lays down a large sheet of absorbent paper onto the surface of the gel, and the design is immediately transferred to the paper similar to the process of mono-print making. You'll often see these marbleized patterns on the page edges and on the inside covers of large elegant old reference books in libraries, and good fine art shops will often have a large selection of single sheet marbleized papers available for purchase.

In my own spiritual vision I could see the complex reality of the world as if projected overall within a transcendental living marbleizing gel with each living being simultaneously being held as a suspended element within it, continually undergoing an artist's skillful transformations. I could see that all these flowing ongoing changes were being incorporated and were also responding to, and were wholly embraced by all the other flowing living participants that simultaneously existed as freely floating members of this one vast living cosmic gel. All these entities were forever engaging in the process of flowing and interacting with each other's presence and responding to motions in kind within their own local dynamic and ever changing environs. All of them were actively transforming into ever slowly evolving unique space filling patterns. I was suspended in awe above this living gel, fully perceiving and bearing witness to its totality and its deeply moving both spiritual and visually captivating panorama. But there was even more to it than that.

Amazingly, through the power of the living presence of a pure transcendent shining light brightly illuminating this constantly evolving scene, not only could I witness the overall interplay of these freely floating beings with each other, but I could also see right through them and directly into the essence of each one's individual character. Their true natures were now being fully revealed to you, and you could see and know their normally hidden inner motivations – the deeper truer realities of their own spiritual beings were also clearly on display. You knew at once whether they were acting and reacting from pure and honest inner motives, or if they were cunningly playing a mutually fraudulent game with each other performing an ongoing "dans diablo" of short sighted ego driven and goal oriented mutual manipulations. Both of these processes were simultaneously and seamlessly working together within this ever-transforming living gel.

Overall this riveting ecstatic luminous experience really consisted of having the overwhelming clarity of full God-knowledge all at once bestowed on you. And you also must then realize that this profound level of awareness that you're now experiencing is actually the highest possible level of understanding of the current state of the one true living reality, or in fact, even of any other possible conceivable future realities. There's no separateness or duality present in this whole consummate all-that-is-ness that you are now witnessing within the transcendent realm of this overall bright shining spiritual illumination. All of it quite simply is only the full totality of our normal reality as perfectly experienced through this unencumbered gift which is now momentarily being shared with you.

Now you are clearly seeing the total all-that-is-ness for the first time, which previously you have only vaguely suspected, and imperfectly experienced hints of, just very small separate parts of it in your own personal ego-driven life. All of it is now being fully revealed to you in its own full nondual completeness, while in the midst of pursuing its ever actively ongoing evolving course throughout time. This continuously advancing progression along its own unbroken self-directed living multifaceted creativity is now lying fully revealed to you. And somehow unaccountably by grace you are now being given this rare holistic glimpse of its full true living presence. Wow, absolutely amazing! This full vision of reality is profoundly and totally mesmerizing. And wholly holy.

You will then deeply understand and know that there is ultimately nothing that you or anyone else needs to do or add to this consummate self-actuating fullness that already contains every living thing in existence. And even if you possibly could, any action of yours would become totally absorbed in the subsequent movements within this cosmic living evolving gel. That everything will still remain always constantly interacting in this ever ongoing process of its continually overall advancing development that is simultaneously occurring all the time, everywhere, all at once – just as it always has been, as it is, as it was, and as it always will be. And you will also realize that this all will extend on in this unbounded infinitely dynamic way well into the future, far past your own limited horizons. And that your possessing this deep transcendent knowledge and understanding does not trouble you in the least. In fact having this overwhelming spiritual experience has actually given you a profound sense of serenity and has finally put your own troubled mind at rest.

Then as the consummate result of all this, you will deeply appreciate the grace that has been bestowed upon you in being able to witness this totally integrated consummate dynamic wholeness –

this holiness – of your being in the presence of this grand clear vision of the root active transcendent forces of the real and ever ongoing creation. And now this is all happening right in front of you, and you are fully in its presence and witnessing it all for the first time clearly illuminated and actually in its purest totality of form.

Finally, you will be able to look away and remain totally satisfied with the fullness and completeness of this experience that has been revealed to you and the knowledge has only been bestowed upon you through the vehicle of spontaneous grace. At the same time as you are actively holding the profound beauty of this overpowering spiritual vision completely within yourself, you will directly feel the deeply reassuring total physically embracing and joyfully profound quality of pure true inner peace being bountifully poured right into the hollow emptiness of your now cleansed being and filling you totally up. Your cup will overflow with this profound sweet ultimate peace. You will then humbly realize that you are among the chosen, and you will then know and understand that this experience that has just been freely given to you is The Great Benediction:

"May the Lord bless you and keep you,
May He be gracious unto you, and
May He cause his countenance to
Shine upon you and give you peace."

This has been my best effort to communicate to you one of my own true spiritual experiences... Even though I know that trying to capture insights of this transcendent nature in words will necessarily always be sadly inadequate ...and even though I also know that it is probably a foolish thing to even attempt to do this. I have ignored these prudent thoughts and I have done it nonetheless, in an attempt to share this deep true experience of my own inner life with you in the hope of a more intimate and personal spiritual communion.

Here once again I am reminded of the greatness of Lao-Tzu's ancient commentary:

"The Tao that can be spoken of is not the Tao."

Chapter 12
Zen, Chan, Huang, and Me

Throughout this book I have used many historical Zen stories that have appeared in the collection "Zen Flesh, Zen Bones" compiled by Paul Reps as illustrations of an idea or to help drive home a point in the arguments presented. These all are actual translations of historical Chinese and Japanese Zen literature covering many centuries of Zen's development in China and Japan. Zen came to Japan via Chan from China. Chan is just the Chinese name for it.

"All know the way, but few actually walk it!"
– Bodhidarma

Chan developed in China from what that old feisty and controversial Buddhist patriarch Bodhidarma brought with him as his legacy from the already developed early Buddhism of India when he traveled on his own 1,000 mile journey to China somewhere around 450 A.D. Bodhidarma is considered to be the 28th patriarch in a direct lineage from Gautama Buddha himself and is said to have symbolically received the Buddha's actual historic bowl and robe of succession.

Chan and Zen are later outgrowths and advanced developments springing from the earliest roots of Buddhism in India. Both Buddhism and Zen/Chan consider the historical Gautama Buddha to be their founder, and they both have a strong tradition of sitting in meditation to clear and concentrate the mind.

The central ideas of Buddhism are The Four Noble Truths - the main point of which is that we are living a life of delusion and suffering, and that this suffering is self-created by your own selfish desires; and The Noble Eight Fold Path - the practical way to end this suffering and to overcome your desires which are generating it. For a Westerner to truly understand the subtlety of Buddhist thought it is almost necessary to learn another whole language – words like karma, dharma, samsara, maya, bodhi, nirvana, dharmakaya, sunyata, dhyana, mantra, yantra, shangha, Mahayana, Hinayana, and many others which are mostly from the Sanskrit language. Many of these words have no direct equivalents in the English language. But to summarize it here in the simplest possible terms, as revealed by Siddhartha Gautama, the historical Buddha's teachings consist of a deeply profound vision of the human condition, and also an accompanying very practical guide for a psychological self-help program – both of which have been handed down directly to us from the India of the 5th century B.C.

But there is one big difference between traditional Buddhism and Zen Buddhism. You can become a good practicing Buddhist by accepting the Four Noble Truths and by following the Buddha's Noble Eight Fold Path of right thought, right livelihood, right actions, right intentions, etc… mainly by behaving decently, by not acting on selfish impulses, and by practicing mindfulness and engaging in regular meditation, which all help with maintaining this self-control of the Buddha's middle way. While in Zen Buddhism it is not enough to become just another obedient believer and follower of the Buddha's deep revelations, but you must actually aspire to become the Buddha himself. The goal of the Zen student is to attain full personal enlightened Buddha consciousness for oneself, just like the historical Siddhartha Gautama did as a result of meditating under the Bodhi tree in the Deer Park so long ago. It does not focus all its energy and attention on an external proper life path to follow, but instead directly on an internal revelatory one whose goal is to somehow directly transform the ordinary self into lofty Buddhahood.

"Zen points directly to the human heart,
See into your nature and become Buddha."
– Hakuin Ekaku

Somewhere I have read that when Albert Einstein died a copy of "Zen Flesh, Zen Bones" was found on the night stand by his bedside. I don't know if this is true but it does make me smile and feel good to think that it just might be. Zen and Zen Buddhism study is truly one of the highest exercises of pure thought that the human mind can engage in, and it is not just the rational part of the mind only, but the whole total mind. It is an abstract spiritual pursuit in the purely inner non-stuff realm, that same mental terrain which Einstein was so very familiar in working scientifically while performing his many "thought experiments" during his own theoretical endeavors. In his later years he had become very frustrated by not being able to complete the oft speculated upon Holy Grail of the physical sciences, GUT, or the "Grand Unification Theory" of all of physics. Einstein was Jewish and this scientific quest that is still on going in the field of physics is actually philosophically very similar to that first Jewish patriarch Abraham's religious quest of joining all of polytheism's many different nature gods into monotheism's one transcendent "God of Everything" or GOE. Of course Abraham's endeavor was much easier! Einstein's similar scientific quest was the mathematical and theoretical combining of all of nature's physical forces, those of electro-magnetism, gravity, the strong force and the weak atomic forces, into one Grand Unification Theory in physics, or the TOE, the "Theory of Everything." If he died having been frustrated in reaching this supremely difficult goal, but was also thinking about Zen Buddhism perhaps he found some amount of inner solace at the end of his very tumultuous and productive life…I do hope so.

As for me, I simply fell deeply in love with Zen. In it I saw a true purity of mind with little to no stultifying dogma attached to it. In fact, Zen has the habit of quickly destroying all fixed and inflexible ideas that have any dogma-like qualities to them. Zen is a way of seeing clearly, a crisp way of cutting through the Gordian knot of existence. The spirit of Zen is always brief and directly to the point, as direct and immediate as the Zen master's staff whacking the student. Not a religion, not a philosophy, but a way of facing reality head on with no illusions. For me Zen was truly a breath of fresh air. For a while I couldn't read enough of Chan and Zen literature, their exotic oriental flavor was infectious and I was infected and deeply under its spell. Eventually "Zen Flesh, Zen Bones" found its place on my night stand too. Thankfully there are now many original Zen and other Buddhist works available in English translations and Zen Buddhism has now also come to the West and is flourishing as a living spiritual discipline here in America today. Perhaps D. T. Suzuki or Alan Watts played the pivotal role of being our own modern day Bodhidarmas by bringing Zen to the West through their spirit and writings.

But I have always remained an outsider and never sought to join the initiated. I never became a formal disciple or a monk in a monastery studying under a Zen master, for this is not my way as I am not by nature a group joiner. Using Zen as a basis also seems to me to be one of the very oddest possible clubs of them all to join. But by seriously maintaining on your own, the right discipline of mind there is much in Zen that can make its own way directly into your life and will take root and grow in the fertile ground of an open mind. I can surely attest to that.

I continue to pick it up, "Zen Flesh, Zen Bones," often after letting it rest for long fallow periods, years really, just to check up on myself and to see how much I've changed in the meantime. It is a wonderful book, and I basically know most of it by heart, yet how I view and understand the various things presented in it can still undergo radical changes for me. Zen stories are one thing, but Zen koans are something else again. The seeds of many of its onetime inscrutable koans have taken root and grown to bloom in my mind over the years, sometimes in a glorious spontaneous sunburst of suddenly grasped understanding, and other times without my even consciously knowing anything has happened at all.

These koans are all like little Zen time bombs ticking away and marking milestones in your own spiritual growth. The first time you come in contact with many of these koans you can't believe that they mean anything at all. But there is something about them that lets you know that they are not meaningless, and they can stick in your craw for years. Many of these classic Zen koans are completely unknown to the casual intellectual in the West, but for one very notable exception; Hakuin Ekaku's "The sound of one hand clapping" koan for some strange reason has a life of its own and is almost universally known. But it is often very ignorantly treated as if it were merely some kind of a funny joke. I've even recently seen a video online of someone who was so very loose and double jointed that he was able to flail his hand about back and forth in midair so quickly and forcefully as to actually make it audibly clap against itself repeatedly over and over again. By doing this it actually physically produced the acoustic sound of one hand clapping, which by the way for those interested in this freakish oddity happens to be exactly the same as the sound of two hands clapping! But this is so far from the point of the Zen koan that if it were presented to any Zen master he would probably laugh out loud and immediately hit the fellow over the head with his staff.

In classic Zendo study a periodic one-on-one audience with the Zen master is required of the resident students who are studying Zen under him. In this private conference the master would examine him and then among other things present him with a personal koan to consider and meditate upon. Eventually the student would be asked to demonstrate his understanding of it to the master. These koans are not logical puzzles with strictly defined answers, but require a leap of the inner spirit to comprehend them in any way whatsoever; often they will reveal themselves in very idiosyncratic ways appropriate only to the individual. "What is the sound of one hand clapping?" Is one of them. "Does a dog have Buddha nature or not?" is another one. "What did your original face look like before your mother and father were born?" Try that one on for size. There are many classic historic Zen koans retold in their original historical settings in the section of "Zen Flesh, Zen Bones" called "The Gateless Gate."

There is a kind of informal code of honor among the Zen community of not discussing personal realizations derived from individually facing off with these logical conundrums of classic Zen koans except while in their master's own private interviews. I suppose it is somewhat analogous to the society of performing magicians not sharing their trade secrets with the general public – it would spoil all the fun! As I mentioned, in my Zen practice I am soloing, so the temptation of blabbing all about my realizations is even that much greater for me. At one point I was definitely going to discuss at length and in great detail in this chapter several of my own deeply personal revelations that I have attained from focusing on some important classical Zen koans. But I have come to the conclusion that no matter how great, powerful and universal I believe my own understanding of them to be, they are all still firmly rooted in my own individual spirit. That by "spilling the beans" so to speak, I would perhaps be lessening the possibilities that you on your own would experience new, original, and perhaps even more truly profound personal understandings of them in your own meditations on these stubbornly fruitful historical Zen riddles. I would thus also be interfering with and spoiling the potential of your own fresh experiencing of the still living ongoing spirit of Zen in your own lives through your own work with them. So, I've changed my mind about it and I have decided not to share any of my own koanic realizations with you, and so not to pollute the clear water of your own inner vision and perhaps burden you with mine. Basically I decided to go along with tradition and not be a spoil sport – and that's just the way it is, folks. You must cut up, chew, and digest your own spiritual food for yourself, or it will not provide any nourishment for you. This is not a cop-out on my part, and you should be grateful… Duck!

Be forewarned though, if you do venture into this esoteric area alone there are many thorny problems awaiting you, not the least of which is language itself. Many of these ancient koans originally employed highly sophisticated word play and often used local metaphors and also may contain many lost idioms from a different culture long since past. Also consider the fact that these have been recorded often many years after they actually occurred, by means of ancient Oriental brush script which by its nature is a complexly visual and a very poetic multi-level language. When you then add on top of all that their translations into modern English sometimes by non Zen masters you will very often come up with prose that is inadvertently densely obscure and inscrutable for all the wrong reasons. Much of it can often wind up sounding like idiotic non-sequiters. And I say this advisedly – especially because I also realize that sometimes in these Zen dialogues idiotic non-sequiters were just what was required of the Zen master's response, especially when his students are presenting him with obviously foolish questions. For example in response to some tortured hypothetical spiritual question from a new student, a Zen master may often simply totally ignore the question and just respond with some unrelated concrete fact, often poetic; such as, "In Spring the flowers on Huang Po Mountain smell sweet."

So Zen koan study can be especially difficult since, cross-culturally, cross-temporally, and cross-linguistically there can be so many different levels of possible pitfalls and introduced errors that can very often occur in so many compounded and essentially unknowable ways. I have found these problems to be more evident in "The Blue Cliff Record," another compilation of early classical Chinese Chan koans. You should not be too put off by this inherently difficult situation as there are many different varieties of historical koans in existence some of which may not really be your cup of tea. They may have been specifically designed to engage other types of mentalities than our current Western mode. With this complex linguistic situation being acknowledged, there are still many scattered gems that will shine through. As an added treat many will often still have an underlying thread of enlightened very high Zen humor running through them, which although it is surely an acquired taste, I know will grow on you as you experience more of it.

Here's one such example:

"Joshu's Zen" *

A student once asked Joshu: "If I haven't anything in my mind, what shall I do?"

Joshu replied: "Throw it out."

"But if I haven't anything, how can I throw it out?" continued the questioner.

"Well," said Joshu, "then carry it out."

**from "Zen Flesh, Zen Bones" compiled by Paul Reps.*

Also much of Zen writings and sayings often contain multiple levels of negation upon negations of many widespread common sense ideas, especially strong negations of anything that smacks at all of dualistic thinking, and often there are also negations expressed of even many of the basic tenants and beliefs of well established classical Buddhism. Those old venerable Buddhist sayings and memorized parts of holy Sanskrit sutras when viewed through the bright light of Zen practice can sometimes actually be seen as obstructions and needless impediments to the goal. Zen does not stand on ceremonies nor does it brook rote memory and repetition in place of true realization. This is a sure avenue to being whacked by the master's staff. In this fierce method, finally, when everything is negated you are left alone with only yourself and the universe and not a shred of dogma or anything else remaining in between to grasp on to or to hide behind. This finally will bring you fully into the present moment, and it can be either fearfully devastating or ultimately joyfully liberating. The Chinese Chan Master Huang Po circa. 850's A.D. is a consummate master of this basically iconoclastic teaching technique. Many of his powerful historic dialogues have survived and been preserved and are now available in English translations. Reading them can become an exhilarating and personally overwhelming exercise in enlightened positive Zen Buddhist nihilism. See if you can swallow that one whole…

By the way, Huang Po was not his original name either, but one he acquired from his local environment as it was the actual name of the Huang Po Mountain in China where he lived and taught for many years and maintained a Zendo there. To have acquired that name he must have been viewed locally as the living embodied spirit of that real Chinese mountain. Throughout its colorful history Buddhist culture and its enlightened sages are often linked for some deeply spiritual reasons to actual mountains, especially in Tibet and China, and Chan Master Huang Po is yet another example of this.

"In the beginning, a mountain is a mountain,
In the middle, a mountain is not a mountain,
In the end, a mountain is again a mountain."
– a Zen saying

For several personal reasons thinking of Huang Po and his mountain reminds me of my very own first true encounter with living Buddhism which occurred while I too happened to be on an oriental mountainside, engaged in hiking with a good friend of mine who also just happened to be named Huang too! It all took place quite unexpectedly while we were both out mountain climbing together on a beautiful autumn day. But it was not in China; it was while we were enjoying ourselves doing a weekend recreational climb of an altogether different mountain in South Korea, and it was truly one of the peak experiences of my life.

Something Truly Amazing

I had left college in the late 60s during the Viet Nam War era, and had been drafted and was serving in the U.S. Army at the time near the small South Korean rural town of Kwang Chon. We were stationed at a separate Army radar outpost of about 150 soldiers that made up the Headquarters Company of a Hawk anti-aircraft missile battalion with five other Hawk Missile Company sites spread out on other mountains all along "Mig Alley." Our units were an ongoing part of the occupying U.S. Armed Forces in South Korea serving in that country long after the Korean War had ended. Mig Alley was our informal name for a very long north-south running central valley that cut through the countryside. The Korean War was the first war in which supersonic jet fighter planes were flown in combat, ours were called the F-86 Sabrejets and the enemy's were the Soviet Mig-15 jets. During the war the enemy's Mig-15 jets had flown straight through this valley at very low altitudes and high speeds to avoid being detected by radar.

After the fighting war was over, our radar site was established on a high mountain range on the west side of this valley, but there was another even higher single mountain standing alone on the east side of the valley which was always very interesting for me to watch in the morning when we were all standing daily reveille. While the bugle was blowing and we were all in formation and saluting as Old Glory was being raised, I would often look over at this other mountain to see just how it appeared that day. It often caught the early morning light in very beautiful ways and its peak was quite often shrouded in wind blown clouds. I was somehow always emotionally drawn to it and I enjoyed very much watching its different moods unfold over time. I had decided to myself that before I left Korea I would one day make an effort to climb this mountain that had so captured my imagination.

At the time I was living in a green camouflage painted army Quonset Hut built on a concrete slab, one of five in a row going up the hillside of our own mountain post radar site. Inside the hut's open interior were two long rows of green metal army bunk beds going down each side wall with free standing metal lockers, and several diesel oil fired space heaters running along through the middle of it. This was our barracks. My bunk mate, Huang, was about my age and he was a Republic of Korea regular enlisted soldier. He had gone through a special selection process to become a Katusa soldier. "Katusa" was an acronym that stood for Korean Augmentation to the United States Army, and it was a limited and highly honorable and sought after duty for any ROK soldier. However, once selected and attached to a US Army company they usually tended to pull all the duties that we Americans didn't want to do ourselves, like permanent KP. That didn't seem to faze Huang at all, and he was always very upbeat and cheerful.

Huang was a nice fellow who wanted to understand everything he could about American culture. Having just been thrown together by circumstance, our own surprisingly compatible natures soon made us good friends. He was trying to learn English from a very worn and outdated book he had with him that was largely focused on teaching English through the use of American slang idioms. So instead of saying he wanted to go to bed, in his own heavy Korean accent, Huang would say, "It's time to hit the sack." This was fine and kind of funny, but the real trouble was that most of the phrases in this very old book he was studying from were hopelessly out of date and had long since gone out of regular usage. He would say things like "23 skidoo," which his Korean definition explained to him, but which was opaque to me since that expression had gone out of style along with the raccoon coats of the 20s. There were many others, a book full of them, that even though I could readily understand all of the words he used, I still had absolutely no idea of what he was talking about, and he of course had no other way to explain it to me. This would always result in a very plaintive look from Huang and he would repeat himself even more forcefully, but all to no avail. It must have been difficult for him to realize that he had learned so much apparently useless stuff. So I tried to update him by teaching him some new popular slang of the day. One of the words I remember trying to teach him was "groovy," which I soon found out was not that easy of an idea to explain to a foreigner either! I remember trying to use the analogy of a wavy groove in an LP vinyl record of good music, but I'm not sure he ever really got to understand the broader more general implications of the whole "groovy" concept.

It's funny, but now that I'm thinking about it, although "groovy" was very popular at the time, it's hardly ever used anymore today and very soon it will be totally obsolete too like most of the old clichés in Huang's book! It's also interesting to note that all these expressions like "cool, hot, hip, bad, groovy" etc. linguistically speaking have only a very short lifespan. I think that's because the more people who are using them, the less "cool, hip, groovy" etc. they inevitably become. By their very nature they seem to contain a built-in "sunset clause"– strange too that they all seem to be talking culturally about that one same largely ineffable quality.

But I also learned some interesting linguistic things from him too. For example, I discovered that what most of us GIs thought were real Korean words that we were using when we spoke to the Korean locals, were actually mostly derogatory words in pidgin Japanese! The Japanese were the previously occupying enemy forces who had earlier conquered Korea and then had treated the Koreans very harshly, with all their usual brutal raping and pillaging, and whom all the Koreans therefore intensely hated. So that when the American GIs became the next newly occupying forces they just continued to speak to them in this same oddly disrespectful doggerel form of Japanese! This was probably their own way of maintaining a meaningful separation between these two artificially war created simultaneous cultures. Of course all of the GIs quickly picked up this phony lingo that was being spoken to them which also contained some newly made-up pseudo-Japanese words in it too just for the Americans, like "mama-san" and "papa-san." But the really funny part was that they didn't actually realize that it was all mostly hokey made-up stuff, and they all just thought that it was the real Korean language that they were actually learning. So that while most of the American GIs racially looked down on all the Koreans and derogatorily called them all "Slopes," at the same time the Koreans were also able to distance themselves from the Americans and were able to look down on them too through their use of this clever made-up linguistic artifice. Who knew? Huang knew. And now I knew too!

In spite of this omnipresent antagonism between the races, after a while Huang and I soon became very good friends. Then one long fall weekend when we were both off duty, I asked him if he would like to go with me and climb that special mountain across the valley. He jumped at the opportunity and very happily agreed to go out for a day of mountain climbing with me. It was often still very beautiful fall weather as we readied ourselves to have an exciting new out of the ordinary adventure together. Next day we packed up some food in our knapsacks and started out together early in the morning for the mysterious mountain across the valley, and we got a lucky lift right up to the rice farms at its foothills. There were no existing roads that went up to this starkly beautiful mountain so we had to walk along the low dirt dikes between all the rice paddies and sometimes on local peasant farmer's property. It would have been a very rare sight for them to be seeing any American soldier alone out walking on his own right through their village and rice fields, so it turned out to be a very good idea to have brought Huang along with me, and of course he was a native and spoke flawless Korean and most of the people were really quite friendly to us.

They all lived right in the midst of their rice paddies in cottages all made of the same universal materials. Their homes were made out of dung and dirt in a kind of mud adobe plastered over hand woven stick walls, with roofs of thatched rice straw on the top. So, from an artistic point of view their villages were all naturally very aesthetically unified with mud and straw houses in the midst of mud dykes and rice fields that were everywhere else all around them. But the insides of their small cottages were usually finished off quite nicely and often had white washed walls, a few pieces of nice lacquered mahogany furniture, and tile or linoleum floors. There was very little wasted land, and what wasn't cultivated rice paddies were cottages; no one had very much of a yard for they couldn't afford the luxury of not using any of the arable land to grow their crops.

When we finally made our way out of the farming lands towards the mountain, the walking became a lot harder with much more tangled underbrush to negotiate our way through. It was a hot clear sunny autumn day and we hadn't even made it yet to the base of the mountain. We were both sweating a lot and were getting scratched up and already starting to get tired too. Pretty far ahead of us where the foothills stopped and the mountain really began there was one last stand of trees in a small wood growing in a little valley cove in the side of the mountain at the tree line. There were no more trees above it. So we decided to head for that area, thinking that at least there would be some shade there and we could relax and have a snack before we began what we came for, the real ascent up the mountain.

As we approached the trees, suddenly the tangled underbrush opened up and gave way to a cleared narrow footpath that was heading right toward the place where we wanted to go. This of course made the going much easier; and we didn't stop to question why there was such a nice clear footpath right here in the middle of nowhere – we were just happy to find it. And as we approached the trees and turned a corner before us stood a round stone walled artesian well filled with cold spring water complete with a half cut drinking gourd floating on top of it. This was a very welcome sight indeed, as you can imagine. Using the drinking gourd thoughtfully provided we greedily drank our fill of the cool sweet refreshing spring water coming from the well. We also splashed the water on our hot heads to cool us off. This made us feel immediately a whole lot better. Then as we went on deeper into the still naturally looking grove of tall trees the foot path turned into a well made wide flat cut stone stairway and around the next turn stood something truly amazing.

There before us, totally hidden from the outside world, stood an amazing Buddhist Temple and Shrine. In front of it, sitting on a wide polished wooden veranda were four monks in orange robes in the midst of preparing their lunch. They were creating a vegetarian meal, by rolling a mixture of sticky rice into small balls and placing them on the big round straw mats that surrounded them. The surface of the two story building behind them was very richly carved and ornately decorated all over in gold leaf with many different glossy red lacquered Buddhist motifs winding around its columns and lintels. It was elegantly finished off with deeply sculpted and brightly gilded eaves of a classically upturned Oriental-styled tiled roof. This lavish sacred building was structurally laid out basically in an overall open square design that contained within it an unroofed central courtyard. This inner enclosure consisted of a meticulously raked square white gravel field. At the peaceful center of this open temple surrounded area, calmly sitting all by itself, being warmed by the bright midday autumn sun, was a really very large beautifully carved and polished stone Buddha, fully engaged in his own silent ongoing everlasting deep meditation. It was all incredibly beautiful, it was all extremely well maintained, and it was all totally unexpected.

I bowed and smiled at the sitting monks and made a universal pantomime gesture to them asking if it was OK for me to enter the shrine. They smiled back at me and made a similarly silent gesture indicating that, Yes, it was OK. But there was something wrong with Huang who sank back and held his head down and didn't even try to communicate with the monks at all. Instead he just went off by himself and sat down outside the Temple on a big rock and patiently waited for me to return. I kneeled down before the entrance gate to the Temple and unlaced my army combat boots, took them off and left them outside. I entered the shrine and sat down silently cross legged in the central courtyard before the meditating stone Buddha for some time. I don't really know for how long I sat there, but I do know that it was the first time ever I truly experienced Peace on Earth. When I was done and left the shrine I smiled and again bowed my head to the attending monks, and they bowed back to me, a foreign stranger in their midst whom they had openly welcomed – a GI, an unannounced occupying force in sweaty olive drab fatigues.

We then continued on to climb the mountain. On the way up I asked Huang what was wrong, and why he didn't go in? He shrugged and just said that it was "the old religion." Huang was a Christian now and he did not relate to Buddhism anymore. That was all there was to it. We made it to the top of the mountain on a beautiful clear fall day. It was hard climbing, but it wasn't really a technical climb and when we got all the way to the top it was totally worth the effort. The view down Mig Alley was spectacular. Huang and I sat down at the summit of the mountain for a while and we rested together and we had a small meal of what was left of the food that we had brought along with us. The weather was still great and it was soon going to be harvest time and the rice nearly everywhere was tall, mature and golden. Sitting at the elevation of the mountain top we seemed to be suspended about half way between a few scattered cumulus clouds in the sky that were drifting by and their cool slowly moving shadows they were casting across the warmly illuminated rice fields below. We both enjoyed the view as the light winds came down the valley. It was just like being alive in the middle of the song "America the Beautiful." There before us were grand vistas full of purple mountain's majesties and amber waves of grain. But I guess this song must really more appropriately have been called, "Korea the Beautiful."

This was all happening basically during the Viet Nam War era, and in America at that time there was what the media called a "generation gap" going on between the young Hippies and the older Establishment, not to mention the Red Necks too, etc. I guess I was more temperamentally aligned with the Hippies at the time even though I was now a soldier... but in Korea at that same moment there was what I would call a real "generation chasm" opening up. In the still traditional culture of the countryside, the women stayed at home or worked in the fields. If they did go outside in public they always walked several feet behind their husbands in flat straw sandals, wore long drab dresses and purposely tied down their breasts in an effort to minimize them; while in the city the girls dressed in colorful miniskirts, walked around in ultra high heels, and wore figure enhancing padded "falsie" bras, and they danced the night away in bars to poorly mimicked imported Western rock & roll music. There were still a few Buddhist monks in orange robes to be seen in public, but the Korean people were now 90% converted to Christianity, and were in many other ways greatly influenced by our Western Culture. In the centers of many small towns which consisted mostly of mud and grass roofed cottages with no electricity, large lit up brick Churches complete with bell towers and spires were to be seen, while Buddhist Temples and Shrines like the one I had just been in, were ensconced and totally hidden from view located far away from the cities in beautiful natural mountain settings without even a road leading up to them.

What could possibly be more culturally opposite than that? Perhaps the difference between the seated robed figure of the blissfully meditating Gautama Buddha and the nearly naked hanging suffering figure of Jesus Christ nailed to a wooden cross? Siddhartha Gautama, the historical Buddha, had originally been a pampered prince from the ruling upper classes of the Indian aristocracy. He was from noble lineage and his teachings were "noble truths," and a "noble pathway." So there is also this great social class divergence between the two, as Jesus Christ was a man of the people who sprang up from the blue collar working classes of carpenters and fishermen. His teachings did not consist of "noble psychological insights," but were couched in simple parables that were easy for the common man to understand. Christ and the Buddha were both in their own ways, working for the betterment of mankind, and they have both had very positive and far reaching effects. Were their nearly totally opposite fates also mainly culturally determined by their social class differences? I wondered… The footpath Huang and I had walked on was still being trod by the local rice farmers who were hand delivering food and humbly supporting the traditional Buddhist monks at the wood hidden Temple and Shrine on the mountainside. But, I wondered to myself — how long would that last?

"Not Far from Buddhahood" *

A university student while visiting Gasan asked him: "Have you even read the Christian Bible?"

"No, read it to me," said Gasan.

The student opened the Bible and read from St. Matthew: "And why take ye thought for raiment? Consider the lilies of the field, how they grow. They toil not, neither do they spin, and yet I say unto you that even Solomon in all his glory was not arrayed like one of these…Take therefore no thought for the morrow, for the morrow shall take thought for the things of itself."

Gasan said: "Whoever uttered those words I consider an enlightened man."

The student continued reading: "Ask and it shall be given you, seek and ye shall find, knock and it shall be opened unto you. For everyone that asketh receiveth, and he that seeketh findeth, and to him that knocketh, is shall be opened."

Gasan remarked: "That is excellent. Whoever said that is not far from Buddhahood."

**from: "Zen Flesh, Zen Bones" compiled by Paul Reps.*

Although I was already interested in Oriental art, philosophy and culture before the time that I spent in South Korea in the US Army, since my first real life encounter with living Buddhism in that small mountain Temple and Shrine with my Korean friend Huang, I have continued on in my own further pursuit of these interests. I've witnessed myself grown to deeper levels of spiritual awareness and presence of mind through my own independent Zen studies. "Zen Flesh, Zen Bones" has been a real resource, and recently I've even been catching myself once in a while when deeply involved in discussions with friends, of starting to sound a little bit like some of those cagey old Zen masters vainly trying to teach their stubbornly confused and off track students just how to become real life Buddhas in one of those few old and well preserved classics of true Zen literature. But at least so far I haven't actually hit anyone over the head with a stick yet. *(to myself)* Duck!

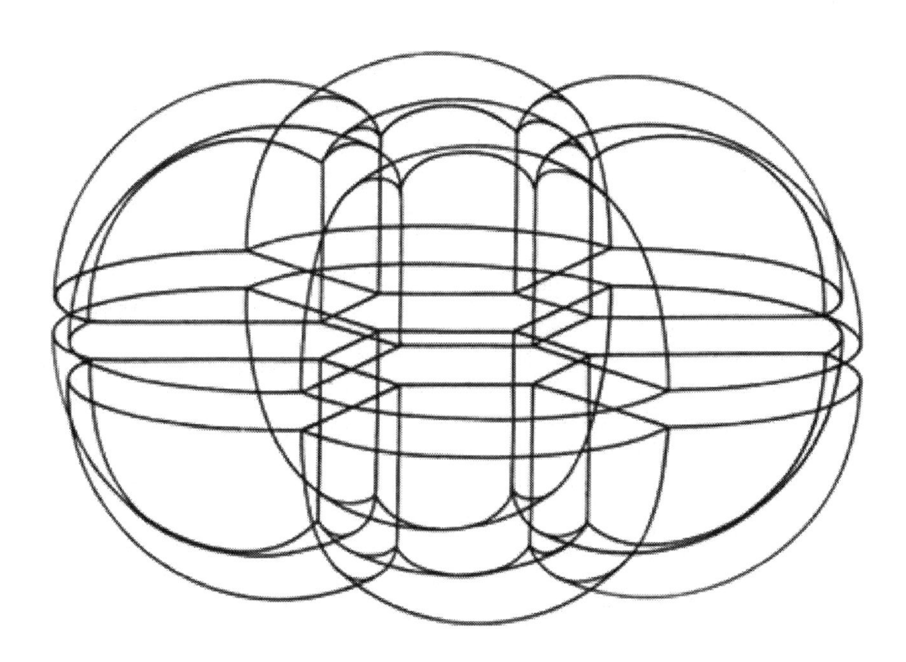

"7 Bubbles on a Mirror Yantra"
from the author's "Bubble Series," an etching

Chapter 13. Clearing House

My son says:

"I've been listening to everything you've said, and I really do like all your different Oriental based perspectives on things. They are really cool! But I'm still not totally convinced of your major "stuff verses non-stuff" premise. I still don't really get it all. I can appreciate your emphasis on how important you think the self-work and all of that is, but what am I actually supposed to do to become a fully conscious unified being? And is this really possible or is it all just another of your big romantic non-stuff ideas based on all your shaky transcendental and mystical logic?"

(Right then and there I should have whacked my own son over his head with my staff... But of course I didn't have a staff!)

I say:

"When we talked about your sticky brain and the process of self-examination like the Buddha sitting under the Bodhi tree, it was all in the spirit of generalization. But what you want to know now is specifically just how is it done?

"How do you actually decide what to keep of your inner random accumulated beliefs and what to throw out and how do you practically even go about throwing out non-stuff anyway? That's what you are asking me right now, is that right?"

My son says:

"I guess so, if this will lead me to a place of less self-doubt."

I say:

"Right, that's exactly it... Look, it's relatively easy to go through your old stuff and decide what you no longer need or want to keep. General criteria are: is it broken, is it old fashioned, is it an embarrassment to me in public, have I just outgrown it and it no longer fits me, is it still useful or does it no longer work right, is there a better newer one I'd rather have, is it the wrong color, size. style, etc, is it no longer "cool," does it still help me do something important in my life, or is it just in the way and I trip over it once in a while but I'll never realistically pick it up and use it again, is it worn out, does it bring back bad memories, did I pick it up just because my friends had one and it was a fad that's now over, or simply do I just not like it anymore?

"You go through a mental check list something like that and decide if you want to keep the thing or not. If you decide not, then there is a garbage truck that comes down the street once a week that will be happy to take it away and you'll never see it again. Here there are also special days, one in spring and one in the fall where you can really clean house and throw out just about anything, really big things too – stuff like old household appliances, beds, couches, refrigerators, old tires, etc. How easy and conveniently organized is our world of stuff.

"However, there are also those special cases that exist of people who have what I call "the warehousing syndrome." They are compulsive hoarders, who when they run out of space to store their old stuff, think nothing of going out and renting an additional self-storage bay to put more and more of their old stuff in that they will never use again, but they are still so emotionally attached to that they just can't throw it out or give it away.

"But what happens in the inner world of non-stuff? It is not quite so simple as in the outer world of stuff, is it? How do you go about throwing out old, bad, useless, hindering, non-stuff? How do you even recognize it, or know that it exists if you can't even see it? And how can you then possibly be able to rid yourself of it? These are not so easy questions to even ask, and there aren't any obviously easy answers to them either, but we will answer them."

My son says:
"Go ahead, I'm listening..."

I say:
"You must begin by cultivating your sense of self-awareness.

Don't just automatically respond to things that happen to you and then go right on to the thing that happens next. This is what most people do throughout their entire life. They live in an overactive state of constantly acquiring new experiences often without ever examining or directly questioning anything that's been happening to them. In doing the self-work it is very necessary for you to be able to create a neutral space within yourself and to be able to "stand aside" and "to be a witness" to your own activities and responses. It's kind of like the difference between just eating your meal and really tasting the food with each bite. You need to taste deeply your ongoing experiences. How does it make you feel when this or that happens to you, and even to question why is it happening to you in the first place? Is it a good strong feeling, or do you feel a little squeamish about the whole thing? Why? Only you can answer these questions.

"After cultivating this internal sense of self-observation for awhile you will then have a basis for recognizing and understanding the "non-stuff" that's lurking behind these experiences and what influences are creating these different good and bad feelings within you. Then you can go deeper into where in your past you might have picked up this misdirecting troublesome non-stuff and just where it came from. Then you can examine it and judge whether or not to keep it, refine it, replace it, or just abandon and throw it out. Also surprisingly, many of the criteria for making this choice may actually be just the same criteria as those we stated earlier in this section for evaluating whether or not to keep or throw out your old stuff. Isn't that strange?"

My son says:
"OK, maybe I could do some of that, but how exactly do you get rid of it? I just don't see how you can ever really throw it out."

I say:
"I'm coming to that, but first there is something important I want to add. There is also a similar non-stuff equivalent to "the warehousing syndrome" we've talked about of having too much old useless stuff that you are still senselessly attached to and just can't get rid of. Those people with this sad condition continually go over

and review past events in their lives that came out poorly, even events that happened many years ago, with people who may no longer even be alive. They regret what they've done in their past but somehow are blocked and can't resolve it and go forward. So they force themselves to internally replay these bad non-stuff events over and over again, and in their minds, they become prisoners of poor decisions they've previously made in their past. They have become trapped in a vicious cycle, and in fact unknowingly they may revel in it. It is a recurring circle that is hard for them to escape. Perhaps in some strange way they are grieving and doing penance for their own past misdeeds, and eventually by continually re-living it they may be serving out their own self-imposed "emotional sentence." These are all the ongoing long term effects of self-created bad karma.

My son says:

"Yes, that sounds right. I even think I know some cases like that. They are very sad people and I think they need help, and probably should try to get some kind of real professional therapy."

I say:

"Maybe so... OK, so now by cultivating your sense of self-awareness and remaining vigilant in this ongoing introspection over time you've come to the point of being able to recognize some of your own persistent recurring problems, some deeply held belief you have within yourself, that is not life affirming and that causes you difficulty in your own everyday affairs. Something that is just not cool and you want to free yourself of it, or to revise it and by so doing effectively change who you are, and to create a truer, less conflicted more unified self. This is the first necessary step, and besides discovering your own inner conflicted problems, you have now in the process also developed an ongoing good habit of being in daily contact and paying attention to the ever changing emotional state of your own inner living spirit. Really developing and possessing this self-conscious mental astuteness is called "mindfulness," and it will continue to keep you on the right path and it will serve you well throughout the rest of your life...

"OK, so now what? What you really want to know is just how

is it done? How do you go about getting rid of your own invisible chronic troublesome old problematic internal non-stuff anyway, right? What's the answer?"

My son says:

"Yes, assuming I can even do that first part...Go on, this is what I've been waiting to hear. Lay it on me."

I say:

"Yes, right... Well here's the really important thing to understand. The way this offensive non-stuff you've just found and identified got into you in the first place is that at one time or another, probably unthinking, you just automatically swallowed it all whole; through your own continuing karmic actions it became part of who you are, of your own thoughts, and finally of your own beliefs... You were the one who created it in the first place and now you are the one who has to un-create it.

"To understand how this is done we have to go back to our earlier formulated "Circle of Being." Your knowledge of the way this works to create who you are in the first place can now also be consciously used in reverse to free yourself of troubling unwanted non-stuff, and it can be continually successfully used repeatedly in this same way eventually to totally purify and unify the self."

How to Change Who You Are

The goal here is no small matter – it is to become active in your own self-evolution and to effect a permanent change in your inner being. It is to consciously have a direct effect on changing the "who you are" part of your interactive "Circle of Being." To actively engage in this process there are three equivalent access points available to us. If you can effectively change for good some aspect of either – "what you do," – "what you think," or – "what you believe," you will inevitably change by some degree consciously and even unconsciously the resulting reality of "who you are." This will definitely be the end result, as they are all mutually interactive and there are no other possibilities.

Here again is a review of what we have already presented earlier in "Chapter 4 – Who am I? The Circle of Being." The beauty of this is that once you realize its simplicity and that this is truly the active formative engine of the self, it is the only tool you will need to accomplish your goal. Understanding and identifying just what it is that is giving you problems and evaluating the best approach to affect change is the basic preliminary groundwork you'll need to establish. "The Circle of Being" is the underlying basis of what we will be continuing to work with here:

"The Circle of Being"

You are what you do.
You do what you think.
You think what you believe.
You believe what you are.

Since the three ways we have to effect change all interact with each other and are equivalent, let's start out with the easiest way to change who you are, which is to engage the "You are what you think" part of the circle. To change this requires you to consciously re-think from scratch, and from your present perspective, just what was the basis of your originally formulated old thoughts that created a belief within yourself that is now seen to be in error and is troubling you. Once you've done this it will automatically go on to affect your future actions based on your renewed understanding, and then the believing and the becoming aspects will surely follow suit. Remember the totally interactive nature of our Circle of Being; it is a continuously self-referential always interacting system, and that all of its parts are not separate but interact and influence all the other parts in a continually automatic and dynamic way that naturally combines to constantly create your own overall character.

You are what you think.

Here's a simple example of performing this re-thinking transformation from my own recent life experiences. When I was a small boy a bat came into our summer lake house one night. It fluttered around the rooms and it seemed ugly and threatening to me. I had heard that bats get tangled in your hair, bite you and suck your blood, and can give you bad diseases like lockjaw and rabies. My father caught the bat and trapped it under a large clear glass vase and left it on the dining room table near a bright light so I could observe it closely in its captivity, which I did. The bat was still alive and unhurt and it now was securely imprisoned, so I could safely observe it for as long as I wanted before my Dad released the live bat back outside again into the dark night air.

The bat was all black and he was not a happy camper. He was very restless and he stalked around the inner circumference of the glass vase, stood up often on his two hind feet and pounded as hard as he could on the glass with his two fists trying desperately to find a weakness in his prison to make an escape. There was none. I could watch him very closely without any fear, and in the bright light I could see him quite clearly. His face looked very demonic to me with terrible pointy teeth in a short snout with whiskers which he opened and closed often as he glared directly back at me with his intensely threatening beady red-black eyes. He had two very large pointy ears all covered in a short velvety black fur, and from his thin arms his long black velvety wings hung down in folds looking exactly like the movie vampire Count Dracula's black cape. It was all right there directly in front of me, and it was all very real and very spooky to me. I thought to myself: "Bats are evil and bad." It is a common belief and it stayed with me for many years. Every time I saw a bat I was repulsed. This idea was also culturally much reinforced on every Halloween with its black paper bats all over the place. They always reminded me of that real demonic looking bat of my youth and they were just not a lot of holiday fun for me.

Now I am about as old as my father was when he caught that bat and put it under the glass vase. I live in the country in a house near a stream with a deck on its western end where I often like to relax lying in a lounge chair on warm summer evenings and watch the changing sunset happening until the stars come out. Sometime around mid-sunset the local bat population comes out too. There are quite a lot of them. I lie there still and enjoy watching their intricate flights. They are masters of a strange soundless fluttering flight and can make astonishingly quick mid-air turn-on-a-dime directional changes at will in order to capture the small bugs that they eagerly seek out and eat for dinner. They have never once swooped down on me, and I do not feel threatened at all in their natural presence. In fact I enjoy watching them and feel blessed to be in the presence of one of summer's local natural wonders that I can see regularly and experience it all right from my own back deck.

I have also learned a lot more about bats recently. Bats are very beneficial animals in the ecosystem, eating up to one-third of their body weight in insects every night, which is a much better way of controlling them than using insecticides or bug zappers! They also help in the pollination of many plants. Bats do not intentionally attack people. Of the about 1,240 different species of bats worldwide only three are actually hematophagous, that is they eat blood, mostly from small mammals, usually rodents. These are the vastly over emphasized true vampire bats of Central and South America. By far, most bats eat insects or fruit, not blood. Bats developed true flight on their own and this is an example of convergent evolution, where the similar trait of flying in birds and bats developed independently and it is not based on the same body structures.

I have now changed my thoughts, attitude, beliefs, and actions towards bats. In my home region recently the bats have been dying in great numbers from a condition called white nose syndrome, a fungal infection that attacks their respiratory systems and saps energy from them during their long winter hibernation. This has resulted in a great bat die off. To help out the bats I recently built and installed a large duplex bat house on a high pole right next to my deck and so do what I can to help foster my local bat population.

As you can see from this short narrative, I have consciously transformed myself from being a bat-hater into being a bat-lover! The change occurred after watching bats in nature and learning new and better information about them, and re-thinking my earlier baseless childhood prejudices. It resulted in my deep and permanent change of heart towards bats. This began in the thinking zone and then progressed to the believing and doing realms when I did something real and helpful for bats in my own area by actually building them shelter on my property.

This is a rather mundane and easy to understand example of self-awareness and change through right thinking. In my bat story I was able to remember just what the experience was that started me off on disliking bats. I still had access to a clear and specific memory from my past. This made it easy to understand just where my prejudices came from and enabled me to throw out this no longer satisfactory non-stuff fearful belief in the negative and threatening nature of bats.

This is an example from my own true personal self-work done by consciously re-thinking some conclusions I had reached in the past. I began to question the basis of these negative beliefs and this led me to reconsider just how they had come into being in the first place. I was then ready and able to effect an internal change within myself that began in the *"You are what you think"* part of my own Circle of Being. This is presented as one of my own successful personal experiences of how to throw out bad non-stuff, and getting rid of it for good.

You are what you do.

But more often than not, you just don't know where or how your problematic non-stuff belief system developed. You can see no clear beginning point like I had in my early encounter with bats. In this case you can just skip re-thinking the *"you are what you think"* part of your Circle of Being, because you really have no access to it, and you can go right on to the doing part of the Circle of Being. This other way of getting rid of non-stuff that you have identified as a hindering negative element is to pro-actively change the *"you are what you do"* part of your Circle of Being. You can simply consciously decide to change your own behavior and actions in any of your current related life situations.

Here are two different examples of changing yourself by simply changing the *"you are what you do"* part of your Circle of Being from two different starting points. This first one is again a simple instance from my own upbringing. When I was young and visiting relatives and friends of the family with my mother, she trained me to always refuse anything that was being offered to me. I thought that's what you were supposed to do and it became another automatic behavior of mine. I was just expected to say politely "No thank you" which I always did and I never really questioned or thought much about it at all. It just became an automatic reflex and I would say it often without even knowing what was being offered to me or if it was a new food, just what it might taste like. A quick simple "No thanks" would just pop out of my mouth and effectively stop them in their tracks.

Even when I grew up and was living on my own, I continued to repeat this imprinted behavior. But then when someone was visiting me and I wished to share something I liked with them, often I would hear this same thing coming right back at me... but not always. It soon became clear to me that the people who accepted my offers of sharing were really warmer and more emotionally open and basically friendlier folks than the others. These were the people who more easily became my real friends while the refusers remained emotionally closed off and were actually knowingly or unknowingly snubbing my friendly advances. This became an easy psychological litmus test for me. Suddenly I saw my mother in a new light that she was also one of these emotionally crippled beings, and after that I changed my behavior completely and I began accepting things more openly without any guilt and freely enjoying them too. I changed the *"you are what you do"* part of what I did. By just stopping to automatically say "No thank you," and instead starting to say "Yes thank you." or better yet, "OK, sure." I quickly became more emotionally open and at ease with myself and others. I believe this simple change in attitude and behavior has led me to many good warm friendships in my life that might not have happened otherwise.

Sometimes, however, unlike the case of the emotionally stunted behavior my mother fostered in me, you can also find yourself functioning almost like an automaton in certain situations without really any understanding of why you're doing it. Suppose, for example, while doing your inner self-work you come to realize that you have incorporated within yourself an irrational deep-seated prejudice against some whole entire social group. You now realize that you must have taken this up unconsciously from your early upbringing and the cultural and community values that surrounded you at the time. Yet these unwelcome hostile feelings still have a total hold on you. Now you understand that this has become a negative limiting prejudice and that in fact, you have no real basis for harboring these unfavorable feelings against a whole diverse category of people. You realize you can no longer justify it, and now you've started to feel uncomfortable and badly about yourself when these feelings do spontaneously arise in you and you wish to set yourself free of this irrational adverse limiting part of your being.

Often these type feelings will just pop up automatically in the triggering situations and you will have no idea of the real cause or where they have actually come from. It is just another long ingrained behavior pattern you've never questioned before. Instead of having your usual knee jerk negative reaction, or just avoiding interactions with the members of this group, you can consciously change what you do and actively seek ongoing opportunities for friendly contact in your normal everyday settings. It may begin with an act as simple as just saying "Hello." Of course you will need to be emotionally ready and open to it, you'll need to listen well and maintain your sense of humor all the while. It may not feel natural or be easy in the beginning, but the more often you interact and do this the more comfortable you will become and your irrational prejudiced feelings will surely lessen and may totally subside over time, as your continuing social interactions will slowly become more relaxed and meaningful.

Instead of being firmly locked out of any real interactions by your previous overall inflexible irrational attitude, your direct new experiences will definitely affect your developing thoughts on the matter. You will certainly begin creating more realistic beliefs based on what these new real life experiences bring. You may even develop new friends and acquire richer and more nuanced perspectives on many other aspects of your own life at the same time. When you begin to open yourself up to new interactions there is no way of telling what else may result. If you have made progress in becoming a unified empathetic spiritual being who can remain comfortably in the dynamic Tao of the moment, this will surely result in many new growth experiences and unanticipated opportunities. In time you may totally outgrow your earlier prejudices and then begin to feel sorry for others whom you can now see in a new light and who still have these same problems and are automatically reacting as you yourself might have done earlier. You will have done the self-work to acquire a deeper understanding and compassion for others and in the process will have broadened the scope of your own life.

This is presented as an example of the process of developing yourself by consciously changing your external behavior – the *"you are what you do"* part of your Circle of Being.

You are what you believe.

Of course it is also possible to have a sudden epiphany and to "see the light" and immediately change one of your long held beliefs. This is an activity of your inner spirit that somehow abruptly changes the *"you are what you believe"* part of your Circle of Being.

This kind of sudden deep being change is often precipitated by some random mundane, but often deeply symbolic external trigger. Something apparently commonplace and otherwise without deep meaning will occur, and because you are internally primed and already at the brink of a spiritual breakthrough it will unaccountably possess a great deep spiritual significance for you. It will start an automatic spontaneous internal cascade of events leading to an immediate higher quality of being. This is called "satori" or sudden enlightenment in Zen practice and is the ultimate goal of studying under a Zen master the logic destroying "koans" in the old traditional Rinzai school, such as the most famous one – "You know what the sound of two hands clapping is, but what is the sound of one hand clapping?" There are many other just as stubborn and worthwhile koans to confront.

Here is a short story that illustrates a Zen nun's satori experience:

"No Water, No Moon"*

When the nun Chiyono studied Zen under Bukko of Engaku she was unable to attain the fruits of meditation for a long time.

At last one moonlit night she was carrying water in an old pail bound with bamboo. The bamboo broke and the bottom fell out of the pail, and at that moment Chiyono was set free!

In commemoration, she wrote this poem:

In this way and that I tried to save the old pail.
Since the bamboo strip was weakening and about to break
Until at last the bottom fell out.
No more water in the pail!
No more moon in the water!

**from "Zen Flesh, Zen Bones" compiled by Paul Reps*

Although these spiritual breakthrough moments are rare and cannot be predicted, they can apparently come on suddenly and often at unexpected moments. They usually are very powerful and have a profound and long lasting effect on the individual experiencing them. However they are also invariably preceded by long ongoing periods of much unresolved inner mental turmoil. The autonomous inner spirit has been unconsciously working upon itself for some time and it has often repeatedly run into some insurmountable road block to its path. Then all at once it spontaneously leaps over the barrier, the road block disappears and you arrive refreshed at a completely new place of deeper understanding.

Here's another one:

"Joshu Washes the Bowl"*

A monk told Joshu: "I have just entered the monastery. Please teach me."

Joshu asked: "Have you eaten your rice porridge?"

The monk replied: "Yes, I have eaten."

Joshu said: "Then you had better wash your bowl."

At that moment the monk was enlightened.

**from "Zen Flesh, Zen Bones" compiled by Paul Reps.*

These two potent little Zen stories are examples of what I call "maha-satori" or "great enlightenments." These are the main reason for which Zen masters exist, but it is also possible on your own to have many "mini-satori." This same type of sudden belief/being change can also occur over a more mundane set of circumstances that may not be so profound as to be considered a genuine life changing enlightenment event. It may involve such everyday things as finally having a deep insight into a friend's true character, resolving a nagging problem that has stumped you for a long time, or suddenly seeing the bigger picture of the family or community situation which you are involved in, etc… Some people have informally described these sudden realization events as "Aha moments." They come upon you all at once as unannounced gifts to your consciousness that are not at all the results of the work of your rational mind, but are the pure product of your inner spirit that is always at work in the background. It has the same overall affect on your Circle of Being as the two other different methods we've described above. They will still follow the same pre-conditions, and will result in a free immediate understanding and resolution of one of your deep-seated belief conflicts, and this will also result in effecting some real change in who you are, and therefore in what you think and what you will do too.

These are presented as examples of the process of developing yourself by the autonomous work of your inner spirit in suddenly changing your internal belief structure – the *"you are what you believe"* part of your Circle of Being.

"If you can correct your mind, the rest of your life will fall into place." **– Lao-Tzu**

Obviously if you are open-minded this process of mindfulness, self-examination, and change can go on throughout your whole life. However the sooner you start it the better, because the longer you live with unexamined unconscious erroneous limiting beliefs and autonomous uncontrolled behaviors the more natural they will start to feel and the harder it becomes to objectively see and overcome them.

I believe the late teenage years are the best time to begin this work – and you should start with the big questions. Some good starting topics when they come up in your everyday life are: Your opinions of others – are you prejudiced in any way and why? Racially, economically, religiously, sexually, etc.? Examine how you habitually treat others and how they treat you. Why? What has real intrinsic value to you regardless of what other people think about it? What is your calling in life, and how can you best pursue it? What is its quality in the big picture? Is it only a self-serving thing, or does it have a greater significance? Why? Your diet – what do you eat, why do you eat it, could it be healthier? Examine your seriously held attitudes towards your own and other people's religion, money, altruism, our capitalist culture, nature, drugs, popular music, social status, new fashions, art, etc. Do you simply conform to social pressures or do you have your own ideals? What are they? Are you comfortable with them and are you always working towards those ends? Why not? And many other similar existential issues.

You should continue daily your practice of this kind of introspection and self-awareness and be able to feel clearly the moment when anything happening makes you anxious. Pay close attention to this. This is a message from within, and you need to stop and listen to it and understand that it is trying to tell you something important. That within you there is something askew… Look deeply into anything that disturbs you – why does it have this effect? How can it be resolved? Be flexible but be relentless. Do this with dedication until you feel that you have truly become whole, a fully conscious and empathetic spiritual being firmly walking your own true path in your own way.

Some smug people naturally resist change and never do start this self-examination process. They are content to remain essentially chimeric automatons based on the accumulated random circumstances of their birth, early life experiences, family, and local community values. These are the people of whom Socrates thought that their life was not worth the living. They are thoughtlessly totally set in their ways, and will always self-justifyingly remain so, and will not even listen to or seriously consider anyone else's different ideas. Strangely enough they are usually very loud, bellicose, and often very stubbornly opinionated people and are generally to be avoided or quickly dismissed if at all possible, unless of course you happen to be a true teacher like Socrates.

****

My son says:

"You keep using parts of all sorts of eastern religions and philosophies to support the many different aspects of your arguments, but again you are totally cherry-picking to suit your needs and you don't seem to really support any one Eastern philosophy totally. Some people might be justified in calling you a spiritual dilettante, which as you must know is not a great compliment.

"And besides the way I understand it, most of these Eastern religious disciplines focus on destroying the ego, which to me is the same thing as the self, with their highest goal of becoming ego-less. I've been led to understand that their belief is that the ego is the main problem and it is what is standing in the way of becoming a better higher being. While all you are constantly preaching about is the purifying and building of a more unified larger self. Doesn't all this obvious glaring inconsistency bother you at all?"

I say:
"Very Good! Congratulations… You are using your intuitive analytical mind very well. I was hoping you wouldn't notice these apparently inconsistent things, but since you have, you are absolutely right to bring them up!

"Since I myself do not believe totally in any one religious tradition, this is one of the very reasons that I didn't give you any specific religious training during your upbringing, and unfortunately I fear it is the reason you went off on your own with no guidance from me or any of the great world spiritual traditions in developing your own materialistic, scientific, and essentially atheistic world view. I should have known this would happen, but I just hoped that somehow through some form of parental osmosis, my spirituality would automatically rub off on you. I guess it must ultimately be my fault that it didn't, and now I am trying my best to fix this problem by helping you broaden your own outlook on life by developing a fuller and more complete understanding of the deeper and subtle nature of your own living spirit.

"Let me be very clear here about what I mean by your own living spirit. We are not talking here about what standard religions call your immortal soul that may or may not exist, and may or may not continue to exist after death, and may or may not stand trial on Judgment Day, and then may or may not be forever after assigned to an eternity in either blissful Heaven or horrendous Hell. But what I mean here is the more common everyday usage of that same word "spirit" — unfortunately spirit is the best word we have for it.

"Every being has a spirit and many non-beings do too. You've heard of the "*Zeitgeist*" or spirit of the times. Your spirit consists of all the non-stuff operatives that you have internally absorbed and that direct your activities in your everyday life. Everyone who comes in contact with you can feel its presence and can perceive something of its quality and nature. It can fall anywhere in a range from being strong and inner directed, to being weak and amorphous, filled with self-doubt and subject to many random external influences. It also can be characterized by having many qualities such as being artistic, shy, trustworthy, outgoing, practical, idealistic, generous, inventive, materialistic, loving, etc. Recognizing and interacting with these spiritual qualities in everyone else around you is being an empathetic spiritual being. It is not really anything mysterious or magical that only exists in another dimension. Spiritual beings are not all transcendent glowing rosy and positive things either — there can be very negative spiritual beings as well. These are people whose spirit can be characterized as being vindictive, selfish, greedy, nasty, lazy, gluttonous, brutal, uncaring, etc. As I've said, we are all in essence spiritual beings in that we all naturally possess our own unique living spirit whether we admit it exists or not.

"The real issue here is that you don't really understand just what is causing your recurrent deep spiritual problems. In fact you don't understand or even recognize them as being spiritual problems at all. Just because you don't believe in the reality of the inner spirit doesn't mean that you don't have one. Now we are trying to play catch-up and give you some heavy spiritual ballast to help you keep your ship upright and sailing on course and to prevent you from broaching to in the often tumultuous sea of life."

My son says:

"Oh no! There you go again. It's your "Captains Courageous" maritime romanticism pop-up coming online again! You sure do like to use a lot of corny old seafaring metaphors in your imagery when you're describing life's dramatic conditions, Matey! But come on now, Dad – what does sailing really have to do with what we are talking about right now?"

I say:

"You know I love sailing, and to me it is the perfect metaphor for life's journey. We are each metaphorically the captains of our own ship – it's kind of like a corollary of the mind/body problem, if you think about it, only easier to grasp and more direct – the captain and the ship! I use metaphors because I am an artist and metaphors are poetic images that carry a lot of extra subjective presence and deep meanings. They enrich my speech. I don't really think that much about making them up, they just come out, yeah, I guess like pop-ups on the internet – your metaphor. The trouble is that you don't relate to them because of your inner materialistic non-poetic purely objective scientific bent. You just haven't yet realized that in fact you're an artist too. In some sense we're all artists deeply involved in the art of creating our own lives. And you're missing out on some of life's deep and rich experiences by denying it, or maybe you just didn't come with that emotional module factory-installed on the mother-board in your internal hard drive. Maybe you really ought to go back online and check for the latest software updates and manually download and install it!"

My son says:

"Come on Dad, give me a break!"

I say:

"But here's a real assignment for you to do that comes from my old artistic days. You should go down to the National Gallery of Art in Washington D.C. sometime, where among a lot of other great works, you'll find a small square room just dedicated to Thomas Cole's masterpiece series "The Voyage of Life." There hanging are his four large paintings of the four stages of a man's life: childhood, youth, manhood, and old age. Each stage is depicted separately on a very large canvas as part of a long allegorical boat journey through a lifetime. It's also really displayed very well with just one painting hung centered on each of the four walls. When you're in that small square room, you're completely surrounded by Thomas Cole's life journey. Just stay there for a while and stand in front of each one of the four paintings in their natural order and see what thoughts spontaneously come to you and how deeply his symbolism touches you. Look at how all the different things change from painting to painting. Look at the child, the youth, and the man, look at the way the boat changes, look at the different landscapes the boat passes through, and observe the overall lighting in each canvas. If you really don't get it and you come away feeling nothing, let me know, and then I'll know that it's hopeless and I'll just get off your case for good.

"Of course, Thomas Cole was a great original American master landscape artist who studied and then broke away from the old European traditions. As he matured in life and in his art, he became the founder of the very influential 19th century "Hudson River School" of painting. This gave America its first own truly native art aesthetic that continued on after his death with many notable artists continuing his ground-breaking work, like Frederic Church, Asher Durand, Jasper Cropsey, and Albert Bierstadt among others. These four great allegorical paintings are major works by Cole at the peak of his artistic career, and it's a powerful and poetic masterwork of art and very good in a 19th century sort of way. When you're there you should also check out Winslow Homer's work too. He's another revered 19th century American maritime artist, and his nautical painting "Breezing Up" is another of my favorite sailing art works. You'll definitely recognize it because of my own revised version of it that I painted in 1984 called "Breezing Up Again" that's been hanging on our living room wall since you were born. Compare the two in your head and see what you think of your old man's artistic work!

"To continue on in this same vein though, I've also always greatly admired our recent sailing presidents FDR and JFK. You and I know what it's like to have to depend on your own judgment and courage during a rough ocean passage even when you're puking over the rail to leeward, like that time we were deeply into it between Cuttyhunk and Newport. Remember? Any president who can handle the helm of a sailboat at sea in any weather to me is a very reassuring presence to have in the White House. When a president gets inaugurated they don't call it taking the helm of the ship of state for nothing, you know."

My son says:

"Ahoy, ahoy! Captain, I've cut my colors, I surrender! OK, OK, give me a break, I concede already... Sailing references do have a certain metaphoric relevance... But for heavens sake, let's get on with it! I've been patiently waiting here all through this whole endless romantic nautical rant of yours to finally end, so that we can continue on and you can then address my two serious questions that we started out with a while ago, which although you've been off on a tangent again, I haven't forgotten about. I want to hear just how you are going to defend yourself against my charges of your actually being a rampant spiritual dilettante, and also explain to me just how your definitely enlarged Western sized ego/self fits in with all this esoteric selfless Oriental philosophy you've been espousing?"

I say:

"Touché! Your suggestion that I may be a spiritual dilettante does hurt and bother me. A dilettante is a dabbler, someone who takes up an art or subject matter merely for amusement and doesn't have any deep connection, knowledge, or commitment to it, or any other one true focus in his life. A dilettante's behavior is very flighty and often bounces around between many superficial areas of art or knowledge that in some way or another may promote or support whatever current point of view he is espousing at that moment. And you are right; it is a very derogatory criticism of someone else's character.

"To go on and seriously answer those two pertinent questions that you have just raised again. First of all, I am not a spiritual dilettante. What confuses you is that my belief system is somewhat like Harvard University's Seal. On the seal's shield in the center of a red field there are three books. They are all open and displaying different syllables of the Latin word for truth "Veritas." This is a beautifully designed graphic symbol that cleverly illustrates in a direct symbolic way that you can't find the whole truth in any one place, but only parts of it in many different works. It is up to you to put it all together and discover the real truth for yourself. This is a great symbol for an academic institution that encourages taking many different courses while studying and pursuing a broad liberal arts college education.

The Harvard University Seal

"It is the pithy symbol for Harvard University and it is also a very good symbol for what I have come to believe about the spiritual truths contained in the world's many great religions. The meaning being I believe that you can't find the whole spiritual truth in any one religion either, but only parts of it in its many different forms.

"This is why I choose different aspects of different religions to focus on in my discussions with you. These parts are what I have found through my own experience to be the kernels of deep spiritual wisdom I recognize as being relevant, true, and important to illustrate the specific spiritual ideals I am trying to impart to you. I repeat, I am not a spiritual dilettante because these are not superficial things that I espouse merely for my own amusement or for the simple convenience of supporting the ongoing arguments of the moment.

But on the contrary, they are spiritual aspects that I have found to be true for me by my own deeply personal experience of them, and I find them truly useful in my own inner spiritual life. Simply put, I've come to believe in them. It just so happens that they are not all contained in any one spiritual tradition, but are scattered about in many, just like the "Ve - ri - tas" in the Harvard University Seal. I am not trying to turn you into a Buddhist, a Hindu, a Taoist, a Christian, a Jew, or a Zen acolyte, although being any one of these is a fine thing to be.

"Your other shot across my bow about the ego/self problem is a little more difficult and uncomfortable for me to explain to you. At one point in my life's study I was on the road to this eastern ideal of transcending the ego and becoming ego-less. Perhaps because I was working without a teacher and doing it on my own (which is my usual way of going about things) that I got into some peculiar personal and also rather embarrassing ground level trouble. In trying to be totally immersed and responsive to the present – to give up all ego control and trying to live spontaneously in the Tao of the moment at all times, I found that I was also becoming in some very basic and unanticipated ways more and more like a newborn baby. In some ways this was actually the goal – to experience reality in its fullest, to be in the present without any adult ideas, pre-conceptions, and prejudices – to cultivate what the modern Japanese Zen writer D. T. Suzuki calls the ideal of attaining "the beginners mind." But to my astonishment and consternation, I was at the same time also beginning to lose my own conscious self-control of my normal bodily functions! Just like a baby too, and this is definitely not a pleasant state of mind to be in especially when you're not near a bathroom! This surprising unanticipated unpleasant ground level development quickly brought me to an abrupt turn around in my own thinking and practice.

"Now I understand that it is not all together desirable at least for me, to be ego-less. For us Westerners this Eastern ego-less ideal is not all that it's cracked up to be. I've come to understand that the problem is not really with the ego itself, but with the common small closed-minded chimera ego, the unexamined ego in its natural haphazard state, the totally greedy self-centered I, me, mine ego. I came to realize that for me, the self must not be abandoned but it must be deeply examined, purified, unified, and greatly enlarged to also include empathetic trans-personal positive spiritual values, and all those other aspects we have already discussed in our earlier self-examination chapters. That is:

(mainly from the earlier chapters)

> *You need to begin the self-work – of examining your own inner core being, of getting rid of the contradicting randomness of some of life's early clogging dross that you may have picked up unintentionally. Of asking yourself, "Is this a valuable piece of my being, is it real, or is it a random piece of dross that has unconsciously stuck to me and is holding me back and needs to be pulled off, looked at once more and finally discarded? Why do I do what I do, does it help me or others? Why do I think what I think, where did it come from, what is its basis, is it good, is it useful and true, is it life- affirming? Does it not only help me, but does it address the greater good for other people and the world too? Why do I believe what I believe? Is it only what I have been told to believe from others? Does it have any true value and basis in my own real world experience?"*

"This is all part of the self-work process I recommend that one needs to individually go through of transcending the small-minded self-centered natural ego that we all start out with. This is what Socrates wishes us to deeply examine within ourselves to live a life worth living. This will not result in ego-less-ness but in becoming a world class "maha-soul," that can, when required also act in a self-less manner and not be one bound by the limitations of the natural uncultured small isolated self-aggrandizing ego.

> *If you can successfully complete this internal self-work you will evolve essentially from a chimera collection of conflicting haphazard randomly acquired personal "non-stuff"*

into a unified trans-personalized and life-affirming empathetic spiritual whole. This inner spirit-work consists of refining and reinforcing your own true nature to create a stable internally defined identity that you can comfortably live and be at peace with. Ideally this will establish a stable unified self that is not riddled with random internal contradictions and will help you make your own life decisions and travel your own true path in life without regrets. As a result you will become a greatly enlarged, internally unified conscious empathetic spiritual being that can withstand the effects of life's constant buffeting by the ever changing outside world. You will have developed your own self-created stable vantage point, and you will be able to comfortably view, and be able to actively take part in the great on-going theater of time and creation which contains us all.

"Mahatma Gandhi is a prime example of a "maha-soul," in fact that's actually what his name means. His given first name was Mohandas, not Mahatma, which was an honorary title bestowed upon him. Mahatma comes from two Sanskrit words "maha" meaning great, and "atman" meaning the essential self."

My son says:
"That's a good answer. OK, you've succeeded in talking yourself out of the corner I put you in… all in all it's not a bad response to my accusations… and now that you've fully explained yourself, I can better accept just what you've been saying all along.

"Gee Dad; did you really start pooping in your pants?"

I say:
"Yeah."

Chapter 14. Shiva's Dance and Resolution

In a previous chapter I have already mentioned the Hindu god Shiva's dance of bringing life and the universe into being by means of a drumbeat in his one hand (vibrations, the big bang, the heart beat?) and its fiery destruction by means of the all-consuming flames held in another of his hands (cremation, nuclear war, super nova?). The drum and fire are really just another symbolic set of our previously discussed omnipresent dualistic pairs of opposites, Creation/Destruction, Life/Death, two of the biggies. These are of course serious things that in our normal life most people are really fearful to directly confront.

This again inappropriately reminds me of a funny old Jewish Borscht Belt joke:

Terrible News

Abe is out for a walk and he bumps into his doctor on the street and asks him, "Hi, what's up Doc?"

Dr. Saul for a moment looks very seriously at Abe and says, "I'm really sorry to have to tell you this, Abe, but I only have bad news and terrible news for you."

"OK," says Abe philosophically, "Why don't you just tell me the bad news first."

Dr. Saul says, "Abe, you've only got one day left to live."

"Oh my God! That's really terrible news!" cries out Abe, "What could be worse that that?"

Dr. Saul says, "I couldn't get a hold of you yesterday."

****

Yes, the end of life is, and always will be death – no laughing matter (except perhaps here). No matter how much we progress in the medical sciences there will always be a major cause of death. Let's face it, it's inevitable. "Life is a terminal condition." None of us looks forward to dying, but it should not be feared as it is the way of nature, an essential part of the Tao of existence, and is yet another of the holy seals of creation that cannot be circumvented. It can be argued that it is death that allows us to be here in the first place. What you really should fear is not having lived your life well.

Lord Shiva's Dance

The Hindu God of Creation, Destruction, and Liberation

But to go on and finish my description of the Hindu god Shiva, he is also depicted as a dancing god (Entropy, Brownian motion, Lord of the Dance?). He is dancing on a floating lotus blossom, the standard Hindu symbol of transcendence and enlightenment. He dances within a rhythmic circle of flames that separates him from the material world of stuff, and he also has two more hands and arms, and two legs as well. With his first two hands he has just shown you his fearsome absolute power over life and death. At the same time while he is dancing, he is balancing himself with one leg on a squirming ugly dwarf that symbolically represents his triumph and subjugation over human fear and ignorance. His third hand is held out to you upright palm facing outward in an open friendly gesture to say that, even though this is the dramatic predicament of our existence, "Everything is OK, and you should have no fear." He then shows you why with his fourth hand which he is pointing at his raised other leg that is suspended in the air in mid-dance. "See!" he is telling you, "Although your time here is strictly limited between birth and death, I have given you the freedom to dance and to enjoy creation." Basically, don't be afraid and try to enjoy your life. In the midst of all this you are free to dance with me, or even to create a brand new dance of your own. This is his positive existential message of liberation to us.

These Eastern gods of Hindu, Tibetan Buddhist, other Oriental traditions are often represented with multiple arms usually holding symbolic objects representing their powers, and often having multiple heads too, in some cases as many as eleven piled on top of each other. They more commonly have nine main heads grouped in three tiers of three each, a trinity of trinities. These images often look fearful, freaky, grotesque, or just plain ridiculous to us in Western traditions. But they should not be laughed at and dismissed so easily. They are part of an ancient artistic tradition that developed in the Orient over a very long period of pre-Christian history. These artists were trying to depict in abstracted symbolic human form what divine beings with great miraculous attributes might look like to us. We say that God is omniscient and sees all things. Well, if you think about it, having nine heads looking out in 360 degrees all around would certainly be a great help in this regard.

Avalokiteshvara

The Thousand Armed Tibetan Buddhist God of Compassion

"Ask, and you shall receive, knock and it shall be opened."

– Jesus

…. in Tibet a thousand times over.

There seems to be very few physical limitations imposed on the Eastern artistic imagination as to how Oriental gods can be represented to us in their human forms. For example, the thousand armed Tibetan god Avalokiteshvara is a helpful god of compassion. He is often depicted as sitting on a floating lotus blossom within a circle of his one thousand arms all reaching out to us. On each of his thousand arms there is an open hand, in each of these hands there is an open eye in the center of its open palm. A thousand arms, with a thousand hands, with a thousand eyes, and that's how Avalokiteshvara is able to see and give a helping hand to so many troubled souls at once.

****

My son says:

"So, from the day we are born, we make connections and expand upon our fundamental and innate mental provisions, purely through our observations and interactions with our environment which also includes other humans too. This makes non-stuff and stuff's existence completely reliant and relevant to the era and location of our existence.

"And so, you might be thinking that non-stuff and stuff are exactly the same? But no... well they are both handled the same in relation to our brains... but if there were no observers, no humans, no life, stuff would still continue to exist, but non-stuff wouldn't. Non-stuff does not exist on its own out in the real world – it just exists within us as far as being a sub-set of physical neurological connections that are subjective to and embedded in each person's existence."

I say:

"Yes, that's right. You can think of it in that way if you wish. But don't denigrate it. This unique, transitory, fragile non-stuff that we all create uniquely inside our own minds, and that makes up our inner spirit, that you say "just exists as far as a sub-set of physical neurological connections, subjective to each person's existence" is in the most fundamental sense who and what we are as individuals – amazing intangible non-stuff. It exists as surely as you exist and it is the direct product of what you were, your thoughts, your experiences, and your beliefs. It continually functions as the basic operative element that produces who and what you are to yourself and to the world around you. It creates meaning in your life and it directs your interests and the future actions of what you will do and will become in the great external world of stuff. In the end it's the only truly self-created framework of your individual life – and you are the one person totally responsible for it. You are its sole architect. So as a responsible person, you should examine, clarify, purify, unify, uphold, honor and always try to make the utmost use of it in the best of all possible ways."

My son says:

"OK, I think I get what you have been driving at, and I guess you are right. But when I'm on my own I don't really think about all these things all that much, in fact I hardly pay any attention to them at all; especially not in such detail as we've been having in our discussions here. It all seems to exist abstractly totally on its own, unconsciously and independently lying there quietly just below the surface of my mind, while my real attention is always being directed at everything else that I'm constantly dealing with in my normal everyday life – things like homework, computer programs, scouting responsibilities, and stuff like that… But then sometimes all at once it just unaccountably rises up to the surface and totally overwhelms me with serious self-doubt and the strong negativity of meaninglessness and all of that. Now I understand how you see it all, but I don't know if I can really do the deep self-work ideal that you are saying is so important that you did at one time. I am not the Buddha, or Socrates, or even you, but I will consider what you've said and give it some serious thought."

I say:

"Yes, do that. Right now for you it's just like the problem of the fish in the water. It is not an easy thing for the fish to see and become aware of the water although he has been in it his entire life and it's always been right there all around him. Try to do the self-work we have been talking about and to become a unified conscious empathetic being. You don't have to do it all at once, but you can continue to take it up at different times. It is the most worthwhile spiritual thing you can accomplish on your own. If you succeed in this, it will truly help to guide you throughout your entire life. As you acquire more independent life experiences you'll begin to see these things more clearly. You don't have to believe in "the Magic Old Man God in the Sky" to be a positive empathetic spiritual human being. It's honestly the best kind of person you can become, and other people will silently honor you for it. You have the ability to unify your life and to attain a far deeper and richer understanding of very many things and also to create within yourself a stable center of your being and to find true lasting peace of mind. These are rare and invaluable things that are not easily acquired and can only be attained through deep self-understanding. This is the path of enlightenment – all the rest are just different levels of darkness.

"I'm glad we've been having these serious, ground level of being type discussions here – better late than never! If nothing else, it makes me feel better. I never got to talk like this with my own father, I'm not sure I could have, but if it had happened I am sure that it would have been overall a very different kind of conversation. I remember once when I was a little younger than you are right now; like you, I was also having some very unwieldy emotional problems cropping up in my own young life. When I went to my father for help he just dismissed me and told me to go off and talk it all over with the rabbi. I did this, but our rabbi was not functionally a one-on-one counseling kind of guy, which might actually have been helpful. Instead he was just a "wind-up-and-go-through-the-motions" kind of rabbi with no patience at all for my adolescent situation, and so of course he wasn't very helpful to me at the time. I just had to muddle my own way through it. At least I've shared with you as best I can my own perspective on the big picture of "life, the universe, and everything." And it really does give me a deep good feeling that you, by your honest and persistent questioning have brought all this about. For me it's been a demanding and a very worthwhile time we've just spent together. I'm grateful that we finally made it happen."

My son says:

"Yes, it has been great and liberating for me too. It really does feel good for me too to be able to say all these things out loud to you and in return to listen to what you have to say about them all. I've always wondered just what exactly you believed in. I've asked you about it several times, but you always just dismissed me with some clever remarks. We've never in fact talked about it all so seriously before. You did once tell me that if you had to describe it, that you were mostly a transcendentalist. But I didn't actually understand what you meant by that and I was just looking for a simpler answer. I guess there isn't any. You've always dismissed my ideas as being too simple. Would we even be talking about all these things now if I didn't have any of those very down emotional episodes?"

I say:

"Hey, you're the one who started these conversations; I'm just trying to hold up my end of it. Yes, I am your father and I do really feel badly about those despondent states of mind you can sometimes fall into, and I am trying to give you a broader more spiritual perspective on life in general to help you through it. You've unknowingly walled yourself off from many of the greatest true sources of spiritual solace and inspiration that already exist in the world, and that generations of people have been able to freely draw upon for emotional support. I realize that this may have been partially my own fault, so I've been trying very hard to help open you up to these other enduring deeper paths of the spirit. There are many more wonderful and meaningful things that are possible for you to experience in your own lifetime than just a good job, money, and more and better new stuff.

"You're a very creative person too, but you're still in the shallow end of the pool. I've loved being your father and watching you grow up and have deeply enjoyed the process of being with you and growing too in so many different ways. I'll still be here for a while and I will try to help you out as much as I can, but eventually I won't be here anymore. So I'm just trying to pass along to you some of my own hard won perspective on these things that I've found important and that have helped me out in my own life. Please, just think about them and try to become more fully aware of your own true beautiful inner spirit and be able to accept it and to know it in its fullness, trust it, and faithfully follow it throughout your life. It will give you the fullest and best life possible and in the end this will become its own reward."

My son says:
"Dad, I love you."

I say:
"I love you too, son…very muchly!"

****

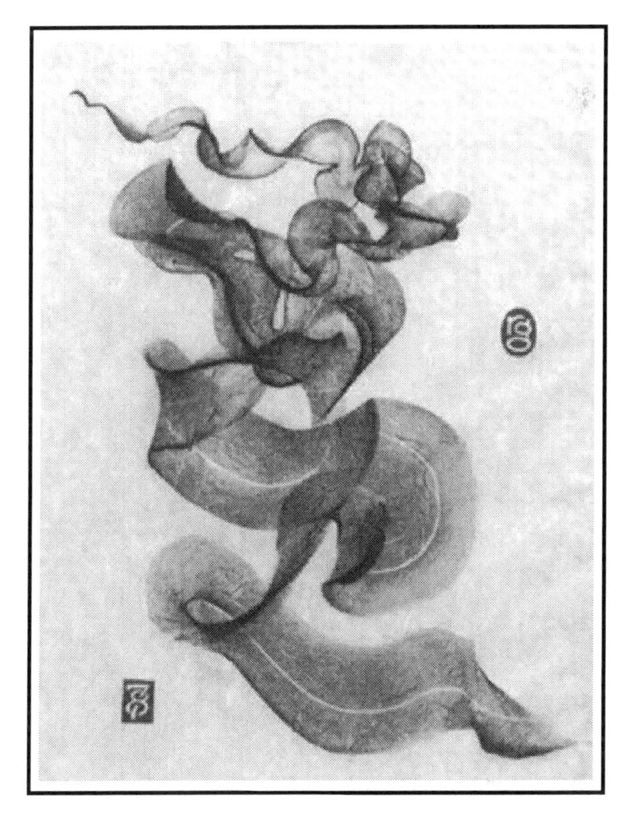

"The Long and Winding Road"
from the author's "Nippon Homage Series"
charcoal on rice paper

Afterward

Additional notes on the text of "Lao-Tzu's Shoe"

As I am writing this my son is currently in college studying to become a computer software engineer. He also has a new found predilection for taking up philosophy course electives. This may have been one of the lasting effects of our discussions. He made me promise that if this account of our conversations ever gets published that I would add a disclaimer to it that states that he never would have said some of the "My son says" quotes exactly as they are written in this manuscript. He objects to some of the word phrasing and emphasis and also some of my own creative additions, and he does not wish to be factually identified with them all in any strictly literal sense.

As I have already indicated, this book is not really an invention, but its genesis was totally an after-thought. It is the result of my trying to put together in a literary artwork many of the salient points from a long extended spiritual dialogue I had with my own teenage son. It was only written down several months after these conversations occurred, because many of its ideas kept returning to my consciousness, and I found them all to be still quite cogent in my own adult life and I felt that perhaps many others might in some way be able to benefit from hearing them all clearly stated as well.

During the course of our conversations we did not have a tape recorder going and this is not presented as a verbatim documentary account of everything that was said. But, dear reader, the overall trajectory of the dialogue is true. Some liberties were taken in making up direct quotes that would help the narrative flow more smoothly and even perhaps more entertainingly. I have just recently re-taken my literary road test and renewed my poetic license and it is now up to date, although my liability coverage may have lapsed...

Where did the title "Lao-Tzu's Shoe" come from?

As I was writing this book I went through many title ideas, such as "The Facts of Life," and "The Infinity Within." Both of these I found out already existed as titles of other books! For a while I was calling it "Stuff and Non-stuff." But as I continued to write more and more I realized that this was only a small sub-theme of the book. Meanwhile my mother-in-law Phyllis Klein had just recently passed away after a lingering illness of Alzheimer's disease. She was a well known local artist and master quilter who had even travelled to China on a textile tour. She brought back many fabric samples, calligraphy, art pieces and other things as well. After she died, my wife and I were going through her stuff and at the bottom of a box we found this one straw peasant sandal. We didn't know what to do with it. What could it mean? Why did she bring this very odd relic back from China? We held on to the shoe for quite a while in a state of wonder. Just when we'd given up on it and my wife Pip was throwing it out as a piece of junk, I said, "Wait, wait, don't throw it out! That's Lao-Tzu's shoe!" and this eventually became my title.

Some notes on the original artworks selected

While engaged in proofreading the final version of this book for typos and grammatical errors, Pip commented that many chapters end with half a blank page or more. She suggested that I add some of my own original artworks in these spaces.

At first I thought that it would detract from the purity of the book. But going along with the idea, as soon as I started selecting some of my earlier graphic images, I began to realize that these "art fillers" having originated from me, also clearly related to the spiritual themes in "Lao-Tzu's Shoe." In a very abstract visual way the "Transformative Figures Series," certainly possess some subliminal relationship to the spiritual self-work themes presented in this book.

The "Soap Bubble Series" also has some roots in Oriental religious philosophy. The two soap bubble graphics selected are both visual yantras. In Buddhism and Hinduism there is an emphasis on meditation to help focus the mind and stop it from wandering. Mantras are fairly well known in the West, especially the great mantra "Om, mani, padme, hum." These are short poetic and spiritually meaningful phrases which are repeated over and over again as an aid to meditation. Yantras are less well known here. They consist of complex visual graphic designs that perform this same function – one focuses on them as another way of stilling the mind. Being a visual artist, I was inherently drawn to these and created several of my own unique yantras within my soap bubble print series. At one level, soap bubble structures have such purity and physical beauty to them that I was temperamentally strongly attracted to them. To have them "pop" in your mind 3-dimensionally from just flat line drawings was a neat trick too. Soap bubbles were also a great source of inspiration for Buckminster Fuller, another one of my heroes.

The "Nippon Homage Series" of drawings were created after my experiences with Japanese Sumi-e ink brush painting. Most of these were done very quickly with just one charcoal stroke drawn on rice paper. The curious visual qualities of elegant simplicity and simultaneous complexity they all possess are a good example of the Japanese spirit of "shibui." In addition, they also directly embody in their making and their viewing, the Taoist concept of naturally free flowing energy. Hence, they can be thought of as being direct visual analogues to the flowing spirit experienced in Tai-chi practice.

So, as a final surprise to me, these "art fillers" were not a distraction at all, but actually enriched and added another meaningful level of purely visual dimensions to the various ideas discussed in the work itself.

****

At the end of the forward to this book I mention in passing, my wonder at the fact that all three of our dominant Western world religions, Christianity, Islam, and Judaism, all stem from that first Jew in the Old Testament, Abraham. The basic lineage is from Abraham through Ishmael, Moses, Jesus, and Mohammad. What would the spiritual structure of our present-day world look like without Abraham? This of course, is yet another one of those questions that just cannot be answered.

Abraham was the original spiritual patriarch of all the Jews who came after him, although Judaism itself was not fully realized as an organized religion until much later when Moses came on the scene, freed the Jews from slavery in Egypt, and wrote The Five Books of Moses, also known as the Torah, or the Pentateuch, or the Old Testament, or the Holy Bible. In it is the Genesis story of Adam and Eve, the Ten Commandments, many religious laws on how to live a holy life, and the detailed history of God interacting over many generations with the Children of Israel and their prophets and kings. Another appellation used for Jewish culture is "the people of the book," and the Holy Bible is that book which is the oldest known, first published, and most widely disseminated book in existence in all of Western Civilization.

Jesus of Nazareth was of course a radical reforming young Jewish rabbi, born as a member of one of the original tribes of Israel and therefore is also a direct descendant from Abraham too. He greatly reformed, preached and worked against many of the problems of the Judaism of his day including throwing the money lenders out of the Synagogue, and he single handedly brought about the hugely important transformation of the Old Testament image of God from a smiting. jealous, and vengeful God, into the loving and forgiving God of the New Testament. And Christianity was not truly formed as a religion until many years after his death, when generations of his followers wrote down the Gospels and other Christian Scriptures in the New Testament Bible, relating his birth and the history of early Christianity. It elucidates the story of Jesus' itinerant life including his preaching in parables, his performing many miracles, and his arrest, trial, crucifixion, and resurrection. It is presented as a continuation of the existing Old Testament Bible, and it also includes the final Book of Revelations concerning the prophesized events surrounding Armageddon and the End of Days.

Ishmael was Abraham's first born son whose mother was Hagar the handmaiden to his wife Sarah, who at that time was still barren. He was the older half-brother of Isaac who was finally born of Sarah only unexpectedly and very late in her life. Eventually, because of Sarah's jealousy, Hagar and her young son Ishmael were sent out from Abraham's family to live their lives separately in the desert. Ishmael is the one from whom the Arabs and Muslims trace their direct lineage as a people, and he is considered the original patriarch of Islam; also included in this line is his father that same Abraham from The Old Testament whom the Muslims call Ibrahim. And Islam could not be considered a fully realized religion until much later when their true founder Mohammad, being a direct descendant from Ishmael, came along and reportedly over a period of 23 years divinely transmitted their own new Islamic Bible, the Koran, to his followers. This was an act of creation on a scale similar to that of Moses and The Old Testament, and Adam, Moses, Jesus and many of the Jewish prophets and other key figures in the Old and New Testaments are included in the Koran and they are also venerated as holy men of God, called Allah, by the Muslims. The Koran is also concerned with Islamic moral law, and how to live a holy life, and it also discusses in its own terms Judgment Day and the Afterlife.

So there is no escape from the fact that we can all trace our religious origins directly back to that same Old Testament first Jew, Abraham, and therefore are all actually descendent brothers and sisters in the one true faith. It is too bad that we can't just consider ourselves to be different branches on the same extended spiritual family tree of Abraham, and so live more peacefully together, if not always in brotherly love at least as respectful relatives... Instead of there being separate Christians, Muslims, and Jews who've often fought and waged war against each other in the past, if we could all unite in the near future and live together in a newly formed, combined, simplified and updated modern religion, perhaps called "The Living Descendants of Abraham" or even just "Abrahamists" or something similar. That really would result in a great spiritual healing, and although it would be an extremely difficult thing to achieve, it would definitely be worth working very hard to accomplish. Then we wouldn't have these three separate ideological centers for focusing our rallying cries around, and perhaps as a result there would be much less conflict in the world... Perhaps...

Well... Those are my speculative thoughts and hopes, but realistically, I guess there is no escape from family infighting. It certainly has been going on for a very long time now and it shows no signs of abating. With today's massively destructive weapons there could now easily be drastic global consequences if things continue to escalate further, especially since the total overall stability hinges on so many separate inherently unstable elements. Unfortunately, there are also many people who claim to be religious, but who seem dedicated to actively promoting massive upheaval and destruction by encouraging and escalating these conflicts in the hopes of actually initiating and bringing about a final Armageddon with fire raining down from the heavens just as it is described in the Book of Revelations. I withdraw in horror form their myopic apocalyptic visions and I consider those people not to be religious at all, but to just be another miscreant group of radical hate-driven terrorists. Hopefully they will not prevail!

From the reading of this book all can see that I have a great love and appreciation for different aspects of many different religions from the living traditions of many separate world cultures of the past and present. I feel that everyone alive today has a birthright to these hard-won deep spiritual truths that have historically been individually forged, often accompanied by great suffering and even resulting in the persecuted deaths of many of the inspired philosophers and mystics who were their originators. And I hope that this work will help in keeping their bright insights alive and well, just like a nourishing fountain of refreshing clear spring water freely flowing through these many profound original expressions of mankind's truly diverse and varied spiritual heritage. It is so sad for me to see each tradition withdrawn and separated out from all the others, with each having its own established protective group of defensive advocates like home team boosters for their own local sports franchises. To me it's all just another tragic instance of that old well worn adage: *"They can't see the forest for the trees."*

Every now and then one sees scattered glimpses of hope, perhaps through some part of a speech given by the exiled Tibetan Dalai Lama, or in the expressions of the newly elected more liberal Catholic Pope Francis, that there will be a great new global awakening and enlightenment coming soon, let's hope so...

In the mean time I give to you all, that heartfelt and beautiful old Hebrew benediction:

"May the Lord bless you and keep you,
May He be gracious unto you, and
May He cause his countenance to
Shine upon you and give you peace."

Shalom.

Bob Grawi, November 2016, Florida, New York

****

The Gravikord Trio

Ben on percussion, Bob on gravikord, Pip on flute

In Performance on Bannerman's Island in the Hudson
October 16, 2016

About the Author

Bob Grawi, a graduate of Cornell University in 1973, holds a B.S. in Biochemistry with a Minor in Fine Arts. At different times in his life he has been a professional musician, a substitute teacher, a soldier in the U.S. Army, a lecturer, a professional fine artist, a writer of poems, a custom cabinet maker, a professional luthier, and inventor of instruments and other original designs.

He has maintained a lifelong interest in world religions, especially Buddhism, Hinduism, Taoism, Zen and Chan. As an artist and an inventor, he is probably best known for his original instrument the Gravikord. His fascination with the polyrhythmic music of Africa and their instruments inspired him to create the Gravikord, which he named after himself and the West African kora. A variable pitched Gravikord is on permanent display in the New York Metropolitan Museum of Art's Musical Instrument Gallery. It has also been featured in a book-CD "Gravikords Whirlies & Pyrophones." He has performed before millions of listeners, and independently sold over 35,000 recordings. Mr. Grawi been interviewed on many radio stations including WNEW-FM and on NPR programs "All Things Considered" and "New Sounds." He holds several U.S. patents on his instruments and has created other innovative products.

Bob Grawi and his wife, Pip Klein, live in a converted onion barn in the Hudson Valley in rural upstate New York. She also plays flute with him in their group The Gravikord Duo. They have performed at the Venice Italy Carnivale, the World Music Concert Series at the Guggenheim Museum of Art, on a Virgin Airlines 747 over the Atlantic Ocean, and at many other festivals and events worldwide. Their son Ben is a software engineer and an excellent drummer who also often joins them in concert. For more information visit www.gravikord.com.

Made in the USA
Middletown, DE
23 December 2018